Blacks and Whites Meeting in America

Blacks and Whites Meeting in America

Eighteen Essays on Race

Edited by Terry White

PAPERS FROM THE 2001 DAVID K. SHIPLER COLLOQUIUM
ON RACE AT KENT STATE UNIVERSITY, ASHTABULA, OHIO

McFarland & Company, Inc., Publishers
Jefferson, North Carolina, and London

Library of Congress Cataloguing-in-Publication Data

Blacks and whites meeting in America : eighteen essays on race /
   edited by Terry White.
      p.   cm.
      Includes bibliographical references (p.) and index.
[Papers from the 2001 David K. Shipler Colloquium on Race at
   Kent State University, Ashtabula, Ohio]

      ISBN 0-7864-1541-X (softcover : 50# alkaline paper)

      1. United States— Race relations— Congresses.
   2. Racism — United States— Congresses.   I. White, Terry, 1950–
   E185.615.B539   2003
   305.896'073 — dc21   2002154477

British Library cataloguing data are available

Cover art: Detail from Howardena Pindell, *Autobiography:
Water/Ancestors/Middle Passage/Family Ghosts,* 1988

Manufactured in the United States of America

*McFarland & Company, Inc., Publishers
   Box 611, Jefferson, North Carolina 28640
      www.mcfarlandpub.com*

T 100314

To the students of Kent State University, 2001–02,
and to students everywhere who have
inherited the world after 9/11

Acknowledgments

Grateful acknowledgment is made to Dennis McSeveney and Paul Monkowski for their suggestion that inspired the conference that produced this book. Also to librarian Sarah Greenberg of the Ashtabula Campus Library. The editor thanks Caryn McTighe Musil for permission to use the chart on pages 28 and 29, which is reprinted from *Diversity Works: The Emerging Picture of How Students Benefit* by Daryl G. Smith, published by the Association of American Colleges and Universities (Washington, D.C., 1997). For reproductions of the art of Elizabeth Asche Douglas and Howardena Pindell (*Phantasm* on page 75 and *Autobiography* on page 77), the editor also expresses his thanks.

Contents

Part I:
Race, the University, and Affirmative Action

Part II:
Race and Identity in the Arts,
Popular Culture, and Sports

Part III:
The Past as Prologue: Race in the Ministry, the Library, the Academy, and on the Campus

Part IV:
Building an Economic Bridge Across the Racial Divide

A line runs through the heart of America. No longer enforced by laws of segregation, it still divides black and whites along a frontier of images and actions.

— David K. Shipler, *A Country of Strangers*, 1997

Despite all my years of roaming the country interviewing people for the book, I had never before heard anyone say to me, "I have considered not having children because of racism." The young black woman sitting across from me rose slowly to her feet. I looked up at her and she looked down at me across a huge gap — a huge gulf — because to feel the decision not to have children forced on you from without — my children are my joy — feels like the saddest thing possible.

— David K. Shipler, September 14, 2001

Preface

These are the papers presented for the David K. Shipler Colloquium on Race on September 14, 2001, at Ashtabula, Ohio, in a conference devoted to the questions and issues of race in society. What began as a formal call for papers in crosscultural and multidisciplinary academic journals and across Internet listservs throughout the world had as its primary aim a desire to explore the problems and solutions of racism in every aspect of life from workplace to home, wherever we gather to worship, become better educated, or play sports or create art. The idea of a conference on race had grown out of a discussion led by Professor Ed Murray of the Kent State University Psychology Department and his wife and colleague Carol Puthoff-Murray, a driving force in the Campus Diversity Advisory Council, recently made a standing committee of all Kent State University regional campuses by President Carol Cartwright, a champion of diversity across our eight-campus system. By then, the Pulitzer Prize–winning book by *New York Times* journalist David K. Shipler had passed from hand to hand among faculty and administration until copies were ordered for all faculty members. A distinguished committee of readers was commissioned to referee the submissions. Psychotherapists Dennis McSeveney and Paul Monkowski, and Richard H. A. Blum, emeritus, Stanford College of Medicine, author, humanist and Renaissance man, were three.

But on September 11 the very idea of normal disappeared from the American vocabulary; a year later it has re-emerged with new meanings, other connotations. One of the concepts most difficult to comprehend then or now is the relationships among the races in the United States. In the year since 9/11, we all have tried to sort out our feelings about ourselves and others in almost every important aspect of life — none more so than race relations and all that those two words connote. On September 14, just mere hours, it seems in retrospect, from the day the World Trade towers collapsed and thousands of lives were extinguished, we met to

1

discuss and present papers on this subject at the Ashtabula Campus of Kent State University in northeast Ohio, a mere speck along the southern shore of Lake Erie across from Canada. By coincidence, we were swept up in 9/11 in a particular way: We know from the computerized graphics of Flight 93's recorder retrieved after the third plane hit the ground near Pittsburgh on September 11, 2001, that we were in the very spot over which those brave passengers attacked the terrorists and prevented their plane from being turned into another horrific weapon.

We were an eclectic gathering of administrators, teachers, religious and community leaders, street activists, journalists, students, college professors and high school teachers, artists, musicians, and business people. We came from all over. And many obviously could not come at all because of closed airports. Two presenters drove here from Alabama. Our keynote speaker was stranded in Washington, D.C., so he had to be driven to the colloquium. Those who could not make it wrote, called, sent emails, and followed through with correspondence in the days after September 14. Another presenter, Bob Widen of Prescott, Arizona, has become a close friend as well as colleague.

I recall how exhausted and drained we were between sessions, eyes bloodshot from hours of being transfixed by the images on television, the one subject always in the background as scholars exchanged papers and people met people throughout the day. Yet it was a day of good cheer and humility, and a day of scholarship and the sharing of thoughts as well as emotions. That day was to be followed by a convocation for the community, organized by Dean Susan Stocker — not about race but about September 11 and what it meant to our community. Yet those same issues of race were never far from the surface.

I saw persons of color come to this building who I know had never stepped inside it before. There was solidarity there, to be sure, but there was real rancor in the air too — unlike the atmosphere at President Bill Clinton's staged production on race at the Akron Town Meeting a few years earlier. I heard African Americans express fear and loathing; I even got a sense from one or two of the more fundamentalist denominations in town that America was getting its just deserts, paying for its sins of the past. But whether the people making these remarks represented many or a few or just themselves, they spoke of one sin — the sin of racism. Wounds so deep could not heal easily. My colleagues and I believed that something else was needed to revitalize a dialogue that had begun in our small environs but needed guidance from intellectual leaders. One of these leaders is the Reverend Neroy Carter, a slender, energetic whip of a man with a diamond-sharp mind. He proposed that we bring to our forthcoming

Martin Luther King, Jr., Memorial Panel, in November, Debra Borstion-Donbraye, a media consultant, who in turn brought to us the lieutenant governor of Colorado, Joe Rogers, the highest-ranking African American to be elected to office at the state level.

The end result was that the conference we had begun in September with such promise before 9/11 had renewed itself in the dialogue that followed. Joe Rogers told an audience of mostly strangers—again comprising people in the community who had never ventured inside our doors—that America was about healing and struggling and finding our way toward equilibrium. He was as passionate on stage as David Shipler had been with the written word in *A Country of Strangers*. As if the conference in September had been reconstituted of the same demographics to achieve a similar cross-section of Americans, I looked out over the stage where our panelists sat facing several hundred people comprised of community leaders, teachers, students, and children, and watched while an auditorium filled to overflowing watched intently and listened to the healing words of Joe Rogers. I saw faces of the young and old, the faces of black Americans, Caucasians, Latinos and Latinas, Puerto Ricans, Hispanics, the faces of biracial Americans—so many nationalities and ethnicities blended into this American fabric—and I knew then that the terrible aftermath of September 11 was finding its way toward a new equilibrium. On September 10, 2002, we presented our second convocation "September 11th—A Year After" in this room. We kept this discussion going again with calmer deliberation and more seriousness of purpose, without rancor and with hope.

Terry White
Fall 2002

Opening Remarks of the David K. Shipler Colloquium on Race

Kent State University Ashtabula Campus,
14 September 2001

Susan J. Stocker

On behalf of everyone here at the campus, I would like to welcome you. I am going to ask that we start our day together by taking a moment of silence to remember those whose lives were tragically lost this week, to remember those who were left behind and remember and give thanks to the police, the firefighters, health-care providers and other rescue workers who continue to work tirelessly in the face of this horrific tragedy and finally to ask our political leaders and fellow Americans to see through their hurt and anger to find the courage and strength to seek, not revenge, but understanding.

I want to recognize the members of the Diversity Advisory Council, especially Carol Murray, former dean John K. Mahan as well as the members of the Ashtabula Area College committee and Dr. Noah Midamba of the Office of Institutional Diversity for his leadership. Finally, certainly not least, to David Shipler for honoring his commitment to be with us today in this most extraordinary, life-changing, and difficult week in American history.

As I read *A Country of Strangers*, I found the book to be filled with oppositions, polar opposites, dualities and paradoxes of all sorts. Here are some that struck me most vividly: "Country of *Strangers*"; Blacks and Whites; Integration versus Separation; "Together or Separate"; "Progress/

Decay"; "Pain/Hope"; "Minority/Majority"; "Love the individual" ... "Hate the group"; "Every American an expert on race" ... "No American an expert on race." And as I stood Tuesday morning surrounded by students and coworkers transfixed by the incredible images of September 11, the pragmatist in me began to wonder what this would mean for our Shipler Colloquium on race relations in America. Will the speakers be able to get here? Will David himself be able to make it from Maryland? Will we, should we, cancel? These selfish thoughts quickly vanished and I returned to David's extraordinary book itself and its promise of hope in a world so complex with tangled nationalisms and ideals that now, in our very own home, we find ourselves so much maligned and misunderstood by others in the world. Suddenly the conference took on a whole new meaning and I returned to a passage in chapter nine that had moved me when I first read it, but in the light of this terrible week has become illuminated with a profound importance:

> Americans make choices constantly as they try to navigate through the racial landscape. They hear, or they do not hear. They speak, or they remain silent. They keep a racist thought to themselves, or they translate it into behavior overtly or covertly. They select one or another mechanism by which to control the prejudices inside them. They confront or evade, question or teach, learn or regard themselves as above learning. They are not helpless in all of this, not mere prisoners of the past or pawns of the present. They are shaped by their surroundings, to be sure, but they also have free will. They act. They choose. And their first choice is how they listen [447].

We come together today as a community and a nation in grief and sorrow, shocked by terrorism in our country, to begin the dialogue and that dialogue must begin with truly listening.

1
Ideology versus Historic Truth: The Concept of Equality of Educational Opportunity for African Americans

JEFFREY J. WALLACE

Introduction

Nearly a century ago, the great African-American scholar W. E. B. DuBois predicted, "The problem of the twentieth century is the problem of the color line, the relationship of the darker to the lighter races of men in Asia and Africa, in America and the islands of the seas" (9). As we move into the new millennium, the prophetic words of Dr. DuBois still ring true — the problem of the twenty-first century is *still* the problem of the color line. While we have made some tremendous strides toward improving the quality of life for certain segments of the African-American population, we still have not resolved the basic promises of freedom, equality and social justice for all citizens in America. With all the intellectual genius, social theories and attempts at social engineering, America has still not been able to solve one of its most pressing social and philosophical dilemmas. In the words of Cornel West, "race matters," and within the social context of American society, race continues to be a dominant factor in American life.

7

The foci of this discussion will be on the illusionary concept of equality of educational opportunity, the false dichotomous assumption of a race-neutral/color-blind society, ideology versus historical antecedents, and the current challenges to affirmative action and diversity in society and in the academy. The challenges, which are currently mounting in the legal environment, are premised on the assumption that civil rights have been achieved in American society, that there is no need for further action on behalf of African Americans or other minority groups, and that all people are now treated as equals under the law. Affirmative action and diversity initiatives are no longer necessary since everyone now has an equal and competitive chance for success.

Higher education stands at the pinnacle of our social order and is viewed as the fount of knowledge. It is assumed that higher education, as a socializing institution, is free of bias, discrimination and the social maladies which plague segments of our society in general. The academy has been revered as the citadel of knowledge and objectivity based on its emphasis on empirical research and data collected to substantiate a position or decision. History has proven that the theories and assumptions regarding race, many of which were advanced through the academy, have been tainted by subjectivity and bias. Higher education has viewed itself as being above the muck and mire of racial bias, discrimination, stereotyping and subjective feelings or opinions. Higher education in recent years has become the locus of high profile debates and attempts at social engineering on the issue of race.

Colleges and universities are extremely powerful agents for social change and they are uniquely situated to promote the values, norms and ideals of democracy and equality. While higher education has the power to shape public opinion and direct discussion, it appears to follow the attitudes and mores of the social, legal, and political climate of its time. The primary emphasis in the following section will be on the role of higher education in the struggle to live up to our democratic ideals of freedom, equality and social justice.

Ideology and Historical Antecedents

Higher education is a microcosm of society in general. The historical antecedents of society in general, and higher education in particular, are rooted in the laudable concepts of equality and racial neutrality. The Declaration of Independence states: "We hold these truths to be self-evident, that all men are created equal, that they are endowed by their Creator with certain unalienable rights, that among these are life, liberty, and the pursuit of happiness."

The Constitution further states: "We, the people of the United States, in order to form a more perfect union, establish justice, insure domestic tranquility, provide for the common defense, promote the general welfare, and secure the blessings of liberty to ourselves and our posterity...."

While these documents espouse a race-neutral ideology, the founding fathers and those who interpreted them clearly had race-conscious attitudes. *The American Heritage Dictionary*, 3rd edition, defines ideology as a body of ideas or ideals reflecting the social needs and aspirations of an individual, group, class or a culture. It is a set of doctrines or beliefs that form the basis of a political, economic, or other system. In America, that ideology is democracy — the American Dream. The grand experiment known as American democracy is rooted conceptually in the principles of social equality, individual rights, government by the people and for the people, and the exercise of political power for the common good.

While the ideology of democracy suggests that "all men are created equal," the reality is that all men are *not* treated as equals. Here, ideology juxtaposed with the historic truth reveals that America and higher education have not lived up to the lofty goals of a race-neutral and color-blind society. At the time the ideas in the Declaration of Independence were developed and the Revolutionary War was being waged, the colonists argued for their freedom from Great Britain while at the same time enslaving Africans in America. African slaves (and free Africans) were not considered as part of the body politic and not thought of as a part of the discussion of freedom. The Constitution, while espousing equality and social justice, was created as a compromise document with clear racial/color conscious sections. Article I, Section 2.3, identified African slaves as three-fifths of a person; Article I, Section 9.1, refers to the extension of slavery in America through the year 1808; and in Article IV, Section 1.3, reference is made to the presence and status of Africans in America. Further, the U.S. Supreme Court in its landmark Dred Scott decision of 1857 articulated the attitude of white supremacy and black inferiority as a national agenda and part of the public policy in America. Africans (whether free or slave) were not considered citizens and certainly not the social equals of whites. Chief Justice Roger B. Taney in his infamous court opinion raised the question:

> Can a [N]egro, whose ancestors were imported into this country, and sold as slaves, become a member of the political community formed and

> brought into existence by the Constitution of the United States, and as
> such become entitled to all the rights, and privileges and immunities
> guaranteed by that instrument to the citizens? [qtd. in Finkelman 57–58].

Taney further stated:

> The African race in the United States even when free, are everywhere a
> degraded class, and exercise no political influence. The privileges they
> are allowed to enjoy are accorded to them as a matter of kindness and
> benevolence rather than right.... They are not looked upon as a citizen
> by the contracting parties who formed the Constitution. They were evi-
> dently not supposed to be included by the term *citizens* [qtd. in Finkel-
> man 56].

Blacks were evidently not supposed to be included in the term *citizen*.
These statements made by Justice Taney established the principle of white
supremacy and black inferiority, in which he proclaims that "on the contrary, they [blacks]

> were at that time [1787] considered as a subordinate and inferior class
> of beings, who had been subjugated by the dominant race, and whether
> emancipated or not, yet remained subject to their authority, and had no
> rights or privileges but such as those who held the power and the gov-
> ernment might choose to grant them... [35].

The language of this document did not suggest the inclusion of
African Americans as part of the "we" in the Constitution and clearly estab-
lishes a race-conscious public policy in America. The social attitude of the
times supported a race-conscious rather than a race-neutral or color-blind
society — for example, regard the social status of blacks asserted by Stephen
Douglas in 1858:

> I am opposed to [N]egro equality. I repeat that this nation is a white
> people — a people composed of European descendants — a people that
> have established this government for themselves and their posterity and
> I am in favor of preserving not only the purity of the blood, but the
> purity of the government from any mixture or amalgamation with infe-
> rior races [qtd. in Finkelman 49].

While Abraham Lincoln may have opposed slavery and in fact eman-
cipated the slaves, he still held firmly to the rejection of social equality for
blacks:

> I am not, nor have ever been in favor of bringing about in any way the
> social and political equality of the White and Black race. I am not nor

ever [have] been in favor of making voters or jurors of [N]egroes, nor of qualifying them to hold office, nor to intermarry with white people … and inasmuch as they cannot so live, while they do remain together, there must be the position of superior and inferior, and I as much as any man am in favor of having the superior position assigned to the white race [O'Reilly 43].

The Thirteenth, Fourteenth, and Fifteenth amendments to the Constitution are clearly race-conscious statutes, granting citizenship, due process, freedom from slavery and the right to vote to African Americans. The Civil War Amendments, the Civil Rights Act of 1866 and 1875, and the First Reconstruction Era, were attempts at remedying the past and an effort to bring African Americans into full citizenship. These attempts at social engineering failed miserably and resulted in the backlash leading to the *Plessy v. Ferguson* decision of 1896 and the era of Jim Crow, one of the darkest periods in the history of America.

Plessy v. Ferguson is important to this discussion in that it continued the race-conscious attitude in its majority opinion, but also established the concept of a color-blind society in its dissenting opinion. This latter opinion is important to the current debate of affirmative action, in that opponents used color-blindness as a rationale for ending affirmative action. Chief Justice Henry Billings Brown rendered the majority opinion and reinforced the ruling in Dred Scott of racial separation and white superiority. Additionally, the decision in *Plessy v. Ferguson* was in line with the social milieu of the times. The backlash of the First Reconstruction Era and anti-black sentiment was further institutionalized and made a part of the public policy in America after *Plessy,* which established the public policy of "separate but equal."

There is nothing surprising in the majority opinion, which took race into consideration in rendering its decision. Justice Brown asserted, "The object of the amendment [the Fourteenth] was undoubtedly to enforce the absolute equality of the two races before the law, but *in the nature of things* [author's emphasis] it could not have been intended to abolish distinctions based upon color, or to enforce social as distinguished from political equality, or a commingling of the two races upon terms unsatisfactory to either"(qtd. in Brooks 32). The ruling relied on racial distinctions and color consciousness as a principle. The distinction between political versus social equality was firmly established along with the notion that *the nature of things* meant necessarily the separation of the races. Thomas Brooks, a scholar of *Plessy,* argues it thusly:

When the government, therefore, has secured to each of its citizens equal rights before the law and equal opportunities for improvement and progress, it has accomplished the need for which it was organized and performed all of the functions respecting social advantages with which it is endowed. Legislation is powerless to eradicate racial instincts or to abolish distinctions based upon physical differences, and the attempt to do so can only result in accentuating the difficulties of the present situation. If the civil and political rights of both races were equal, one cannot be inferior to the other civilly or politically. If one race is inferior to the other socially, the Constitution of the United States cannot put them on the same plane [51].

The dissenting opinion pronounced by Judge Harlan laid the foundation for the concept of color-blindness and has been used in the twentieth century to promote equal opportunity, integration, diversity and the justification to eliminate affirmative action. His now-famous quote reads:

Our Constitution is color-blind and neither knows nor tolerates classes among citizens. In respect to civil rights, all citizens are equal before the law. The humblest is the peer of the most powerful. The law regards man as man, and takes no account of his surroundings or of his color when his civil rights as guaranteed by the supreme law of the land are involved. It is, therefore, to be regretted that this high tribunal, the final expositor of the fundamental law of the land, has reached the conclusion that it is competent for a state to regulate the enjoyment by citizens of their civil rights solely upon the basis of race [qtd. in Brooks 57].

A very telling statement in the majority opinion speaks to the sentiment or attitude of the social climate of the times, again, to quote Brooks:

This end can neither be accomplished nor promoted by laws which conflict with the general sentiment of the community upon whom they are designed to operate. When the government, therefore, has secured to each of its citizens equal rights before the law and equal opportunities for improvement and progress, it has accomplished the end for which it was organized and performed all of the functions respecting social advantages with which it is endowed [51].

What lies at the heart of the civil rights initiatives of the 1950s and 1960s is the assumption that America can rid itself of two centuries of anti-black sentiment, racial hatred, and the subordinate status of African Americans without recognition that those atrocities occurred in the land of the free and the home of the brave. While laws have changed, the anti-black sentiments and the uneven interpretation and implementation of laws continue to leave the treatment of African Americans at the whim of white America.

The History and Fallacy of Equality of Educational Opportunity in Higher Education

In the mid to late 1960s, higher education became a part of the egalitarian movement coined "equality of educational opportunity." The principles which underlay the concept of equality of educational opportunity, are rooted in the Declaration of Independence, the Constitution, and two Supreme Court decisions, *Plessy v. Ferguson* in 1896, and *Brown v. Board of Education* of Topeka in 1954. In *Plessy*, the concepts of "separate but equal" and the principle of a color-blind society were established. The *Brown* decision continued the color-blind notion, adding integration as the process by which equality would be attained. Both Supreme Court decisions were clearly race-conscious, and both documents highlighted the fallacious assumptions of equality of educational opportunity.

There is no doubt that the second half of the twentieth century has witnessed significant changes with respect to civil rights and the legal environment for African Americans. The period from 1896 to 1954 is a low point in the history of American society in that the official U.S. public policy made African Americans second-class citizens. The *Brown* decision of 1954, the Civil Rights Act of 1964, the Voting Rights Act of 1965, the Civil Rights movement of the 1950s and 1960s, Lyndon Johnson's Great Society programs and policies, the Higher Education Act of 1965, and Executive Order 11246, all have had a significant impact on the development of the theory of equality of educational opportunity and all had a race-conscious orientation.

To understand the creation of the concept, one must understand the social and political context of the 1960s. Having come through a period in which America was confronted with the contradictions of democracy vividly portrayed in living color on television, there was a sympathetic reaction to changes in the legal status of African Americans. Within this social upheaval, John F. Kennedy's "New Frontier" and Lyndon Johnson's "Great Society" were the foci of the federal government's attempts at social engineering. Historically, the federal government always played a significant role in the lives of African Americans during this time period, which some have classified as the Second Reconstruction, the second possibility to live up to the principles of democracy. President Johnson stated:

> This nation, this people, this generation, has man's first opportunity to create the Great Society. It can be a society of success without squalor, beauty without barrenness, works of genius without the wretchedness of poverty. We can open the doors of learning, of fruitful labor and rewarding leisure, not just to the privileged few, but we can open them to everyone. These

goals cannot be measured by the size of our bank balance. They can only be measured in the quality of the lives our people lead. Millions of Americans have achieved prosperity, and they have found prosperity alone is just not enough. They need a chance to seek knowledge and to touch beauty, to rejoice in achievement and in the closeness of family and community [qtd. in Andrew 20].

The Great Society programs were a radical vision of reform, an attempt at changing old societal agendas to be inclusive rather than exclusive of African Americans. It was believed that the problems which prevented America from itself becoming a "great society" were fundamental and only required adjustments in the system. In retrospect, we have come to realize that transformation and not reform was necessary. The problems facing American society were endemic within the fabric of the nation. The public policy espoused democracy while the social attitude practiced inequality and injustice toward African Americans. This is a part of the classic debate by scholars on the differing tactics of Dr. Martin Luther King, Jr., reformist, and Malcolm X, revolutionary. The early pronouncements of the Great Society expressed the idealism and the hope for the future. As the egalitarian pronouncements of the early 1960s developed programs that impinged on individual rights of white Americans in the late 1960s, the reactions and backlash started to occur:

Because the problems that the Great Society sought to address were fundamental, not only to life in the United States but to the lives of its citizens, in any reconsideration readers need to keep in mind several questions. Did the Great Society test the limits of legislation to induce change? Can government really do anything significant to remedy pervasive social problems? Did expectations of change accelerate so rapidly during the 1960s that legislative machinery and government bureaucracy were unable to keep pace? Is mere reform sufficient? Or are the problems structural, requiring more fundamental changes? In short, is the American system basically sound except for the provision of help for the unfortunate, or is a more radical transformation needed? And was it possible to accomplish either within the context of Lyndon Johnson's consensus politics? Because the problems challenged in the 1960s remain largely unresolved even today, contemporary critics of the Great Society such as Newt Gingrich can plausibly use these problems to criticize the efforts of the sixties liberals [Andrew 4–5].

The problem plaguing society from its inception has been the inability to understand the depth and complexity of race in America. America has failed to deal with domination and subordination as factors; this failure, in turn, has governed the relationship between African Americans and white Americans. It is deeply rooted in our conscious and subconscious beings. In spite of this, President Johnson believed the system was fundamentally sound, requiring merely

> mild reforms and technical adjustments so that [the nation] might provide opportunity for everyone. The government could balance the interests of various social and economic groups and sustain a consensus. Within liberal ranks, however, a division arose over what it meant to provide opportunity — ameliorative reform to alleviate the symptoms of distress, or structural change to eradicate the causes of pervasive problems? This confusion later became most evident in the Community Action Programs of the War on Poverty:
> The Great Society eventually discovered the limits of consensus: it could be maintained only by avoiding divisive issues. But the issues addressed by Great Society programs were so important that they were bound to be divisive. The problem came with success, civil rights leader Vernon Jordan later observed, when privileged groups had to share their rights and privileges with the newly empowered. Stability and change did not go easily together. Conservative critics later commingled the left and centrist positions in an effort to discredit the Great Society, blaming the decade's race riots, social violence, antiwar activities, and inflationary economics on LBJ's efforts to redress inequities in American society. (8–9)

From a theoretical perspective, equality of educational opportunity rests on the faulty and dichotomous assumption of the existence and possibility of equality in American society. Equality is a lofty goal with a color-blind presumption. In reality, however, equality given the historical evidence has never existed in America. Building theoretical presumptions on a faulty and nonexistent reality calls into question the stability and reliability of such a concept and its ability to actualize its desired outcomes. In the case of equality of educational opportunity in higher education, what were the desired outcomes? Was the outcome integration, desegregation, elimination of inequalities, affirmative action or diversity? In attempting to answer that, a definition of equal educational opportunity is necessary. Herein lies the first problem — that is, as one tries to define in some measurable way the goals or intent of equality of educational opportunity in the 1960s.

The premise in this context is that higher education, as a socializing institution, had no clear vision, plan, or goal other than the presumed notion or possibility of equality. The very social attitudes—the social milieu of the 1960s—promoted the idea that if laws were changed that integration and equality would follow. Words are inadequate to convey the meaning of a concept in that there are multiple perspectives dependent upon the individual, group or institution attempting to craft a definition. The new lexicon of the second half of the twentieth century attempted to convey a point of view based on the social attitude of the times. Such terms as *integration, desegregation, equal opportunity,* and *affirmative action* were new to the language of the times and were consequently defined by groups within society dependent on their own semantic bias and point of view. Liberal-versus-conservative perspectives varied in how such terms came to be defined at large. From a liberal perspective, equal educational opportunity had an expansive definition focused on desired outcomes. The conservative point of view was more restrictive in its definition. This latter thinking corresponds with the view of the neo-conservative today who believes that laws are sufficient and that the responsibility for achievement of results rests with the aggrieved groups. This places no responsibility on society and makes no acknowledgment of past discrimination and racism. From a legal perspective, the evaluation of equality of educational opportunity in the courts suggests that

> [t]he legal construction of equality in education always began with the assumption that school inequality did not exist and that it was the plaintiff's responsibility to produce contradictory evidence. Using this method, the court constructed a model of equality by validating educational inequality. There was, and still is, a limitation with using an indirect mathematical proof to achieve equality in a social context. It is a very static process, making it nearly impossible to capture and change dynamic social realities.... Under our system, the courts assume that inequality does not exist, and thus the burden of providing contradictory evidence, or in essence, the construction of a new model of equality rests with the citizen who is compelled to challenge the school system's policy. The use of an indirect mathematical proof to both legally and socially construct equality was, and continues to be, a time-consuming and restrictive process. Further, the indirect method is not an expansive process that initiates the construction of equality in education or anticipates policies that promote inequalities and prevent their implementation. Nor has this method framed equality as a result. Rather, equality is viewed as a process [Grant 100].

The same is true in defining the term integration. There is an expansive view held by some liberals and many African Americans who look for both process and results. The restrictive view of integration deals with desegregation and not true integration.

Higher education, similar to the larger society, has a history of racism, discrimination and exclusion of African Americans. This history is well documented in the seventh chapter of Meyer Weinberg's *A Chance to Learn: A History of Race and Education in the United States.* Entitled "Guarded Preserve: Black Students in Higher Education," it outlines the exclusion and discrimination against African Americans prior to 1954 and the movement toward desegregation in the 1960s. To understand the present and to plan for the future, there must be some knowledge of the past. To open the doors of colleges and universities without understanding the historical perspectives did not allow a full understanding of the issues and the ability to develop a plan to achieve the desired goal.

The second problem is that higher education, as an institution, did not have a coherent plan or pedagogical concept by which to achieve equality of educational opportunity. The promotion or intention to open colleges and universities to African Americans and other minority groups in the 1960s did not come through the university, but was rather imposed by external forces. There was no pedagogical concept to provide access and opportunity. In this context, higher education was reacting to the sign of the times and public policy, but with no investment or plan as to how to achieve equality of educational opportunity. With neither educational plan nor articulated definition, the concept of educational opportunity was launched.

The new lexicon of terms, along with a paradigm shift away from blatant, overt racism and anti-black sentiment, trends toward a subtler, less overt action — in a word, *neo-racism*, which word suggests that, although the tactics have changed, the attitude still remains. This neo-racism, while softer in its approach, has the same devastating impact on the lives of African Americans as the overt racism of the past.

The new terminology includes words such as *integration, desegregation, equal educational opportunity, affirmative action* and *diversity*. Each of these terms has as its etymological root a semantic assumption of racial neutrality and color-blindness. Hopefully someday, our society would be devoid of the social construction of race. The presumption is that laws will somehow end the inequality in our society and that everyone is now on an equal footing to succeed or fail.

The term equality of educational opportunity can be traced back to the Coleman Report of 1967. The impetus of the concept of equality of educational opportunity was imposed on higher education by external forces. There was nothing endemic to the academy which fostered the recognition of inequality or the need to provide open access to African Americans and other minorities. The *Brown* decision was basically directed at the public school system. The Civil Rights Act of 1964, Title VI, prohibited discrimination in any program that received federal funding. The Elementary and Secondary Education Act (ESEA) of 1965 provided federal funding to the states. This act created funds for library textbooks, instructional materials, and the construction of buildings. The Higher Education Act of 1965 for the first time provided federal scholarships (EOG grants) for undergraduate students, funds for the construction of classrooms, monies for libraries and instructional support, and funds to improve undergraduate courses. It was the infusion of federal dollars into colleges and universities which prompted access to African-American students. Colleges and universities, which were enclaves of segregation, began to open their doors to qualify for federal dollars. Just as elementary and secondary education began to apply to receive federal dollars, colleges and universities followed suit. As historian Allen Matusaw has argued, "[M]ost local districts accepted the money but not the objectives it was meant to fulfill…" (qtd. in Andrew 126). Higher education accepted federal funds, but did little to deal with the substance and intent of equal educational opportunity.

The issue of race in the latter part of the 1960s shaped the agenda of equality of educational opportunity. The Coleman Report (Equality of Educational Opportunity) identified racial segregation as a major factor in the access and opportunity for African Americans:

> Coleman's summary traced the complexity of the problem: the sources of inequality of educational opportunity appear to be first in the home itself and the cultural influences immediately surrounding the home, then they lie in the schools' ineffectiveness to free achievement from the impact of the home, and in the schools' homogeneity which perpetuated the social influences of the home and its environment [124].

From this scenario, the concept of "educational opportunity" was born, which blamed the family and the environment for the educational deficiencies of African Americans. The initial programs in higher education focused on the educational and cultural disadvantagement of African-American students. The plethora of programs which emerged on college campuses in the mid to late 1960s centered on helping the poor and ill-equipped "disadvantaged student" to attend college.

The Higher Education Act of 1965 provided a great impetus to the enrollment of African Americans on campuses across the country. It ushered in the promise of access and opportunity not only to African Americans, but also to all groups in higher education. "Passage in 1963 of the Elementary and Secondary Education Act … dramatically changed education in [America]. Central to that change was not only the availability of federal monies but also a new philosophy that endorsed access and opportunity for all who qualified. No longer should poor but bright students be denied a chance at higher education" (Andrew 130). The assumption by many Americans is that equal educational opportunity benefited or advantaged African Americans over whites. The facts are that the Higher Education

Act of 1965 provided tremendous benefits to middle-income and poor whites in greater numbers than African Americans and other minorities.

Higher Education, Race, Affirmative Action and Diversity

The original intent of equality of educational opportunity in the 1960s was focused on the "poor." This intent was changed to some extent in the latter part of the 1960s to focus on race rather than purely socioeconomic conditions. It was this change in focus which became problematic and divisive in America. Was the intent integration, desegregation or affirmative action? With no historical background or understanding of historical records, higher education moved forward with enrolling larger numbers of African Americans and others under the guise of affirmative action. In that record, the focus was on increasing the number of African Americans in higher education. The questions which challenge higher education are whether the goal of equality of educational opportunity was integration or desegregation. If the goal was integration, we have fallen short of that goal, and if desegregation, we have made some progress in attaining the goal. The paramount vehicle by which that goal has been achieved is affirmative action. While the process of affirmative action is fraught with misconceptions and misinterpretations, it is the only legislative action that has produced results. Affirmative action has had a greater impact on higher education than any other single initiative in the history of American higher education.

The quest for the vision of equality of educational opportunity in higher education was part of the public policy and public sentiment in the mid to late 1960s. As we move into the twenty-first century, what is the public policy and public sentiment in America and higher education today? Has higher education achieved its goals of equality of educational opportunity or is there still work to be done to realize true equality, freedom, and social justice?

Higher education, as a socializing institution, has made significant strides toward providing access previously denied to African Americans prior to the 1960s. There is unprecedented evidence that the inclusion of African Americans in higher education has changed drastically over the past three decades. The question to be asked and answered is what was the goal of equality of educational opportunity — integration or access — and to what degree has either been achieved? If simply access was the goal, then higher education has made significant advancement in realizing its goal. However, if integration within American society and the academy was the goal, there is still a tremendous gap in the desired goal and the actual outcome.

The mood in the nation as we enter the twenty-first century is different from the sentiment and public policy displayed in the 1960s. The federal government took leadership in setting the tone and direction of the Great Society programs, of which equality of educational opportunity was crucial. From the late 1940s through 1960s there were tremendous improvements in civil rights activities and opportunities for African Americans. While the critics were many, the proponents and advocates were able to move the agenda forward, at least from a legislative and legal perspective. The achievements among certain segments of the African-American community have been dramatic; however, the vision of a truly democratic society has still *not* been realized.

The success of higher education in achieving equality of educational opportunity should be determined by its stated goal and purpose. The historical evidence and the present circumstances clearly suggest that the academy had no specific goals or objectives, other than providing access to African Americans. In fact, the impetus for including African Americans on college campuses came from external forces and not from within the academy. There were no specific plans, no pedagogical underpinning, and no specific outcomes desired. The public sentiment of the times, the public policies and laws enacted, and the desire for colleges and universities to obtain significant amounts of federal dollars, was the engine which drove the inclusion of African Americans on college campuses. Fiscal support and resources rather than a firm commitment and understanding of true equality and integration prompted college and university officials to create programs to enroll students and to hire faculty and staff. At the time, these measures were seen as the process by which desegregation on college and university campuses would occur. Today these efforts are categorized as affirmative action measures and are viewed with some skepticism. The academy has never been clear in its position on affirmative action, given its philosophy of merit. The special programs to enroll black students on various campuses have always been an issue for some, in addition to hiring of African-American faculty and staff. Because higher education has not fully acknowledged its deeds of the past and has not recognized the social, political, economic and educational realities of African-Americans' lives and existence in America, it has failed to embrace these students, faculty and staff in a truly integrated, welcoming campus environment. True integration

> is about the realm of life governed by behavior and choice, not by statistics and institutions. It should not be confused with desegregation, which means the elimination of discriminatory laws and barriers to full

participation in American life. Although desegregation is a necessary pre-condition for integration, it is entirely possible to desegregate without integration — for Blacks and Whites to attend the same schools without ever learning about each other or becoming friends, or for Blacks and Whites to work for the same employer without mixing much on or off the job. Desegregation may unlock doors, but integration is supposed to unlock minds... [Steinhorn and Diggs-Brown 5].

While black Americans are allowed to be a part of the higher education enterprise, they have never been truly accepted or integrated into the fabric of institutions. They have been tolerated, viewed as anomalies, and patronized at best.

In searching for a definition and meaning for equality of educational opportunity, there are two views: expansive and restrictive. The expansive view stresses equality as a result, while the restrictive view looks only at process. The former stresses "equality as a result and looks to create real consequences for oppressed people. It interprets the goal of antidiscrimination law as the elimination of substantive conditions of subordinates, and it seeks to incorporate the power of the courts to achieve the goal of eradicating the effects of oppression" (Grant 99). This view supports the vision of true equality and the elimination of inequality. The results of this view should be an integrated society. The restrictive view of equality of educational opportunity "treats equality of opportunity as a process, minimizing the importance of actual results [whereas] antidiscrimination law ... is to prevent further injustice rather than to redress current products of past wrongdoing" (100). It is this latter view that American society and the academy have adopted as public policy. Professor John Hope Franklin states in *The Color Line*:

It was at this juncture — when public policy generally, and the work of the three branches of government in particular, had created a climate so favorable to racial justice and equality — that many white Americans began to talk about our society as being color-blind. And if we had not arrived at that happy state, conditions were in place that would be especially helpful in rapidly advancing us to that state. Indeed, some argued, the surest way to becoming a color-blind society was to assume that we were already in one [42].

The point of view or perspective that African Americans now have the same rights and privileges as all Americans (as a result of civil rights initiatives, laws and statutes) negates the need for affirmative action or "special programs" or protections. The Fourteenth Amendment to the Constitution was written specifically for the newly designated African-American citizens. These new citizens needed protection given the previous conditions of servitude and exclusion prior to the Civil War. The Civil Rights amendments and all of the Civil Rights acts were written to protect the rights of African Americans. It is the perception of some that the laws and statutes enacted to protect African Americans from the actions and reactions of public sentiment have been shifted to protect everyone, which is now preventing a solution to the racial problems in America. This ebb and flow of attitudes toward African Americans in society is predicated on the absence of understanding of historic truth in favor of hollow pronouncements of the societal ideology of a democracy. Today the myth of a color-blind society dominates the thinking and attitude toward African Americans. The attitude that the laws, legislative statutes all are color-neutral and have no racial consciousness attached is a fallacy. Professor Franklin furthers asserts:

> Thus, they reasoned now that African Americans enjoyed equal protection of the laws, and they needed no special protection of the laws. Those who had counseled the social engineers not to go too fast seem willing overnight to embrace the concept of a color-blind society that offered neither favors nor even protection based on color. The consequences of such a position were dire indeed, for the view was vigorously advanced that it was even improper to offer protection to those entering a period of transition leading to genuine equality [43].

The argument today surrounding affirmative action and diversity initiatives is that opportunity is all that is necessary, and to confer special status on African Americans is discriminatory and akin to reverse discrimination against white Americans. Here lies the dilemma which faces American society and the academy today: whether to end affirmative action, which has been the only implementation process which has fostered some positive results for African Americans and other groups (i.e., women, persons with disabilities, etc.), or accept the fallacious notion that in a color-blind and race-neutral environment, the desired goals will be achieved without any additional support and direction. The history of America does not support the latter position and in fact, the former statement supports the status quo or a reversal of positive advancements for African Americans. The legal environment now dominates the thinking on affirmative action and diversity.

The notion of a color-blind society and a race-neutral environment is now dictating the direction and attitude of the American public. The academy, which could take a leadership role, is ambivalent at best on the issue of affirmative action.

The Supreme Court's decision in *The Regents of the University of California v. Bakke* (1978) began the downward spiral of affirmative action in higher education. There were two important directives which came out of the decision. Justice Powell suggested in *Bakke* that a race-conscious policy is justifiable if it serves a compelling interest or goal. He believed in a color-blind constitutional standard, but also argued for some guidance for affirmative action. He believed that there was a compelling argument for colleges and universities to achieve a diverse student body, and that race could be justified as one of a number of factors to admit students to a university. The issue is the public good. Is diversity in the best interest of society and the academy? While the laws may be color-blind, the implementation, treatment and actions of society do not support the reality of a color-blind and race-neutral society. Race *does* matter, and our laws and statutes, in fact, have a color-conscious reality. The language from the *Bakke* decision is currently being used to justify a diverse student body. Race can be used as a factor, but not the sole factor in admitting students to a university:

> The Court's concession to race-conscious affirmative action programs in higher education reflects the Justices' awareness that Blacks have already made some strides through such programs and that great progress is needed. The elevation of "reverse discrimination" to the protective status of a judicial concern is, in part, an expression of the belief that Black progress in higher education has reached the point of threatening the majority [Morris 3].

Bakke exhibits a radical shift in public policy and sentiment from *Brown* in 1954. The *Bakke* case struck a death knoll for affirmative action in higher education and opened the door to constitutional challenges by students and others in the legal profession. The ambiguity of the *Bakke* decision leaves much to interpretation. The challenges to *Bakke* and its interpretation have led to the plethora of recent cases, such as Hopwood, University of Georgia, University of Michigan, University of Washington. The opponents of affirmative action use this ambiguity to argue against special support for African Americans. In the 1870s, Justice Joseph P. Bradley argued in the Civil Rights cases that a time "must come when a black citizen should stop being the 'special favorite of the law,' and when his rights as a citizen or a man are to be protected in the ordinary modes by which other men's rights are to be protected" (Brooks 174–75). This same view is being expressed today as we move into the twenty-first century. Race should not be a factor in determining opportunities and that it should not be used to make decisions.

Justice Harry Blackmun in the *Bakke* decision stated that to get "beyond racism, we must first take account of race. There is no other way

... in order to treat persons equally, we must treat them differently" (Regents 2806–08). While blatant racism has declined, there is still evidence that demonstrates the subtle and unconscious racial bias that persists. If a color-blind society existed, there would be no need for affirmative action. Americans must begin to deal with the historic truth that race, racism, and color-consciousness is a fact of life in this nation. No attempts at ignoring the reality will solve the problem. Dialogue on race is vital to understanding and a search for a solution. If America and the academy continue to hide their collective head in the sand hoping that racism or color-consciousness will go away, they are in for a rude awakening. A color-blind society does not exist and has never existed in America. When opponents of affirmative action raise the banner of integration and a color-blind society, they use Dr. King's dream of a society in which the content of one's character, rather than the color of one's skin, is a deciding factor in life experiences. It is clear that King was expressing a hope for the future when he said he had been to the mountaintop and seen the promised land. Yes, the promised land is out there, but the goal is still a distant hope, which needs to be realized. Assuming that this dream will be achieved with hard work and dialogue is a hope without foundation.

Higher education as a socializing agency has the potential for leading the struggle to eradicate inequality, injustice, and racism. To take a leadership role, higher education must rid itself of its own complicity in white supremacy and black inferiority, acknowledge its role in support of that ideology, clearly state its position on affirmative action as a common good, and begin the difficult but necessary dialogue on race. There is nothing more patriotic or defensible in an educational environment than the search for truth, honesty and expansion of knowledge. Contrary to the position of the opponents of affirmative action, a diversified student body is important to the full development of a well-rounded citizen. Diversity enriches education by providing all students with the opportunity to learn from those who are different from them. Diversity promotes a healthy, civic development in all students and strengthens community and workplace cooperation in an increasingly diverse society.

Colleges and universities can support diversity as a common good for the future and as an educational benefit for students, faculty, staff and society as a whole by promoting diversity in course offerings and teaching methodologies and by supporting student, faculty and staff dialogue outside the classroom. The ultimate goal is to eliminate discrimination in principle and practice, encourage intergroup relationships and destroy artificial barriers such as skin color and racial classification, which cause inequality and denial of social justice. Diversity is *not* affirmative action, but rather the result of affirmative action. If we are to eliminate the reality that America and the academy are a country (campus) of strangers, we must work together to accomplish that goal. There must be a plan with stated objectives, strategies, timelines and some manner of evaluation to determine if the goals are being met. The work is not easy; it will create some chaos, but out of the struggle can come a positive result.

Dr. King stated, in one of his most famous sermons, "All men are caught in an inescapable network of mutuality, tied in a single garment of destiny. Whatever affects one directly affects all indirectly. I can never be what I ought to be until you are what you ought to be, and you can never be what you ought to be until I am what I ought to be" (7). This is the goal, this is the vision of a democratic society in which all people are created equal and treated as equals and that the principles of equity are applied to enhance opportunities to secure true equality.

References

Andrew, John A. III. *Lyndon Johnson and the Great Society.* Chicago: Dee, 1998.

Brooks, Thomas. *Plessy v. Ferguson: A Brief History with Documents.* Boston: Bedford, 1997.

DuBois, W. E. B. *The Souls of Black Folk.* 1963. New York: Dover, 1994.

Finkelman, Paul. *Dred Scot v. Sanford: A Brief History with Documents.* Boston: Bedford, 1997.

Franklin, John Hope. *The Color Line: Legacy for the Twenty-First Century.* Columbia: University of Missouri Press, 1993.

Grant, Carl A., and Gloria Ladson-Billings, eds. *Dictionary of Multicultural Education.* Phoenix: Onyx, 1997.

King, Martin Luther, Jr. *Strength to Love.* Philadelphia: Fortress, 1963.

Morris, Lorenzo. *Elusive Equality: The Status of Black Americans in Higher Education.* Washington, D.C., Howard University Press, 1979.

O'Reilly, Kenneth. *Nixon's Piano: Presidents and Racial Politics from Washington to Clinton.* New York: Free, 1995.

Regents of the University of California v. Bakke. CA Super. Ct., 1978.

Steinhorn, Leonard, and Barbara Diggs-Brown. *By the Color of Our Skin: The Illusion of Integration and the Reality of Race.* New York: Dutton, 1999.

2
Building a Diverse and Respectful Campus Community: A Systematic Approach Model

Noah O. Midamba

The dramatic transformation in the composition of the student population of American colleges and universities over the past generation is unparalleled in the history of Western higher education. In the early 1960s and with the exception of students attending historically black colleges and universities, only a relative handful of Americans of color went to college in the United States; today, upward of one in five undergraduates at four-year schools is a minority.

This multicultural revolution, which arose in large measure alongside colleges' and universities' efforts to recruit minority students, played a major role in the social and economic advancement of millions of Americans of color. In addition, the contribution of these individuals has made college and university campuses more diverse communities.

For many years, higher education has assumed that having a diverse campus community contributes to the "robust exchanges of ideas on campus," but it has not attempted to articulate or examine the relationship between the two (Alger, 2000, p. 57).

This section is intended to provide a systematic approach to how colleges and universities may best serve a growing diverse campus community. At the conclusion, major elements of a campus community transformation

26

model will be outlined and developed from an institutional and individual faculty and staff process.

How Does One Create a Diverse Campus Community?

A community confers upon its members an identity, a sense of belonging, and a measure of security. It is in communities that the attributes that distinguish humans as social creatures are nourished. Communities are the ground level generators and preservers of values and ethical systems. Gardner (1989, p. 73) notes that ideals of justice and compassion are nurtured in communities.

Theoretical Paradigm

To create community one must be able to understand, predict, and change behavior where

$B = f (P \times E)$
B = Behavior, f = function of, P = Characteristics of the person, $\times$ = degree of subject's interaction, and E = Characteristics of the environment.

This cultural change model places emphasis on the shaping of the environment through the building of a community. A diverse campus community is more, however, than a list of communal traditions and experiences with which individuals may identify and to which others may react. The expression "diverse campus community" has also come to refer to the variety of strategies higher educational institutions have developed to address the consequences of earlier homogeneity at a particular institution of higher education. Adelman (1997) noted this variety when he observed that a diverse campus community means different things depending on the observer. For some it is code for the presence of designated and previously excluded groups; for others it is a climate that welcomes heterogeneity; for still others it is a range of programs designed to influence what and how students learn. For many it is all these simultaneously.

Given the variety of diversities on campus (and in society) and the disparate action that higher education is taking to address diversity, it is clear that we cannot use one-dimensional conceptions to define a diverse campus community. For example, does diversity refer only to African-Americans and Latinos, or does it include white women? How inclusive should a definition of diverse campus community be? What role do Asian Americans play in diversity conversations? Are gay and lesbian concerns integral to issues of a diverse campus community? When we talk about campus diversity efforts, are we describing programs for particular groups? For any group that feels distinctive or marginal? For all students? For everyone on the campus community — faculty, staff and administrators, as well as students? How do communities outside the campus relate to campus diversity issues and groups?

In the diagram below, Smith (1997) used four distinct though interrelated dimensions to define a diverse campus community.

Representation: Focuses on the inclusion and success of previously underrepresented groups. This is the most commonly understood element of diversity initiatives, and it has emerged from a social and historical context of exclusion and resulting underrepresentation.

Campus Climate and Intergroup Relations: Addresses the impact of the collegiate environment on institutional and student success. It includes activities which prevent students from experiencing campus as alienating, hostile, and "chilly."

Education and Scholarship: Involves the inclusion of diverse traditions in the curriculum, the impact of issues of diversity on teaching methods, and influence of societal diversity on scholarly inquiry.

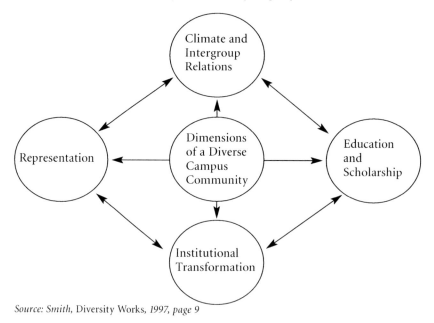

Source: Smith, Diversity Works, *1997, page 9*

Institutional Transformation: Refers to deep, reorganization questions, which build upon the many changes prompted by the earlier dimensions, developed by Smith.

What Is the Emerging Operational Definition of Diversity on College and University Campuses?

The emerging operational understanding about diversity and higher education has evolved from remarkable experimentation on campuses in a wide variety of diversity programs, focused especially on the first three dimension outlined by (Smith 1995, p. 5). In this model, Smith refers to four key dimensions of campus diversity: (1) access and success, (2) climate and intergroup relations, (3) education and scholarship, and (4) institutional vitality and viability.

The richest diversity initiatives with the strongest impact have moved far beyond the question of access, while never losing sight of centrality. Colleges and universities are paying more attention to how well new students succeed and how effective institutions welcome faculty, administrators, and staff from underrepresented groups. They are also recognizing

Dimensions of Campus Diversity

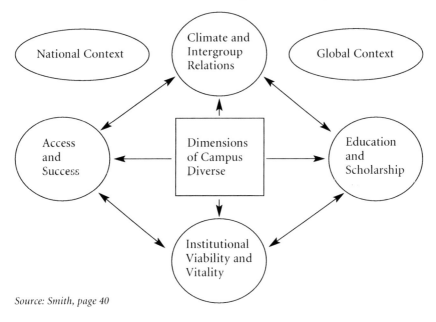

Source: Smith, page 40

the influence of campus climate and intergroup relations on retention and responding with innovative programs. They are examining traditional structures and practices that have created barriers to a diverse student population. They are also encouraging new scholarships among formerly ignored groups and issues, thus adding to and revising the knowledge base of our disciplines, stimulating innovations in curriculum, and bringing renewed attention to improving teaching and learning.

At the outset of any diversity initiative, every member of a college or university campus community, faculty, staff, and student body needs to raise a question: "Can I see myself in the definition?" According to Lee Gardenswartz and Anita Rowe (1998, p. 24), principals of Gardenswartz and Rowe, a California-based diversity consulting and training team, the trend seems to favor a broad definition, one that goes beyond the visible differences such as race, ethnicity, age, and gender. For many people, a narrow definition focusing only on a few visible characteristics is not only too exclusive, but also too closely linked to affirmative action.

A broad definition of diversity includes more than race, gender, and sexual orientation. A broad definition includes differences in personality and work style, religion, disabilities, ageism, socioeconomics and education, and work-related diversity, such as membership in management and union, functional level and classification, or proximity/distance to head-quarters. While initially these latter diversities may seem much less impor-tant than race, gender, or sexual orientation, they can matter a great deal. Among the issues that frequently damage an organization or workgroup are factors such as education, socioeconomics, and work experience. Such factors are relevant to the assumptions that people make about one another and the collaboration, openness, and trust that people feel in working together. Thus, a broader definition of diversity will help faculty, staff, and students find a place or places to connect with one another. A broad definition offers chances to create and fortify relationships that will enable every member of the community to deal with specific diversity issues that will arise later. On the other hand, we must keep in mind that to those who have been excluded from career opportunities, whether through entrenched systems or individual bias, either unconscious or intentional, a broad focus can seem irrelevant and meaningless.

What is crucial for college and university communities is a definition of diversity that all faculty, staff, and students can relate to. Such a defini-tion will withstand the test of time. If we can all see ourselves in it, we will be more likely to invest in the initiative. This investment is important since resistance to diversity initiatives often surfaces with time. Accord-ingly, Kent State University (2001) defined diversity in the broadest term possible: "the existence of differences within individuals or groups of people in our society." To further reinforce Kent State University's definition of diversity, UNESCO's 31st General Conference recently declared: "Cultural diversity is an ethical imperative, inseparable from respect for human dignity. It implies commitment to human rights and fundamental freedom, in particular the right of persons belonging to minorities and those of indigenous peoples."

The Major Differences between Affirmative Action and Diversity Programs

Recent legal challenges to affirmative action and increased public scripting regarding the use of race in college admission now make it imperative that colleges and universities publicly relate how diversity benefits their campuses and helps fulfill their educational missions.

The recent study by the American Council on Education (Milem and Hakuta, 2000, p. 6) examines existing data that shows how diversity benefits students, campuses, and society. The study also calls on institutions to conduct and publicize research on their campuses that shows how diversity benefits higher education. Affirmative-action programs, the study states, were designed to undo the damage that has been done by discrimination in American society. However, "today opponents of affirmative action criticize it for being inequitable and discriminatory, thus reinforcing a number of myths about racial dynamics in higher education" (p. 67). Misconceptions regarding affirmative action include a belief that past inequalities in access and opportunities for students of color have been sufficiently addressed; that test scores alone define merit, and thus diversity programs benefit only students of color who participate in them.

The figure below will explain the differences between Equal Educational Opportunities, Affirmative Action and Diversity.

EEO/AA	*DIVERSITY*
Government Initiated	Voluntary
Legally Driven	Productivity Driven
Quantitative	Qualitative
Problem Focused	Opportunity Focused
Assumes Assimilation	Assumes Integration
Internally Focused	Internally and Externally Focused
Reactive	Proactive

Why Diversity Is Central to the Mission of Colleges and Universities

As pervasive as diversity is in American culture today, there are some who see diversity as a distraction from a more important issue, as a threat to national unity and local communities, or as a collection of special interest groups. In the context of higher education, such criticism has led to heated debates over the content of the curriculum, resistance by some to programs specifically designed to attract or support populations newly included at colleges and universities, and insistence that focusing on particularities of one identity group is at best irrelevant and at worst divisive. Some people worry that only difference is valued, not commonalities. They see groups clustering together and fear that disunity will be the consequence. So much new scholarship has been generated that some fear that what they regard as classic tradition will be lost. Others believe that minorities and women get special privileges at the expense of more qualified people. A portion believe that colleges and universities have gone too far in accommodating new populations on campuses and sacrificed excellence in the process (Musil, 1999, p. 8).

Higher education is the academic laboratory for defining new democratic practices of equality, opportunity, and inclusion, and for the most part it has taken on the challenges, motivated by a series of compelling arguments that it should do no less. These arguments include the academic, moral, civic, demographic, and economic.

Academic argument— Several arguments have persuaded the majority of the academic communities to begin to evaluate campus policy and practices in order to foster deeper learning, create more inclusive communities, and to prepare students to assume responsibilities for sustaining a diverse and robust democratic society. Many believe that diversity is deeply linked to ensure academic excellence; just as many are imbued with the conviction that knowledge suffers when differing perspectives are ignored.

Moral argument—A second argument that has motivated many in the academic community to support diversity is a moral one. Many support diversity because they believe it is simply the right thing to do. It directs the academy's attention to unfinished national business. A commitment to diversity is seen as a commitment to equality and equal opportunity.

Civic argument—Closely related to the moral argument is a civic one. Based on the belief in the civic importance of an educated citizenry, democracy depends on the meaningful participation of and practice of deliberate dialogue among its people with the corollary that citizenly responsibility is an essential part of the infrastructure of a democratic society.

Demographic argument— The fourth argument for addressing a diverse community rests on a simple mathematics. Colleges and universities understand that they need to educate current and projected generations of college students. The majority of these students are female and nearly 30 percent of them are students of color. Another 40 percent of future students are older adults, and nearly half of these are first-generation college students.

Economic argument— The demographic argument is tied to another compelling reason for making diversity integral to the academy. It is a matter of economic opportunity and economic justice. Research indicates that educational attainment of the family head is directly related to the income and living standard of a family (Elway Research, 1998, p. 10).

A Systematic Diversity Model for Higher Education

Many colleges and universities in the United States have developed their own distinctive models for addressing issues of campus diversity. The model described below certainly does not represent the only choices a campus has. New models emerge every day as colleges and universities continue to engage in vibrant dialogue about appropriate diversity models to address their particular campus communities.

Whatever model an institution chooses, consensus is definitely emerging that the model represents the best example of an institutional transformation as well as the level of an individual learning process necessary for every staff and faculty to go through in order to build a highly functioning, diverse and respectful campus community.

An Institutional Transformation for Diversity

An Institutional Transformation Process:

(1) *Institutional Leadership and Commitment*

Vision, commitment and leadership (by example) are essential for systemic change at college and university campuses. Diversity and democracy challenge us to move beyond our individual and institutional comfort zones of assimilation (cognitive, affective and behavioral) to engage, understand and respect differences and similarities among people and cultures. An inclusive institutional vision encourages a nurturing and challenging intellectual and social climate for all members of a campus community.

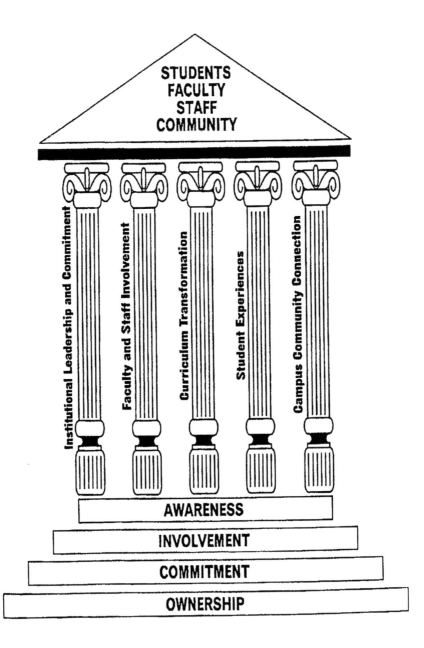

STUDENTS
FACULTY
STAFF
COMMUNITY

Institutional Leadership and Commitment

Faculty and Staff Involvement

Curriculum Transformation

Student Experiences

Campus Community Connection

AWARENESS

INVOLVEMENT

COMMITMENT

OWNERSHIP

(2) *Faculty and Staff Involvement*

Examples of faculty or staff involvement include opportunities designed to support faculty or staff in the areas of pedagogical change, curriculum transformation, sexual harassment, antiracism and anti-homophobia.

(3) *Curriculum Transformation*

Higher educational campuses are changing their curricula to address issues of diversity. This initiative focuses on American Pluralism "across the curriculum," special studies programs on designated communal traditions, new interdisciplinary programs, traditional disciplinary majors that have systematically addressed diversity in their course offerings or requirements, with additional focus on diversity requirements, credit-bearing service learning programs and special institutes.

(4) *Student Development and Experience*

Faculty and staff on college and university campuses build relationships with students that make valuable and lasting differences in their lives. Student experience and development is a priority, focusing on students as a diverse group at the center of the classroom, the campus and the community. These are activities designed to address residential life, programs to work on inter- and intragroup relations on campus, and programs designed to attend to students' transitions among their own communities and within the campus community.

(5) *Campus-Community Connections*

The campus-community priority is about campus-community partnerships. These partnerships include active commitments from staff and student who recognize their responsibilities for participating in multiple communities (including, but not limited to, on-campus communities) and efforts to work with local community leaders and groups in solving particular problems or conducting community-based research. This priority aims to address disparate perceptions of the nature and meaning of U.S. diversity on campus and in the community.

Individual Faculty and Staff Learning Process:

(1) Awareness: All faculty and staff need to know where they currently stand, where they are going (and why), how they are going to get there and who can assist them regarding diversity. It is important at this stage to:

Perform a personal audit
Determine educational support needed
Communicate your need to others

(2) Involvement: All faculty and staff must be involved in making diversity happen. This second stage of the process requires that one:

> Develop a support structure
> Develop a personal mission
> Develop training needs
> Conceive a quality diversity environment
> Communicate his or her vision

(3) Commitment: Commitment doesn't just happen — it is built over time. Ingredients include strong participative leadership, vision, enthusiasm, and continued training and teamwork fueled by the development of a recognition and reward system. At this third stage one needs to:

> Demonstrate commitment
> Promote change
> Be an active member of university teams
> Solve problems
> Make suggestions
> Energize the quality diversity environment

(4) Ownership: You feel ownership as you are empowered to improve the organization, see your suggestions lead to performance improvement and are recognized for your effort. This is the highest stage of the faculty and staff learning process. At this stage one:

> Encourages team improvements
> Recognizes achievement
> Rewards success
> Shares benefits

Suggestions for Faculty Actions

These questions promote self-reflection and discussion among faculty:

Have I created an environment that is equally welcoming of all students or have I made some students feel uncomfortable and isolated?

Have I developed a pedagogy (regardless of course content) that allows students with differing experiences to be successful in my classes?

Have I reviewed the content of my courses and of my advising of students with an eye to promoting the institutionís diversity goals?

Have I engaged in faculty development activities related to diversity, given that my formal training may not have exposed me to diversity-related issues?

Have I worked with my departmental colleagues and with my profession to create an environment that promotes diversity?

Many people in the United States express discomfort dealing with diversity-related issues and with people different from themselves. What have I done to reduce my own and others' discomfort?

Have I created an environment that is equally welcoming of all students or have I made some students feel uncomfortable and isolated?

Use language to describe students and their relationships that is equally applicable to all students who may be enrolled in your class. Many students may be younger than you are, but many students are not "kids."

Students use time at the beginning of the semester to figure out what their new professors are like. If you want to be welcoming to a diverse group of students, try to use examples that draw on diverse peoples and cultures early in the semester.

While faculty often view their offices as private or personal space, the décor of offices can communicate messages of inclusiveness or exclusiveness to students. The same holds true with dress. Dress and other forms of decoration can, students tell us, accentuate or reduce the social distance between faculty and students. Posters reflecting diversity strike some faculty as silly or faddish; faculty need to recognize that some students read such artifacts as statements in support of a diverse student body.

Students report that faculty sometimes unintentionally make offensive comments in class (about, for example, women or people of color or gay people). We as a faculty will only know this if we make it clear to students that we are willing to discuss with any of them events in class that they find disturbing. We may find it necessary to apologize for statements we have made, even if they are made with the best intentions or in an effort to use humor to clarify a complex point.

React decisively when you see instances of prejudice or discrimination. Some people believe that silence is neutral, that silence is simply not acting. It is, in fact, acting to perpetuate that prejudice or discrimination.

Have I developed a pedagogy (regardless of course content) that allows students with differing experiences to be successful in my classes?

Do not expect any one student to enjoy being asked to speak for the entire group. While some students seem to be proud of or grateful for the chance to introduce the "minority" perspective to class discussion, others are altogether uncomfortable when additional attention is drawn to them.

Further, no one — regardless of the level of sophistication or knowledge — can speak for an entire group.

Do not expect your students to perform well (or poorly) as a function of their group membership. Most, if not all of us, developed group stereotypes as we grew up. We need to be mindful of those that work to undermine students' learning and success. (For example, do we communicate to female students our expectation that they will have difficulty with quantitative material? Do we expect Asian-American students to have no difficulty with the same material?)

As appropriate to your content area, develop differing teaching styles. Even though evidence on differences in learning styles by group is not conclusive in many disciplines, varying the way in which class time is used (e.g., not always lecturing) may help ensure that a course does not favor one way of achieving mastery of content over another.

Develop assignments or class projects that promote discussion and interchange among a diverse group of students— for example, panel discussions, group discussions. Create an environment where all students can learn from one another and can acknowledge the contributions that are made to the discussion.

Find ways of humanizing your classroom so that individual students see one another as individuals rather than as merely the representatives of groups (with whom they might not feel comfortable). For example, consider icebreakers that encourage students to know other names and encourage them to know something about one another's backgrounds and interests.

As you ask students for evaluations of your classes and your teaching, ask for comments related to diversity. For example, ask students for their opinion about your sensitivity to diversity. All of us "believe" that we are sensitive to these issues, but our students may have different perceptions that are real, too. The feelings that students have about our classes and us are never themselves "wrong," but we might not understand them. We need to ask what makes them feel the way they do, and then listen to what they have to say.

> *Have I reviewed the content of my courses and of my advising of students with an eye to promoting the institution's diversity goals?*

Integrate people from diverse backgrounds into the examples you use to explain course content. Before using such examples, however, reflect on whether you are inappropriately perpetuating stereotypes.

No one can be knowledgeable about cultures. Nonetheless, most of us have knowledge about some culture other than the dominant one. Draw on that experience to indicate to students that there are many cultures and that understanding diversity is important.

Create reading lists that draw on the contributions of scholars or practitioners from a variety of backgrounds and lifestyles, as is appropriate to your discipline.

Review the materials that you distribute and that you assign your students to read for bias against various groups. Textbooks, for example, may send subtle messages to students about who can and should pursue particular fields of study and who is and is not valuable and important.

Create assignments that encourage your students to attend university diversity functions sponsored by the university that are appropriate to your classes. Some faculty build such assignments into their course outlines, while others develop extra credit systems for participation in such events.

A variety of resource people exist both within and outside campuses to assist with diversifying the curriculum. Make use of the range of resources that are available such as affirmative action or diversity offices.

The belief that only a small number of people are knowledgeable about a particular culture can be insulting. Is the culture so exotic that it can only be understood by a handful of experts? Further, while individuals or groups are complimented by invitations to speak to classes on areas of their expertise, they often have other and competing commitments. Consequently, assume that there are many knowledgeable people about diversity and do not always rely on the same staff or student groups to speak to classes about given topics.

In introducing students to diverse cultures, recognize the full range of the culture, not just the material culture associated with food and dress. Acknowledge the existence of contemporary native cultures not just historical ones. (That is, Native Americans live among us; uniquely indigenous cultures continue regardless of where Western-style dress is found throughout the world.)

As you encourage students to become involved in campus diversity events, recognize the range of events available — not just the "big" ones. (For example, while Martin Luther King Jr.'s birthday receives considerable attention, academic speakers focusing on contemporary African-American life receive less.)

Encourage student research projects on topics related to diversity.

Give students some choice in selecting projects so that, if your coverage of material overlooks a particular perspective (from the student's point of view), the student will have an opportunity to "fill in the blanks."

As is appropriate to your discipline, provide assignments that help students recognize and challenge the stereotypes and assumptions they make about people different from themselves, with one desired outcome being increased cognitive complexity in thinking about others.

Make use of the diversity-related resources of the library and multicultural videos from the audiovisual services department.

Recommend electives to your majors, minors and advisees that expose them to diversity.

Find out about the diversity resources that are available on your campus, so that you can provide appropriate advice when you cannot solve a problem that a student presents to you. These may include office of diversity, multicultural center, office of campus life, international education office, office of disability services, women's resource center and the office of affirmative action.

*Have I engaged in faculty development activities related to
diversity, given that my formal training may not have
exposed me to diversity-related issues?*

Attend workshops sponsored by the office of campus life or the office of diversity that discuss ways of teaching students from diverse backgrounds.

Attend workshops and presentations at your campus that expose you to diversity-related issues that are appropriate to your discipline.

Consult with experts on campus who can assist you with developing teaching techniques that may be appropriate for diverse student populations.

Share your success stories with colleagues so that each of us is not reinventing the wheel or digging the same pit.

Establish peer support groups within your professional associations so that faculty can learn from one another about successful efforts to incorporate diversity into the classroom.

Attend sessions at conferences that will expose you to diversity-related issues, even if your main reason for attending the conference is the other sessions and events.

Apply for faculty teaching and program development grants to learn more about diversity issues relevant to your field of expertise.

*Have I worked with my departmental colleagues and with my
profession to create an environment that promotes diversity?*

Recruit a diverse faculty. Do not assume that printed material (that is, advertisements) is sufficient; use your social networks to learn of professionals from differing backgrounds in your field who may be on the job market.

Get to know the minority caucuses in your professional associations. They can help you identify resources for the classroom, help you recruit students and help you recruit a diverse faculty.

Support colleagues who experiment by using new teaching methods and who take risks by incorporating new material in classes. The narrative that accompanies a faculty member's application for reappointment, tenure or promotion can be used to explain to colleagues that rationale for using innovative teaching techniques or the logic of introducing new materials.

Encourage your colleagues to develop a multicultural curriculum for your students, as is appropriate to your field of study.

Recruit a diverse student body to your department by developing ties with student organizations, high schools and community colleges that draw on diverse student populations.

Establish a mentoring relationship with a student, faculty member or staff member who belongs to a group that is traditionally underrepresented in your field.

Encourage students from diverse backgrounds to pursue graduate study in your field and support students as they work through the application process.

Seek to broaden the mission statement and goals of your department or profession to make them more inclusive, if they are not already.

*Many people in the United States express discomfort dealing with
diversity-related issues and with people different from themselves.
What have I done to reduce my own and others' discomfort?*

Announce diversity functions in class so that your students are more inclined to view diversity as part of the future of American life rather than an oddity.

Serve as a role model to your students by attending the diversity functions you tell them about.

Attend diversity functions with your students as part of a class project or assignment. Your presence may make them feel more comfortable.

Acknowledge that understanding diversity is hard work. Show staff (and others) that you also learn and that you make mistakes. You can show how you wrestled with these issues— that mistakes can be made and that errors can be corrected.

Suggestions for Staff Action

The following questions are useful in promoting self-reflection and discussion by staff or administrators:

Have I created an environment that is equally welcoming of all staff and students or have I made some staff or students feel uncomfortable and isolated?

Have I engaged in staff development activities related to diversity, given that my background and formal training may not have exposed me to diversity-related issues?

Have I worked with my colleagues to create an environment that promotes diversity?

Many people in the United States express discomfort dealing with diversity-related issues and with people different from themselves. What have I done to reduce my own and others' discomfort?

Have I created an environment that is equally welcoming of all staff and students or have I made some staff or students feel uncomfortable and isolated?

Use language to describe staff of color and their relationships that is equally applicable to all staff at your college, university.

While staff often view their offices as private or personal space, the décor of offices can communicate messages of inclusiveness or exclusiveness to other staff. The same holds true with dress. Dress and other forms of decoration can, students tell us, accentuate or reduce the social distance between staff. The presence of posters and other such artifacts of diversity can help support diversity among and between staff.

Staff of color report that colleagues sometimes unintentionally make offensive comments in meetings (about, for example, women or people of color or gay people). We will only know this if we make it clear to colleagues that we are willing to discuss with any of them events that they find disturbing. We may find it necessary to apologize for statements we have made, even if they are made with the best intentions.

React decisively when you see instances of prejudice or discrimination. Some people believe that silence is neutral — that silence is simply not acting. It is, in fact, acting to perpetuate that prejudice or discrimination.

Have I engaged in staff development activities related to diversity, given that my background and formal training may not have exposed me to diversity-related issues?

Attend workshops sponsored by the office of human resource development that discuss ways of interacting with colleagues of color.

Attend workshops and presentations that expose you to diversity-related issues that are appropriate to your discipline and/or department.

Consult with experts on campus who can assist you with developing communication techniques that may be appropriate for a diverse staff.

Share your success stories with colleagues so that each of us is not reinventing the wheel or digging the same pit.

Establish peer support groups at your campus or within your professional associations so that you can learn from one another about successful efforts to incorporate diversity into the workplace.

Attend sessions at conferences that will expose you to diversity-related issues, even if your main reason for attending the conference is other sessions or events.

Have I worked with colleagues to create an environment that promotes diversity?

Recruit a diverse staff. Do not assume that printed material (that is, advertisements) is sufficient; use your social networks to learn of professionals from differing backgrounds in your field who may be on the job market.

Get to know the minority caucuses in your professional associations. They can help you identify resources that will help you recruit a diverse staff.

Encourage your colleagues to develop a multicultural training program, as is appropriate to your department.

Recruit a diverse staff to your department by developing ties with organizations and schools that draw on diverse populations.

Establish a mentoring relationship with a staff member from a group that is traditionally underrepresented in your department.

Seek to broaden the mission statement and goals of your department or profession to make them more inclusive if they are not already.

Many people in the United States express discomfort dealing with
diversity-related issues and with people different from themselves.
What have I done to reduce my own and others' discomfort?

Announce diversity functions in meetings so that your staff are more inclined to view diversity as part of the future of American life rather than an oddity.

Serve as a role model to other staff by attending the diversity functions you tell them about.

Acknowledge that understanding diversity is hard work. Show staff (and others) that you also learn and that you make mistakes. You can show how you wrestled with these issues— that mistakes can be made and that errors can be corrected.

Conclusion

Despite a small but vocal cadre of critics, there is ample evidence that colleges across America are committed to reinvigorating diversity programs on campuses to address issues of our increasingly diverse and interconnected world. They are doing so to serve the long honored mission of higher education to explore fundamental questions and submit both previous assumptions and established traditions to vigorous examinations. And they do so to serve the societal needs of our nation and our world. Through such transformed institutional leadership, faculty and staff involvement, curriculum, student roles and campus community connection, higher education is creating diverse and respectful campus communities which are vehicles for creating a more equitable society. These new emerging diverse campus communities have become for many students what Maxine Green calls "democratic spaces of possibility" as students learn how to move from a contact zone of a single familiar community to a contact zone of communities, ideas and people that are different. There is growing evidence that these kinds of communities actually help students recognize unfinished agendas of equality and enhance their commitment to forging stronger, more just broader communities. As Carol Schneider has forcefully argued:

> Higher education is uniquely positioned, by its mission, values, and dedication to learning, to foster and nourish the habits of hearts and minds that Americans need to make diversity work in daily life. We have an opportunity to help our campuses experience an engagement across difference as a valued and public good.... Formed as we are by the academy's

strong tradition of intellectual and social pluralism, higher education faces a rich opportunity to put our own commitments to learning at the nation's service.

References

Adelman, Clifford. "Diversity: Walk the Walk, and Drop the Talk." *Change* 29 (1997): 35–45.

Alger, Jonathan R., et al. "Does Diversity Make a Difference? Three Research Studies on Diversity in College Classrooms." Academe 77 (200): 54–57.

Elway Research, Inc. 1998. Campus Diversity Initiative Survey of Washington Businesses, Seattle, WA: Ford Foundation,1998.

Gardner, John W. "Building Community." *Kettering Review* (1989): n. pag. Rpt. Ch. 11. *On Leadership.* New York: Free, 1990.

Gardenswartz, Lee, and Anita Rowe. *Four Layers of Diversity: A Complete Desk Reference and Planning Guide.* Rev. ed. New York: McGraw-Hill, 1998.

Greene, Maxine. "Diversity and Inclusion: Toward a Curriculum for Human Being." *Teachers College Record* 95. 2 (1993) : 211–21.

McTighe, Carolyn, et al. *To Form a More Perfect Union.* Washington, D.C.: Association of American Colleges and Universities, 1999.

Midamba, Noah O. *Kent State University Diversity Implementation Plan 2001–2005 — A Framework to Foster Diversity at Kent State University's Eight-Campus System.* Kent State Univ. 2001.

Milem, Jeffrey F., and Kenji Hakuta. "The Benefit of Racial and Ethnic Diversity in Higher Education." *American Council on Higher Education (ACE).* 7th Annual Status Report on Minority in Higher Education. Washington, DC: ACE, 2000. N. pag.

Musil, Cary McTighe, et al. *To Form a More Perfect Union: Campus Diversity Issues.* Washington, DC: Assoc. of American Colleges and Universities, 1999.

Schneider, Carol Geary, and Lee Knefelkamp. "Education for a World Lived in Common with Others." *Education and Democracy: Re-Imagining Liberal Learning in America.* Ed. Robert Orrill. New York: The College Board, 1997. 327–45.

Smith, Daryl G., et al. *Diversity Works: The Emerging Picture of How Students Benefit.* Washington, DC: Assoc. of American Colleges, 1997.

_____. "Organizational Implications of Diversity in Higher Education." *Diversity in Organizations: New Perspectives for a Changing Workplace.* Eds. Martin M. Chemers, Stuart Oskamp, and Mark A. Costanza. Thousand Oaks, CA: Sage, 1995. 220–25.

UNESCO General Conference. *Universal Declaration of Cultural Diversity.* 31st Session. 15 Oct.–3 Nov. 2001.

3

Veiled Diversity: A New Look at What Diversity Means Within the Academy

Michelle McCoy

As we gain momentum in promoting diversity initiatives regarding race within the academy, we are, at the same time, faced with multiple challenges as our nation becomes more culturally plural. One needs only to conduct a brief observation of our students in order to acknowledge their identifiable differences within the halls of academe. Clearly, one can somewhat ascertain differences in race, physical disabilities, gender and age. But the true challenge lies in recognizing types of diversity that are not so obvious.

Discussion of these other differences is not to undermine race as being at the core of the foundation of the "diversity movement" in this country. Scholar of diversity and women's studies Peggy McIntosh (1989) formulated an important question: "Having described white privilege, what will I do to end it?" (12). Clearly, race remains the dominant issue in facing diversity.

During the earlier years of the American Association of University Women (AAUW), there were no women of color who were registered members. In 1946, the organization was forced to change its membership policies to allow women of color into the organization because one branch refused to accept a membership application from an African-American woman. Since then, AAUW has modified its membership criteria, allowing for more inclusion (Levine 1995).

3. Veiled Diversity (McCoy) 47

During the 1990s, AAUW conducted national studies and discovered that its definition of diversity needed to be broadened in order to accurately reflect its membership population; thus, a more encompassing definition was incorporated, embracing various elements of diversity that are not so apparent:

> In principle and practice, AAUW values and seeks a diverse membership. There shall be no barriers to full participation in this organization on the basis of gender, race, creed, age, sexual orientation, national origin, disability, or class [AAUW].

According to AAUW's executive director, Jackie Woods (2001), this new definition is more inclusive, allowing underrepresented groups to identify with multicultural institutions; however, even as the definition expands, there always will be some constituents who feel abandoned. Nevertheless, if these minority groups can "attach" themselves to one of the terms within the definition, they feel accepted.

Colleges and universities echo AAUW's sentiment. Professor Sylvia Hurtado (1999) of the University of Michigan said, "Colleges and universities that have adopted a proactive commitment to student diversity have done so because they understand how their central mission is linked with the future of a diverse society" (10). Obviously, demographics will vary from one institution to another, but acknowledging the makeup of a university's student body, faculty and staff could be the first step to developing an accurate understanding to creating a more current, comprehensive definition of diversity.

Again, some elements of diversity will be difficult to unearth. For example, a student with a "hidden" impairment such as a learning disability would be difficult for others to recognize because of the current laws in place that protect the individual's privacy regarding disclosure. Conversely, those individuals with more discernible disabilities, such as physical limitations or apparent aging, share a commonality with stereotypes that other underrepresented groups experience.

Program coordinator of dialogues on diversity at the University of Michigan Pat McCune (2001) commented, "Like students of color, those who can be identified at a glance as physically different experience assumptions about inferior intellectual capacity" (9). We can, however, strive to learn about these types of diversity, allowing for us to better understand how the individuals might feel in various situations.

Consider how today's journalism students must learn how to address various groups. Would they write about "Oriental" students or "Asian" students? Should they say "handicapped" or "disabled?" Which is more appropriate: African-American or Black? Would a reporter choose to address someone as an elderly person or as a senior citizen?

This process of understanding how to label various groups is dynamic, and will continue to evolve as society dictates. More importantly, our willingness to recognize veiled forms of differences can be within our own academy's definition of diversity.

The Poynter Institute (2001), known as the think tank for journalists, also expands its teachings to focus on the following "five under-covered issues: Race/Ethnicity, Religion/Faith, Sexual Orientation, Gender and Race Relations" (9). The goal of the institute is to teach journalists how to handle different aspects of diversity so they maintain elements of accuracy and objectivity. Consider that if journalists do not accurately reflect their surrounding communities, including a thorough assessment of the cultural makeup of their audiences, they may be in danger of not only being socially irresponsible, but also inaccurate.

Moreover, the academy should be socially responsible, too, in acknowledging its cultural landscape. A group of researchers of Claremont Graduate University (2000) concluded that enough evidence shows that serious engagement and recognition of diversity within the academy has a positive impact on racial issues and also provides opportunities for those who consider themselves "different."

Perhaps academicians can remove the "veil" from all diverse groups so we can genuinely create and acknowledge a true picture of what true diversity means in the new millennium. In 1997, at AAUW's national symposia proceedings, western states director of "A World of Difference Institute" in Los Angeles, California, Debra Stogel, explained why "A Campus of Difference" program was created. She said some of the program's goals were to examine the stereotypes that prevailed at college campuses. Also, once discrimination issues were identified, dialogue could then be encouraged via faculty, staff and students on how to resolve the problems and discuss how diversity enhances the environment.

Professors Elizabeth Torre Reck and Judith Lewis (1997) of Tulane University comment on the new realities of America's diverse ethnic composition:

> As American society continues to become more racially, ethnically and culturally diverse, so do student bodies in our universities and colleges. As a result, today's students experience escalating pressure in the classroom and outside the classroom to respond to often confusing complexities associated with gender, race, class and culture. An increase in central challenge for teachers in higher education is how to create learning environments and curricula that encourage students to explore

themes and issues arising out of this shift in the ethnic composition of America and equip them for living and working in a multicultural world [139].

Therefore, we must remove our own veils to allow for total inclusion in what could constitute a true definition of diversity, one which actually reflects the landscape of each academy in this nation.

References

The American Association of University Women. Washington, DC: American Assoc of University Women, 2000.

Beliak, Haim, et al. *Diversity Works: The Emerging Picture of How Students Benefit — An Executive Summary.* 6 June 2000. Featured Mono. <http//www.aacu.org/Publications/featuredmono.html>.

Hurtado, Sylvia. "How Diversity Affects Teaching and Learning: A Climate of Inclusion Has a Positive Effect on Learning Outcomes." *Educational Record* 10 (1996): 27–29.

Levine, Susan. *Degrees of Equality: The American Association of University Women and the Challenge of Twentieth-Century Feminism.* Philadelphia: Temple UP, 1995.

McCune, Pat. "What Do Disabilities Have to Do with Diversity?" *About Campus* (May/June 2001): 1–32.

McIntosh, Peggy. "White Privilege: Unpacking the Invisible Knapsack." *Peace and Freedom* (July/August, 1989): 12.

"Poynter Web Site Features Diversity." *Diversity Digest* Winter 2001: 9.

Stogel, Debra. "Combating Prejudice in Campus Communities." Gender and Race on the Campus and in the School: Beyond Affirmative Action. Symposium Proceedings. College/University Symposium, AAUW. June 1997.

Smith, Daryl G. *Diversity Works: The Emerging Picture of How Students Benefit.* Washington, DC: Assoc. of American Colleges, 1997.

Torre Reck, Elizabeth, and Judith S. Lewis. "Lessons in Identity: A Strategy of Cultural Diversity Learning among Social Work Students." Gender and Race on the Campus and in the School: Beyond Affirmative Action. Symposium Proceedings. College/University Symposium, AAUW. June 1997.

Woods, Jackie. Executive Director's Welcoming Remarks. Presentation at the Association Convention of the American Association of University Women. Austin, Texas. June 2001.

4
From Jackie Robinson to Sammy Sosa: Baseball and Race in America

STANTON W. GREEN

Introduction

I would like to begin by suspending time for a moment. Imagine it is July 31st 2001— the inter-league trading deadline in major league baseball. The Boston Red Sox are looking for a catcher to replace the injured Jason Varitek. Dan Duqette is in his skybox on his cell phone with 11 teams. He finds that Josh Gibson is available along with Doug Mirabelli. He signs Doug Mirabelli. The Yankees, trying to compete with the Red Sox and replace some of their injured players, are looking for a starting pitcher. Satchel Paige and Sterling Hitchcock are available. They trade for Hitchcock.

The reasons for these seemingly unreasonable decisions are as obvious as the color of the skin of the ballplayers. Indeed, if baseball were played and managed the way it was through the mid–twentieth century, these decisions would have made sense since the availability of superstars such as Josh Gibson and Satchel Paige — arguably the best catcher and pitcher to ever play baseball — would have depended upon breaking the racial taboo of mixing black men and white men on the ballfield. The strength of the racial divide in American society was strong enough to overwhelm the credo of American sports (and indeed society)— that is to put the best team forward. America as a "Country of Strangers," as David

51

K. Shipler so eloquently describes it, defines the people who play America's pastime — the game of baseball.

In earlier papers (Green, 2001; 2002), I have explored the role baseball has played over the past century in defining what it is to be an American and about the ways in which baseball has contributed to constructing an American Identity. In this paper, I want to extend this into a discussion of baseball and race in America. Most specifically and to the point, I will explore the impacts the game of baseball as America's pastime has had on African-Americans during the twentieth century and the impacts racism has had on baseball itself.

Much is expected of America's pastime. Baseball's past is not only significant as history, but like all history, it affects how we behave in the present. About a month before he was killed, Martin Luther King, Jr. visited Don Newcombe, the great African-American Brooklyn Dodger pitcher and a teammate of Jackie Robinson. At dinner, Dr. King thanked the ballplayers saying, "Don, you and Jackie and Roy [Campanella] will never know how easy you made it to do my job" (Aaron, 1991, p. 194). The symbolic and political power of baseball infuses American culture and this has been especially true with regard to the issue of race.

Mr. Shipler's journalistic perspective in *A Country of Strangers* offers the personal views of people from a variety of places and settings in the United States. I shall complement this approach through an examination of two autobiographies which portray what it was and still is like to be a black baseball player. What immediately struck me as I read the biographies of Henry Aaron and Joe Morgan was how the facts of being black and being a ballplayer were inextricably bound. In simple words, for African-Americans, it is not possible to be simply a ballplayer — it is possible to be only a black ballplayer. Aaron's and Morgan's autobiographies go well beyond the superficial reports of game-by-game, season-by-season accounts. They offer insight into the culture of baseball and the intertwining of baseball and American culture especially with regard to race and racism.

As an anthropologist, my examination of American society focuses on the role of culture as it defines group values, attitudes and behaviors. My title "From Jackie Robinson to Sammy Sosa" expresses the cultural-historical framework of my argument. Jackie Robinson is rightly credited with breaking the color barrier in baseball. Although Larry Doby and many other athletes shortly followed him, Robinson was the point man for the integration movement. He took the abuse hurled at him by those who were mired in segregation and Jim Crow and showed leadership throughout his life to further social justice in baseball and society-at-large (S. Robinson, 2002).

Sammy Sosa's coming of age in 1998 during his home run race with Mark McGwire provides a chronological mark for judging just how far baseball (and American society) has come since Jackie Robinson was rookie of the year in 1947.

Integrating Baseball

It is important to remember that Jackie Robinson was not the first black professional ballplayer and indeed there was never an official ban on black ballplayers in major league baseball. Black ballplayers participated in professional baseball during the nineteenth century. Moses Fleetwood Walker, the last of the ballplayers, played in the American Association, considered a major professional league in the late–nineteenth century. By the turn of the twentieth century, racial segregation had infused baseball so that even owners who were inclined to sign black ballplayers could not do so. There were attempts to get around the exclusion of black ballplayers during the early 1900s. John McGraw tried to pass off Frank Grant, a black man, as Charlie Totkahama, a Cherokee, and Connie Mack apparently considered signing black ballplayers but decided not to fight prevailing attitudes. So in the end, segregation persevered until Jackie Robinson and Larry Doby signed for the 1947 season (Peterson, 1970; Moffit and Kronstadt, 1994).

It is also important to remember that Robinson's breakthrough in 1947 did not lead to a rush to sign black ballplayers. Shortly after Jackie Robinson signed with the National League's Brooklyn Dodgers, Larry Doby became the first black ballplayer in the American League when he signed with the Cleveland Indians. But very gradual integration and much resistance followed these signings. Over a decade and a half was necessary before every major league team had at least one black ballplayer and spring training facilities were integrated. We often think of 1947 as the year baseball was integrated. It is important to understand integration as a slow, long-term and ongoing process as David Shipler does.

The year Jackie Robinson began as a Brooklyn Dodger, he was not allowed to play in an exhibition game in Sanford, Florida. In fact, in 1963, the spring training accommodations in Pompano, Orlando, and West Palm Beach were still segregated. This means that the Washington Senators, Detroit Tigers, and Kansas City Athletics still lived in segregated quarters. Dodgertown itself was only integrated in 1949. The Dodgers were followed a decade later by the integration of the spring training facilities of the Braves in 1959, and the St. Louis Cardinals and Chicago White Sox in 1961.

The integration of spring training in Florida was in large part the result of the work of several prominent ballplayers and the African-American sportswriter Wendell Smith (Carroll, 2001). Smith had worked for the *Pittsburgh Courier* in the 1940s and indeed had set up a try-out for 3 Negro League players with the Red Sox in 1945. The tryout, as it turned out, was a publicity stunt and this was certainly made clear by the fact that the Red Sox were the last team to add a black ballplayer to their team when Pumpsie Green was sent in to pinch run in a game during the 1959 season. Smith had also traveled with Jackie Robinson to help him secure private housing during road trips.

On January 23 and February 6, 1961, Smith published two articles in the *Chicago American* that activated public opinion against segregated spring training. Titled "Negro Players Want Dixie Rights," Smith publicized the indignities black ballplayers had to endure during their training in Florida (Carroll, 2001). Earlier on, in 1959 and 1961, Henry Aaron and Bill White had aired these complaints about the treatment of black ballplayers and their families. Wendell Smith took the story to the public. Shortly after these articles were published, Bill Veeck bought the hotel his team stayed in in Sarasota to integrate it. That same season the Yankees broke their 36-year relationship with their St. Petersburg hotel and facilities after the hotel refused to integrate. They moved their training facilities to Ft. Lauderdale. The point again is that the integration of baseball was a slow and politically charged process that took over a decade and a half to take hold.

The 1971 All-Star Game offers an excellent example of the politics of baseball integration. The rosters for the game indicate the contributions the first generations of African-American and Latino ball players were making to major league baseball. The All-Star roster for that year included 27 African-American and Latino ballplayers including 8 of 18 starters. The teams included such future Hall of Famers as Henry Aaron, Luis Aparicio, Roberto Clemente, Willie Mays, Frank Robinson, Lou Brock, Juan Marichal, Willie McCovey and Willie Stargell. Yet even this celebration was marked by racial tension. After the American League manager Earl Weaver named the African-American pitcher Vida Blue as his starting pitcher, a question immediately arose. Would the National League manager Sparky Anderson name Doc Ellis, another African-American, to start for the National League? The symbolism and honor of starting in the midsummer classic is steeped in baseball history. It is a major honor to be named starting pitcher for the All-Star Game. Pitching is a special position in baseball, which has been beyond the glass ceiling for non-white players (much the same as quarterbacking was until recently in the NFL).

It wasn't until 1965 that Juan Marichal became the first black pitcher to start an All-Star Game. Luis Tiant the first black starter for the American League all-stars followed him 3 years later in 1968.

Doc Ellis, an outspoken all-star that year, confronted the controversy directly in an interview in the *New York Times*. He asserted, "They wouldn't pitch two brothers against each other" ("The 1971 All-Star Game," 2001, n. pag). Ellis received a lot of negative mail for his comments, but among his supportive correspondence was a letter from Jackie Robinson. Robinson told Ellis that he was proud of him for having spoken up. And as it turned out, Anderson chose Ellis to start the game. Anderson insisted that Ellis was chosen not because of the controversy, but "because of his [Ellis'] 14–3 won-loss record." The ambivalence of America's race relations was surely evident in this instance.

Baseball and American Culture

The cultural connectivity between baseball and American culture is why baseball remains America's pastime (*Baseball*, 2002; Hofstetter 2002). Baseball holds much cultural power. It has been played by presidents since George Washington, and credited by America's poet, Walt Whitman, as America's game (Folsom 1994; *Baseball*, 2002). Baseball is not just a passive reflector of American society; it is an active ingredient. It has, for example, played an active and positive role in assimilating immigrants and socializing youth into adults throughout the twentieth century and it continues to do so today (Reiss 1980). It has also played a role in the racial tensions of America between the ideals of social justice argued by our founding fathers and American racism reflected by the founding fathers' ownership of slaves.

In Hank Aaron's autobiography, *I Had a Hammer*, Aaron's co-author, Lonnie Wheeler, charges baseball with the responsibility to live up to American ideals:

> As the great populist sport, baseball has obligations. Its mandate calls for more than reluctant pragmatism; it calls for conscience, vision, and rolled-up sleeves. It calls for the national pastime to be an example, to give back something that really matters, and, most urgently, to deliver on the trust that is bestowed upon an August, metaphoric, and inherently public institution [303].

The 1997 celebration of the 50th anniversary of Jackie Robinson's crossing baseball's color line revealed the mixed results of baseball's last half-century with regard to social justice. The celebration of Jackie Robinson as a civil rights hero was, I believe, genuine and strong. His number 42 was retired in all of baseball — an accolade never before or since given to anyone in the game. His work and life were celebrated in ways meant to pass on his words and deeds to a new generation and new millennium. At the same time several commentators noted that Jackie's team the 1997 Los Angeles Dodgers, had no African-American starting players. Although the irony — some might argue the hypocrisy — of this situation is quite clear, there are several lessons to be learned in this observation.

The first is a benign interpretation: The transition from Jackie Robinson and Don Newcombe and their European-American teammates of the 1947–1949 Dodgers to Jose Vizcaino, Ramon Martinez, Chan Ho Park and Hideo Nomo of the 1997 Dodgers is clearly consistent with the immigration pattern of the later twentieth century. A recent news report indicated that 25 percent of MLB ballplayers are foreign-born, as quoted by *Infobeat.* Today's immigration pattern incorporates large areas of Latin America and Asia and again baseball and culture seem to go hand in hand as Asians and Latin Americans follow the sport into American society. In the current case, it is the immigrants themselves who are playing ball, and in some cases they are coming explicitly to do so. Cuban-Americans cheer Cuban ballplayers, such as the brothers Livan and Orlando Hernandez, in much the same way that Italian-Americans cheered such players as Tony Lazzeri, Ernie Lombardi and Joe DiMaggio (Baldarasso, 1998) and the Jews heralded Hank Greenberg and Sandy Koufax (Dorinson, 1998). Latin American and Asian major league ballplayers and their fans are becoming part of baseball's next generation. Seattle Mariners games are broadcast live to Japan so that Japanese fans can follow Ichiro Suzuki. Indeed the ethnic pride of these ballplayers was emotionally illustrated at the Hall of Fame induction of Orlando Cepeda. Cepeda spoke of how proud he was to be the second Puerto Rican Hall of Fame inductee as well as how proud he was in being a black Latin American.

The second interpretation for why there were no African-American ballplayers in the Dodgers' 1997 starting lineup is less benign. It reflects quite directly the continued discrimination and the diminishing role of African-Americans in baseball during the latter part of the twentieth century (Treder, 2002, pp. 71–101). The decrease in African-American ballplayers and the small number in management indicate how American class structure and racism perpetuates a pattern of immigrants socially supplanting African-Americans. African-Americans are allowed to go so far and no farther into the American mainstream and baseball is consistent with this broader societal pattern. In baseball the management glass ceiling is at first base and hitting coach.

In an ESPN panel discussion entitled *Race and Sports* in 1996, it was remarkable that baseball, Jackie Robinson's professional sport, was the least engaged of all the represented sports in the issue of minority access to sports participation and especially management. Indeed, the one baseball franchise owner on the panel seemed to be taken aback when Joe Morgan, Hall-of-Fame second-baseman of the Cincinnati Reds, brought up the question of why inner-city kids are not being recruited into baseball while those from Japan and Korea were being heavily recruited. The club owner seemed genuine in his surprise that this was an issue and asked Joe Morgan to recommend how the situation could be improved. Joe Morgan responded by suggesting the obvious— support inner-city baseball and recruit American minority ballplayers.

To major league baseball's credit, it has responded to this criticism. Major league baseball is now supporting inner-city baseball leagues. And this year, MLB granted $250,000 to a team of baseball researchers from SABR's Negro leagues research committee to collect statistics from the Negro leagues. This grant will be used to collect and validate the statistics of over 4000 players and 9000 games from the years between 1920 and 1950. This seemingly academic project will have significant political clout because it will for the first time allow people to verify the statistics of Negro league players so that they can be rightly placed and judged within professional baseball standards. As Shipler notes, a history of exclusion is an incomplete and untruthful history:

> Most readers of this book will not have known that black Americans were colleagues of Bell and Edison, invented ingenious machines and labor saving devices, fought at San Juan Hill, helped tame the western wilderness, starred in rodeos, made an early flight from coast to coast, and helped shape American horse racing. And that lack of knowledge simply proves a point: In white memory, which has been the dominant memory, blacks are usually absent. They just do not figure in the American story, except as slaves, as reminders of guilt. And nobody likes to be reminded of guilt [11].

Most readers of Shipler's book are probably unaware that Josh Gibson, Satchel Paige, "Double-Duty" Ratcliffe and Pop Lloyd were colleagues of Babe Ruth, Ty Cobb and Walter Johnson.

The credibility of Negro league ballplayers has always been challenged because of the lack of systematic statistics. Josh Gibson's 800-plus home runs have always been questioned. At best he has been named the black Babe Ruth. Could it be that Babe Ruth was the White Josh Gibson? The verification of Negro league statistics will lend some objectivity to this racially divided debate. Most generally and profoundly it will make our histories more accurate — a requirement for the kind of truly multicultural and complete understanding that historians such as Ronald Takaki (1993) have been calling for in order to break down the walls of prejudice. The Hall of Fame has just this year agreed to await this study in order to come up with a more equitable way to judge Negro league ballplayers for their induction into Cooperstown. It is a great pity that this comes after most Negro league players have passed on (the youngest Negro leaguers are now in their mid–70s).

Culture and Racial Stereotypes

David Shipler's work illustrates the issues of culture and race in America through his interviewing and reporting. As an anthropologist, I want to briefly address these two concepts as an introduction to my discussion of Henry Aaron's and Joe Morgan's autobiographies.

Culture is often used as a catchall (pun intended) term to characterize a group of people. It is more precisely defined by anthropologists in two ways. *Culture with an upper case C* describes the ways people think and behave through symbolic learning and language (as opposed to the trial-and-error and imitative learning upon which most other animal species rely). People can and do construct their worlds through symbols— and quite significantly these can and usually do include ways of categorizing groups of people based on physical and behavioral characteristics. Racial categories are a prime and most pertinent example of a social category constructed via symbols and language.

Culture with a lower case c describes the shared experiences and lifestyles of particular societies and groups within societies. Notions of right and wrong (values), desired qualities (ethics), dispositions toward persons and things (attitudes) and the acceptable behaviors that go along with these serve to define a group's culture.

Racial categories are social categories whether they are externally defined or self-defined. They are ways of defining groups of people on the basis of physical characteristics; but of course they represent much deeper assumptions concerning cultural characteristics relating to values, attitudes, ethics, and behaviors and most significantly, inferred physical and intellectual abilities.

The stereotypes of "smart" white players and "athletic" black players are well known. Shipler cites two of the most notorious cases of racial stereotyping in sports. The first one is Jimmy "the Greek" Snyder's comment on TV that "Blacks are better athletes to begin with because they are bred that way" (271). He also cites the comments of Al Campanis (GM of the Dodgers): "I truly believe they [blacks] must not have some of the necessities to be, let's say, a field manager or perhaps a GM" (271).

Both comments were explosive. It instantly cost Campanis his job and his reputation. The sensitivity of the racial divide in America made his comments totally unacceptable. Campanis tried to argue that he had been talking about professional training and not physical or mental abilities when he spoke of necessities. This argument was given no credence. It could be given no credence given the atmosphere of racial politics. I am not defending Campanis, but only noting, as Shipler does, the sensitivity that so quickly shows up when racial issues are brought to the public forum in the United States. Stereotypes are but a short step away from racial categories.

Henry Aaron, arguably the most talented and well-rounded player to play baseball, was often criticized for his lack of smarts and laziness. As he puts it:

> Because I was black, and because I never moved faster than I had to, and because I didn't speak the Ivy League English, I came into the league with an image of a backward country kid who could swing the bat and was lucky he didn't have to think too much.... After a while, the stories about me all seemed to adopt a similar theme — that I was just a simple colored boy [96].

It is interesting to compare the treatments of Joe DiMaggio and Henry Aaron. Both players were quiet and deliberate. Both were from very poor backgrounds. DiMaggio was known for not wasting any movement. Yet Joe DiMaggio was perceived as dignified and graceful and Aaron as slow-thinking and slow-moving (Aaron 149).

It is indeed a slippery slope between the social construction of race and the political oppression of racism. Let me explore some of these issues through very brief excerpts from two of baseball's best ballplayers who happen to be African-American, Henry Aaron and Joe Morgan.

Henry Aaron

Henry Aaron left his home in Mobile, Alabama, in 1952 when he was 19 years old. He traveled to Winston-Salem, North Carolina, where he was to join the Indianapolis Clowns, a professional Negro league baseball team. Never having been away from home, he was of course anxious. But his reminiscence of this first trip from home reflects much more than the homesickness of a teenager:

> I just sat there clutching my sandwiches, speaking to nobody, staring out the window at towns I'd never heard of. It was the first time in my life that I had been around white people. After a while I got up the courage to walk up and down the aisle a few times. I wanted to see what a dining car looked like, *and I needed somebody to tell me where I wasn't allowed to go* [author emphasis] [1].

It is worth repeating his last line: "I needed somebody to tell me where I wasn't allowed to go."

Henry Aaron, of course, went on to a career that is perhaps unparalleled by any field position player (non-pitcher) in baseball history. He played over 20 years, had a lifetime batting average of over 300 while holding records in RBI's and of course the hallowed career home-run record of 755 home runs. He hit at least 20 home runs in 20 consecutive seasons (no one else has done so in more than 14 seasons). Of course, it was in the early 1970s when he was chasing Babe Ruth's record of 715 home runs that he received most media coverage and when the racial tension in baseball and America hit the headlines. As Aaron put it, "The Ruth chase should have been the greatest time in my life but it was the worst. I couldn't believe there was so much hatred in the world" (4).

Some of you may have seen on television, or subsequent film, Aaron's 715th home run, which he hit in his home stadium in Atlanta. As he crossed home plate, his mother ran out to the field to hug him in what was one of the most moving moments in sports history. What one couldn't realize from watching this event was Mrs. Aaron's perspective on the situation. When she was asked about the incident she said that the primary reason she ran onto the field to hug her son was to protect him from an assassin. She was certain that someone was going to shoot him from the stands.

Throughout his career Aaron reflected on and reacted to American racism:

> Once the record was mine, I had to use it like a Louisville slugger. I believed and still do, that there was a reason why I was chosen to break the record. I feel it's my task to carry on where Jackie Robinson left off, and I only know of one way to go about it. It's the only way I've ever had of dealing with things like fastball and bigotry — keep swinging at them [4].

Hence, his nickname Hammerin' Hank and his self-titled autobiography, *I Had a Hammer.*

Henry Aaron considers himself a second-generation black ballplayer following the likes of Jackie Robinson, Larry Doby, Roy Campanella, and Don Newcombe. He is among the many black players who crossed over from the Negro leagues to the major leagues. The Negro league teams played a regular schedule but also barnstormed around the country often playing white major league teams in major league stadiums. They played in Latin America during the winter where they were warmly accepted into an integrated society. They played almost every day all year long. But the indignities that these players had to deal with when they were playing in "the land of the free" (as we are reminded by the *Star Spangled Banner* before every professional game) were almost unfathomable. Aaron reports on one game played in our nation's capital:

> We were rained out of a big Sunday doubleheader at Griffith Stadium in Washington. We had breakfast while we were waiting for the rain to stop and, I can still envision being with the [Indianapolis] Clowns in a restaurant behind Griffith Stadium and hearing them break all the plates in the kitchen after we were finished eating. What a horrible sound. Even as a kid, the irony of it hit me: Here we are in the capital in the land of freedom and equality and they had to destroy the plates that touched the forks that had been in the mouths of black men. If dogs had eaten off those plates, they'd have washed them [34].

Aaron's reflections on his career as a black ball player are full of these kinds of incidents and his insights into American Society. Early in his major league career he helped propel the Milwaukee Braves to the National League Pennant. He writes:

> The morning after [we won the pennant] there was a picture in the paper of my teammates. Most of them naturally were white. On the same front page was a picture of a riot in Little Rock, Arkansas. It seemed that Little Rock, like much of the South, wasn't leaping into the spirit of Brown vs. the Board of Education. The Wisconsin *CIO News* noticed the irony of both those pictures on the same page, just as I had. "Milwaukee's dusky Hank Aaron blasted the Braves into the World Series only a few hours after an insane mob of white Supremacists took the Stars and Stripes in Little Rock and tramped it on the ground of Central High School. Their cheers that are lifted to Negro ballplayers only dramatize the stupidity of the jeers that are directed at those few Negro kids trying to get a good education for themselves in Little Rock" [126]

Henry Aaron's contribution to baseball goes well beyond his play on the field. He continued his career in management of the Atlanta Braves organization. His work in this area has been largely ignored. Throughout his career as a player, Aaron worked closely with other players and mentored youngsters. He considers his ability as a teacher one of his greatest strengths. After he retired he was appointed director of player development for the Atlanta Braves. But as Joe Morgan (of whom I will be speaking shortly) notes, Aaron is rarely given credit for work in this position.

The Braves were the most dominant team in the National League during the 1990s. The media lauded the work of their manager Bobby Cox and general manager John Schuerholz for transforming the Braves from one of baseball's worst teams into one of its best. And both Cox and Schuerholz deserve credit. But one rarely if ever hears of Hank Aaron's work. As director of player development, he was the executive in charge of nurturing the great young talent that became the Braves of the 1990s. Indeed the Atlanta Braves went from last place to first in 1991 and have remained there for the past decade. The strength of their team relies on a rich farm system. Hank Aaron was the director of that farm system through 1991— the correlation of his work and the Braves' subsequent success seems to have been missed by the media.

Joe Morgan

Joe Morgan began his professional baseball career in 1963, a decade after Hank Aaron. His autobiography, like Aaron's, reflects on life being black and being a ballplayer. His first experience was in the segregated south in Moultrie, Alabama:

> It was always a struggle going from town to town, hotel to hotel, restaurant to restaurant. Even in those places where black people were allowed, there was still an underlying sense of being out of place. It was as though, without anyone saying it, a black player could just feel the silent judgments and objections to his presence. When you stayed in the same hotel with your teammates, why you went to a bar or a restaurant, there was always that unvoiced question, "Why is he here?"

Although he notes this racism as "much more subtle," an incident in the late 1980s, after he had retired from his Hall of Fame career, indicates the potential violence that always underlies this "subtlety."

On his way to a celebrity golf tournament in Tucson, he was waiting to change planes in LA airport. Beyond his celebrity as a ball player, Joe Morgan was by then one of baseball's most respected TV announcers. While his was sitting in the lounge, conversing with fans and signing autographs, he was accosted by an (unidentified) Los Angeles policeman who accused him of being a drug dealer. He was not allowed to get his identification from his baggage, and despite the fact that one of the people in the lounge identified Joe Morgan as a "broadcaster and a baseball star" he was handcuffed and taken into custody. He was eventually let go without apology. "Well, maybe you are who you say you are," the policeman said. Morgan sued LAPD and won.

From Jackie to Henry to Joe to Sammy

Although it is certainly true that things have improved since the days of segregated baseball, racial discrimination persists quite clearly in professional baseball. The decline of African-American ballplayers is one issue; the paucity of minority managers and absence of general managers and owners is as serious. The ideological strength of racial segregation is powerfully described in Neil Sullivan's 1992 *The Diamond Revolution*. Sullivan asserts that during the first half of the twentieth century racial bigotry overwhelmed the objective, the ideal, indeed the passion, of winning in major league baseball. MLB teams gave up the prospect of finding the best talent because that talent was black. I refer you back to my opening and ask you to conceptualize your favorite team without any black ballplayers. I would have to imagine a Yankee team without Derek Jeter, Bernie Williams, Alphonso Soriano, Jorge Posada, Orlando Hernandez, Mariano Rivera, among others. This past year, Barry Bonds would not have broken major league baseball's single-season home run record, nor would Bonds, Sammy Sosa, or Ken Griffey, Jr. be seen as a possible successor to Henry Aaron as the lifetime home-run king. Indeed, the career home run king would still be Babe Ruth.

The power of American apartheid is fictionally tested in Peter Rutkoff's *Shadowball*. Using the license of fiction, Rutkoff's novel explores the tension between racial segregation in baseball and the competitive spirit of Charles Comiskey, the owner of the Chicago White Sox in 1917. In a method similar to Derrick Bell's *Faces at the Bottom of the Well*, Rutkoff allows Comiskey to approach Pop Lloyd, the finest shortstop in the Negro leagues (and perhaps all of baseball), through a Jewish middleman and takes us through the tensions this creates. The primary tension he is exploring, of course, is that of racism and the fictional consequences of this situation. Rutkoff's words paint a real picture of twentieth-century segregation and the consequences are telling. (You will have to read the book to find out more.)

The costs of not integrating professional baseball were great for both black and white players alike. Sullivan notes the differences players like Oscar Charleton, "Smokey" Joe Williams, "Bullet" Rogan, Jose Mendez could have made on Ty Cobb's Detroit Tigers; or pitchers such as Satchel Paige,

Ted Trent, "Slim" Jones, or Bill Jackman could have made for the Pirates of the 1930s that featured the Waner brothers and Arky Vaughn. He notes the Pirates' "inept pursuit" of Josh Gibson at a time when they desperately needed catching help. Of course the same would be true if Ty Cobb were moved to play on a Negro League team (a pretty scary thought given Cobb's virulently racist attitude). Team quality and competitiveness were sacrificed to maintain the myth of white supremacy. Baseball provides a metaphor for the losses American society has taken as a result of being a "country of strangers."

Another issue is the impact of integration on the Negro leagues. Over the course of 30 years, Negro league baseball had become integral to black culture and society. And it was first-rate baseball. Once players started crossing over to major league baseball, the Negro leagues began to fail and many black ballplayers and workers in the industry of baseball lost their jobs. This situation parallels the impact integration had on black public schools, some of which is reported on by Shipler. Integration robbed black communities of their neighborhood schools, deprived many black teachers of their jobs and basically consolidated education into the white version of public schooling. I came across this first-hand. When I first moved to Columbia, South Carolina, in 1971, I noticed a number of abandoned schools. One of these was just 2 or 3 blocks from my home, while my children were zoned into schools several miles away. I came to realize that the abandoned schools were the archaeological artifacts of the segregation period of the South. My neighborhood school had been a black school and hence it was abandoned when integration was forced upon the state of South Carolina.

How Far Has Baseball Come?

How far has baseball advanced since Robinson and Doby broke the color barrier? Let's look at the McGwire-Sosa home run race of 1998.

The quest to break Roger Maris' 37-year-old home run record was lauded as a national celebration. At least part of the reason for this was the relationship that developed between a white American suburban kid, Mark McGwire, and a black Latin-American immigrant, Sammy Sosa, and the leadership they both exhibited. There was much pride taken in the home-run race as a competition between the two talented ballplayers without regard to race or ethnicity. But there always seemed to be tension in the way Americans viewed this relationship between a white man and a black man. On the one hand, the camaraderie between these two players was broadcast as a lesson of brotherhood. On the other hand, the underlying tension of who was going to make it to 62 first — the white man or the black man — seemed always to be lurking. When McGwire broke the record first, the Maris family was present to congratulate him along with the commissioner of baseball and the National League president. But the same did not occur when Sosa crossed the threshold. History seemed to be repeating itself. The commissioner of baseball at the time, Bowie Kuhn, was not present at the games when Aaron tied and broke Babe Ruth's lifetime record of 714 home runs. Rather remarkably, Kuhn begged off from these games to attend an event at the Cleveland Indians' Wahoo Club (another subplot of American racism in baseball).

In 1998, people were attuned to the racial questions surrounding the McGwire-Sosa race. People asked why McGwire was so focused on it. Was it, they speculated, because he was first or because he was white? Was it because he was an American (in the United States-born sense)? Was it because of Sosa's Spanish dialect? Not far beneath the surface of brotherhood was a subtext of race, American-style.

One response to this situation was Sammy Sosa's. During a nationally televised press conference, Sosa was asked who was "the Man" in baseball. He proudly proclaimed: "McGwire is the man in the US and I am the man in the Dominican Republic." His good humor and astute cultural sense diffused the tension by his momentarily "migrating" from the US back to his native country. Sosa made it unnecessary to compare a black immigrant with a white native. His comments reflected both Sosa's genuine desire to keep the home-run race free from the social race, yet his comments also acknowledged the cultural and racial differences between him and McGwire and the difficulty Americans have with race and ethnicity.

Baseball and Chicago responded loudly to Sosa's comment. Sammy Sosa Day was celebrated in Chicago where the Maris family showed up and Sosa was given equivalent accolades (and gifts) to McGwire. The fact that McGwire was first to break the record was ignored (as much as it could be) to acknowledge the incredible feat of both men. I believe that Sosa himself should be given much of the credit for maintaining the positive course of this situation and for finding a way to help white America deal with its racist subconscious.

The home-run race, to my mind, illustrates both the problems Americans have with race as well as the hope that these problems can be worked through if smart and genuine people work to do so.

During the 2001 season, Barry Bonds, an African-American ballplayer, broke McGwire's record by hitting an amazing 73 home runs. After the season was over, Bonds revealed the disquieting fact that indeed his life had been threatened in much the same way as Henry Aaron's had. He received letters and phone calls telling him that we would be killed if he broke the home-run record. America's pastime, to some, remains to this day within the domain of white America. This is why it is so important to understand David Shipler's description of America as "a country of strangers" and to work to repair American history to make this nation inclusive of all Americans. When we bring black baseball into the memory of all Americans, we will finally include the efforts and accomplishments of Jackie Robinson, his Negro league teammates and all of black Americans who have contributed to "*Our* National Pastime."

References

Aaron, Henry, with Lonnie Wheeler. *I Had a Hammer: The Hank Aaron Story*. New York: HarperCollins, 1991.

Baldarasso, L. "Italian-American Baseball Players." Eleventh Annual Meeting of the Cooperstown Symposium on Baseball and American Culture, June 1999. Cooperstown, NY.

Baseball as America. Washington, DC: National Geographic, 2002.

Bell, Derrick. *Faces at the Bottom of the Well*. New York: Basic, 1992.

Carroll, Brian. "Wendell Smith's Last Crusade: The Desegregation of Spring Training." Thirteenth Annual Meeting of the Cooperstown Symposium on Baseball and American Culture, June 2001. Cooperstown, NY.

Dorinson, Joseph, ed. *Jackie Robinson: Race, Sports and the American Dream*. New York: Warmund, 1998.

Folsom, Ed. *Walt Whitman's Representations*. Cambridge: Cambridge UP, 1994.

"Foreign Players in Baseball." *Infobeat* 4 April 2002. 5 April 2002 <http//www.infobeat.com>.

Green, Stanton W. "Baseball and the Next Generation of Americans." *Proceedings of the 10th Annual Cooperstown Symposium on Baseball and American Culture*. Jefferson, NC: McFarland, 2001.

_____. "The Baseball Diamond as American Landscape." *Proceedings of the 11th Annual Cooperstown Symposium on Baseball and American Culture*. Jefferson, NC: McFarland, 2002.

Hofstetter, Vanessa. *America's Diamond Mind*. Thesis. University of the Arts — Philadelphia, 2002.

Moffit, L., and J. Kronstadt. *Crossing Over: Black Major Leaguers 1947–1959*. Iowa City: U of Iowa P, 1994.

Morgan, Joe. *Morgan: A Life in Baseball*. New York: Norton, 1993.

"The 1971 All-Star Game." *Yankee Magazine*, August 2001: 78–80.

Peterson, Robert. *Only the Ball Was White: A History of Legendary Black Players and All-Black Professional Leagues*. New York: Gramercy, 1970.

Riess, Stephen. *Touching Base: Professional Baseball and American Culture and the Progressive Era*. Westport, CT: Greenwood, 1980.

Robinson, Sharon. *Jackie's Nine: Jackie Robinson's Values to Live By: Courage, Determination, Teamwork, Persistence, Integrity, Citizenship, Justice, Commitment, Excellence.* New York: Scholastic, 2002.
Rutkoff, Peter. *Shadowball: A Novel of Baseball and Chicago.* Jefferson, NC: McFarland, 2001.
Shipler, David K. *A Country of Strangers: Blacks and Whites in America.* New York: Knopf, 1997.
Sullivan, N.J. *The Diamond Revolution: The Prospects after the Collapse of the Ruling Class.* New York: St. Martin's, 1992.
Takaki, Ron. *A Different Mirror: A History of Multicultural America.* Boston: Little, 1993.
Treder, W. "A Legacy of What-ifs: Horace Stoneham and the Integration of the Giants." *Nine: A Journal of Baseball History and Culture.* Edmonton: U of Calgary P, 2002. 71–101.

5
Mind + Body = Loss and Displacement: Two Contemporary African-American Artists

Lynda J. Lambert

Significant stories from our ancient past have influenced our present. The ancient stories mingle with the stories of the not-so-distant past, and they merge with our present circumstances, influencing them in diverse ways. David K. Shipler often takes on the role of griot, in his *A Country of Strangers*: The *griot* in West African societies was the village historian who recounted the community's past with a pointed critique of the present, acting as the living memory and conscience of his people: "The *griot* was not only the dynamic element of his tribe, clan and village, but also the authentic witness of each event. It was he who recorded and deposited before us, under the tree, the deeds and exploits of each person" (Clark 144).

Acting as *griot*, Shipler's tales cause the reader to reflect on our history and events and stories that influence the end product of contemporary African-American artists. Today, the telling of stories remains central to the questions of life, death, and origins for those who hear them and for those who tell them. Stories are told verbally in texts, and stories are told visually, through contemporary artists such as Howardena Pindell and Elizabeth Asche Douglas. The effectiveness of ancient stories enables these two contemporary artists to explore truth. As African-American visual artists, they continue to explore their own truth by using images of the body as metaphors in their art, and to cope with the world in which they live through the art making process.

In ancient Old Norse wisdom we find the idea "The mind knows only/What lies near the heart" (qtd. in Hamilton 465). Shipler touches on this historical recurring theme throughout his book, when he comments, "In racial thinking, it is assumed that the body reveals the mind" (275). Let us first look at a story familiar to audiences throughout classical antiquity.

Story #1: A Greek Story

Shipler notes, "Symbols and metaphors that derogate blackness and elevate whiteness are indelibly etched into the great works we read, the words we speak, the images that move us" (232). This tale from antiquity is "told only in a very early poem, one of the earliest of the Homeric Hymns, dating from the eighth or the beginning of the seventh century. The original has the marks of early Greek poetry, great simplicity and directness and delight in the beautiful world" (Hamilton 57).

The setting for this story is a grassy meadow one lovely, sun-drenched afternoon in late April. Earlier in the morning, it had rained gently and the field felt soft and buoyant beneath the feet of the young girls who came to play and pick flowers. They giggled and chatted as they frolicked through the velvety blades of delicate yellow-green spring grass. The girls were gathering flowers "in the vale of Enna, in a meadow of soft grass and roses and crocus and lovely violets and iris and hyacinths." The spring flowers were blooming abundantly and suddenly one girl, Persephone, ran ahead of the others as she "caught sight of something quite new to her, a bloom more beautiful by far than any she had ever seen, a strong glory of a flower, a marvel to all, immortal gods and mortal men." Just on the horizon of her vision, there was a brilliantly exquisite "bloom of glowing purple and silver" (112). It stood alone, near the crest of the hill, just ahead of her: Only Persephone among the maidens had spied it. The rest were at the other end of the meadow. She stole toward it, half fearful at being alone, but unable to resist the desire to fill her basket with it, exactly as Zeus had supposed she would feel. Wondering she stretched out her hands to take the lovely plaything, but before she touched it a chasm opened in the earth and out of it coal-black horses sprang, drawing a chariot and driven by one who had a look of dark splendor, majestic and beautiful and terrible. He caught her to him and held her close. The next moment she was being borne away from the radiance of the earth in springtime to the world of the dead by the king who rules it (qtd. in Hamilton 113).

This particular flower was created by Hades' brother, Zeus. It was placed there to seduce and distract her. Hades was waiting for her, just below the surface of the earth. In an instant, Hades plucked Persephone herself. He came flashing through a chasm in the earth. He was riding in his chariot, drawn by coal-black horses. He grasped her by the wrist and sat her beside him (57). We can envision a light skinned maiden being snatched by the god who is described as having a "look of dark splendor." She was weeping as she was taken down into the underworld. Persephone's abduction and descent was an ancient "Middle Passage" experience. She has been taken to a dreaded, dark place; her childhood was now over. She would from this time forward be the wife of the King of the Dead, Hades. Persephone was now Queen of the Lower World. The king of darkness came to the upper world of sunshine and light to take a mate. "In the end … there is no more potent attribute than the color of the skin. And there is no more powerful color than black" (Shipler 232).

Persephone was instantly transported from a familiar world of light, playfulness, flowers, innocence, friendships, and laughter into another world that was unfamiliar. Demeter's only daughter, Persephone, was lost as she plunged into a dark underworld with Hades. "Persephone was down in the world beneath the earth, among the shadowy dead" (Hamilton 57). From the moment of her abduction, all possibility of communication with family and friends ceased. Along with the loss of a place in the world as she knew it, Persephone also experienced a loss of language.

Eventually, in her grief, Persephone's distressed mother, Demeter, through relentless persistence, would strike a deal with the gods. Persephone was permitted to live three quarters of each year in her former LIGHT world, and one fourth of the year in the DARK lower world with her husband, Hades. Persephone had dual residency in both (light and dark) worlds. Through the abduction Persephone experienced displacement. Complete restoration to her former life would not be a possibility. Persephone, a displaced person, had to negotiate continual shifts through two separate worlds, and with each shift, part of her remained in each world.

Not unlike the mythological Persephone, two contemporary African-American artists, Elizabeth Asche Douglas and Howardena Pindell, are living examples of women who live in two worlds. Each artist uses the "body" as a metaphor throughout her work. Loss of language and displacement are conditions reflected in the art they make. It can be discerned by close scrutiny of their art and their writing.

Story #2: A Hebrew Story

> The concepts and usages of black evil and white goodness, of beautiful fairness and ugly blackness, are deeply imbedded in the Bible, are folded into the language of Milton and Shakespeare, indeed are laced into almost every entwining strand of the art and literature in which our history is clothed. They can be traced down the columns of any dictionary from white hope to whitewash, from the black arts to the Black Mass, from black-browed and black hearted to blacklist and blackmail, aversion to blackness has been the stuff of eloquence and poetry.
> — Harold R. Isaacs, qtd. in *A Country of Strangers* 232–33

The second significant story is from the Bible. Here, a storyteller narrates at a moment in time that was before the storyteller's time. The event dates to the period following the story of Noah and the Great Flood. In the eleventh chapter of Genesis is found the story of the tower of Babel, capitol of Babylonia. This story is significant because it marks "the last episode in which God deals with all of humanity together" (Digest 125). After this event, God would deal with humans and intervene in human affairs only through contact with specific, selected individuals.

The time in which the story takes place must be well before the notorious 70-year exile that began in 586 B.C. when the leading citizens of Judah were taken captive by King Nebuchadnezzar and brought to Babylonia. "Nearby were the famous hanging gardens and, nearby, the Tower of Babel" (Lucado 1531). The "storyteller is quite aware that in his own time the nations did not have a common language, and that the presumed existence of a universal tongue, before the attempt to build the tower of Babel, therefore took place in a different era" (Rogers 201). "Now the whole earth had one language and one speech" (Gen. 11:1). Having one language and one speech was the normal condition, before the time of the storyteller's era.

In this story, there was a vast building enterprise when humanity united and began to build a tower "whose top is in the heavens" (Gen. 11. 4):

> Scholars have long sought an historical precedent for the well-known story…. Most of them propose the second-millennium BC ziggurat pyramids of Mesopotamia as an inspiration. Indeed, the land of Shiner, where the tower was built, has been identified as the Tigris-Euphrates basin, site of the ancient city of Babylon. In the biblical account, the name *Babel* is given the tower because the Lord — displeased with humanity's presumption that it could reach the heavens with the structure — confused their language. The word *balal* in Hebrew means confuse [*Who's Who* 323].

Elizabeth Asche Douglas began to focus her attention on the image of a tower and human faces in a work from 1996 called *Tower II*. She clearly references the ancient story from the Old Testament in this work. Five years later, again Douglas focused her attention on presenting a work, *Reflections*, 2001, that uses the tower as image, along with human faces, intricately intertwined within the cantilevered tower.

Some scholars believe that in this Genesis account humanity was divided. God decided to "confuse their language, that they may not understand one another's speech" (Gen 11.7). The ultimate punishment, in this ancient story, was that a people's language and ability to communicate with each other was taken away. With the confusion of their language, all building operations ceased. The tower would remain unfinished and in ruins. The ancient Babylonians encountered a Middle Passage experience as they were scattered, confused, and completely unable to articulate their condition and circumstances with any other person.

Douglas uses golden picture frames to construct a very unstable tower, which seems to be only a moment away from total collapse. Within the wooden frames, translucent images of a face become a recurring theme in the work. The same face looks back at the viewer from within each of the frames. The face is submerged in both light and darkness—light is necessary to see the image at all when viewing the work. If there is not enough light, the image disappears quickly into the darkness and its presence cannot be seen. The face looks out, through flashes of light, through eyes that are completely void. While the viewer tries to get a better look at this face, it can vanish without warning. Trying to look into the eyes will not reveal any secrets, as the eyes never fully take form. Like Persephone, the face looking out through the golden frames lives in two worlds simultaneously, yet is not fully a part of either world.

Again, in one of her latest works, *Double Vision*, 2001, Douglas intentionally toys with the theme of a tower, using frames, and a transparent portrait image looking out at the viewer. Not only do we see a view of the face encased inside of it, we can also see our own image reflected back at us. This face provides an image for us to contemplate and a mirror in which to contemplate our own reflection within and upon the face that Douglas has provided us. The face in the frame is united with the viewers' own reflection which overlays the image in the frame. There is a merging of two people in the frame, which causes an uncomfortable feeling of being a part of two worlds, yet not fully in either one.

The back-and-forth flashing of the faces gives a visual equivalent of the "call-and-response" style of interaction that takes place among blacks and also reflects the going back and forth from one culture to another, as necessary, to communicate effectively in a culture that requires living in two worlds (Shipler 71).

In *Within and Without the Mask* (2001), Douglas wrestles with identity and worldview questions. "The stories of all the peoples of the ancient world that wrestled with questions of life, death, and origins were true for at least some of those who wrote and heard them. This was not so much an intellectual truth as a truth that enabled the world to be coped with and lived in; the truth of these stories was their effectiveness in enabling those who heard and told them to cope with the world" (Roberson 201).

Mask is constructed of fragments of "found objects." We can look at *Mask*, but in doing so we also look inside of mask and through mask. *Mask* appears, disappears, and changes as we move around it. In looking at *Mask*, we can also see our own reflection looking back at us via the use of mirror fragments within the sculpture. Notice the root that works its way up through the center of the mask, undulating from outside to inside, and deeper into the center of the mask. Mask exists in two worlds, and is created through use of objects from the external physical world, yet gives us a look into the metaphysical, spiritual word of the artist.

Within and Without the Mask is a reminder to those who take notice that it will take time, introspection and contemplation to be able to see beyond outward appearances and basic elements. *Mask* remains silent. The only clues to the nature of *Mask* are the visual elements that we cannot read without study and perseverance. Looking deeply into *Mask* reveals that there are broken fragments of mirrors there, again reflecting our own image back to us. *Mask* invites us to come on a long journey; a lifetime journey. "The journey does not have to be a guilt trip; it is just an encounter with the facts of life" (Shipler 569). It's not an easy journey, but one worth embarking on. Shipler declares that talking about race is one of the most difficult endeavors in America. "Shouting is easy. Muttering and whining and posturing are done with facility. But conversing — black with white, white with black — is a rare and heavy accomplishment. The color line is a curtain of silence" (473). In another of her figurative sculptures, *Playmate* (2001), Douglas gives the viewer a moment in time in the life of a child. Just a glimpse of something that at first appears quite innocent.

As we have seen in the myth of Persephone, good things can and do happen to unsuspecting and innocent young people. At first glance, Douglas seems to give us a lighthearted glimpse into a child's playtime. Playmate hurls her wooden rope into the air. We can immediately get the idea of a child playing on a lovely summer's day. But let's take another, closer, deeper look at *Playmate*. *Playmate* hurls her rope into the air, creating a line that separates her from us. It could also entangle us, if we get too close to her. We have to look at each other from a distance, as Shipler writes, "trapped in each other's imaginations" (562).

Have you ever seen a child playing jump rope with her legs spread wide apart and her feet firmly pressing downward onto the earth? And, with the pressing downward, and the unfurling of the rope, the child's hair flies upward as in terror or the force of a sudden movement. This child has been caught at the moment when something unexpected has occurred during her playtime. She is a reminder that such a child was playing in a church basement in Alabama as a bomb was tossed through the window.

Shipler talks about the children who were growing up when the civil rights movement began in the 1950s and how

> "awful, indelible images" were part of their landscape. He says, "I am haunted still by the cute little white girls who twisted their faces into screams of hatred as black children were escorted into schools. I saw for the first time that the face of pristine innocence could be merely a mask.... Here was the enemy" [4].

He further reminds us that "[i]n racial thinking, it is assumed that the body reveals the mind" (275). Douglas again picks up on the theme of the body as a metaphor in *Phantasm*.

This figure created by bits of fragments, found objects, stands tall. Surrounding the figure on all sides is a rope-like string of wooden beads that flares out in both directions, like a cowboy might fling a lasso. Yet the only thing that is caught in this lasso is the figure herself. Perhaps this whirling line is one that remains as a barrier encircling the figure, separating her from things that cannot be overcome. *Phantasm* is a creation of the imagination of Douglas mingled with her history and the history of a culture. Or maybe, this figure is a lone specter or apparition with the likeness of a person playing a game of tug of war? Let us examine the details of *Phantasm*.

The two "legs" are made of different woods. One resembles a root, the other a piece of sanded sawn wood. Both hold the figure erect and provide a transition from the weight of the object in space to the smaller base on which the sculpture is tenuously grounded. The two slender appendage-type structures appear as roots from two different worlds, yet, both are necessary to hold up and give life to the figure itself. The figure stands amid the flaring of the wooden, beaded ropes in this solo, silent game of tug of war.

After her suicide, Chicago journalist Leant McClain's works were published in *A Foot in Each World*. In an essay written by her in 1980 titled "The Middle-Class Black's Burden," she laments: "I am burdened daily with showing whites that blacks are people. I am, in the old vernacular, a

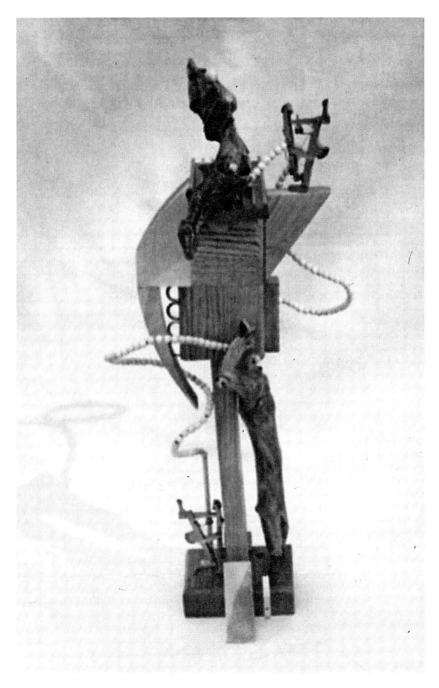

Phantasm by Elizabeth Asche Douglas, wood sculpture (33" × 17" × 13"), 1999.

credit to my race…. I run a gauntlet between two worlds, and I am cursed and blessed by both. I travel, observe, and take part in both; I can also be used by both. I am a rope in a tug of war" (qtd. in hooks 109).

I have looked at a number of works by New York City artist Howardena Pindell in chronological order to show a progression of her use of the body as a motif that reflects a sense of displacement.

Pindell expresses her dilemma, and her keen frustration, about how to appropriately synthesize the two worlds of her ancestry in her life. While her heritage is one of two different worlds, she does not see her art and life as being separate things. They are one and they have become one in her mind by sheer determination and self-direction. Like Persephone who could speak the languages of the two separate worlds, Pindell recognizes and speaks of loss and displacement yet she is able to overcome these things through her imagination and creative invention. Both artists, Pindell and Douglas, use fragments and found objects to mold a new kind of communication structure. It is one that tries to overcome the limitations of those that have broken down. Communication has been established between two previously disparate worlds.

In the introduction to her book in 1977, Pindell wrote, "I sustain myself through sheer tenacity…. The goal of my work is to share knowledge. I do not see art and life as separate" (ix). And the knowledge she shares with the viewer is that she lives in two worlds but that her art enables her to live as a complete and whole person despite her dual heritage.

Ten years after her book was published, she painted *Autobiography*: *Fire*: *Suttee* (1986–87). The image of Pindell's own body floats across a red sea in an expression of empathy with the Hindu widows who are burned alive with the corpses of their husbands. As an act of faith she has laid her own body down on the canvas, traced its outline, cut it out from the canvas, then sewed it back.

In *Autobiography*: *Earth/Eyes/Injuries* (1987), she again traces her own body, over and over, repeating the process. The figures are cut out of the canvas, and then sewn back into it. This work is a response to the pain she suffered in a near fatal car accident in 1979, and the feelings she had when she looked around and saw strangers watching her body being extracted from the wreckage. Eyes float above, on, and below the surface of this painting. They bear silent witness to both the beauty and the horror of her experience as accident victim. Additionally, the eyes remind us of her dual citizenship as though she is being watched from another world.

Once again, Pindell has the starring role in the tale she visually presents us with in her *Autobiography*: *The Search/Chrysalis/Tradition/Positive/Negative* (1988–89). Multiple sets of eyes look back at the viewer, and multiple views of Pindell's own body, and self-portraits of the artist. While the painting is a vortex of centrifugal and centripetal forces, we are reminded that there is still the opportunity for change. She offers hope. Things have not yet been set in stone. Intermingled among the figures and the watching eyes, are the text fragments, the words, indicating a very complex, unstable world.

Pindell says that this painting grew out of her experiences with deep meditation. The process of the work itself is done by laying down layer upon layer of information, using a variety of mediums such as vinyl tape, tempera, photo transfers, and strong color shifts. The weightless, shifting figures seem almost to float across the surface, rising and falling between layers of paint strokes. Body parts are detached, giving the viewer an uncomfortable, claustrophobic feeling.

Howardena Pindell compares her ancestral background "[to] a vast stew." We can see the stew brewing in her *Autobiography: Water/Ancestors/Middle Passage/Family Ghosts* (1988). Here she explicates her references to her own multiracial heritage, "[meditates] on black slavery and its consequences in America" (viii). The painting symbolizes this mixture and the fact that Africans kidnapped and held hostage in this country were massively tortured and sexually abused by their captors" (76).

Detail from Howardena Pindell, *Autobiography: Water/Ancestors/Middle Passage/Family Ghosts*, 1988. An eclectic composition of acrylic, tempera, oil slick, paper, polymer, photographic transfer, vinyl type on sewn canvas.

A close look reveals once again she has put her own image in this work. Pindell has multicultural roots and she uses the image of her own body, body parts, heads, and word fragments. Her body, with eight hands, appears

> in a field scattered with independent images of postcards, photographs and mementos. In this and other compositions, the smaller images, works and phrases and questions written into the surface of the painting refer directly to the artist's "personal experience with issues of abuse, some of which were brought about by encounters with racism, sexisms and issues of class" [Sims 19].

On the lower left, there is the image of a slave ship, which is the site of the Middle Passage. She selectively uses body parts to show a truth. "Eyes throughout the painting represent witnesses, even if silence was the only testimony permitted because of the fear caused by the abject abuse of the slaves by the enslavers"(Pindell 76).

In the upper center there is an exaggerated, elongated head of an African woman. According to her, she represents "the one African woman from whom all human life is traced by scientists" (76).

In her book, she refers to Charles L. Blockson's *Black Genealogy*, in which he describes "enforced illiteracy" as a condition under which African people lived in the South. The inability to communicate with each other occurred when language was scrambled and removed from the Africans during the Middle Passage, and it was further reinforced by "constant name changes by the enslaver of the names of their captives" (76). There-fore, the conditions that existed on the Middle Passage continued on in the lives of the people who were enslaved. Without a common language, and without a name, how can one communicate effectively or at all?

> Generations have carried this pain with them.... An elaborate mythol-ogy has been developed to sanitize the history of the country.... Those who perpetrated the crimes carry the memories through the generations. This may explain the prevalence of addictions, child abuse, battering, and rape throughout all levels of American society. This may explain the demand for silence on the subject [76].

Pindell is a child again in *Autobiography: Scapegoat* (1990), holding a ball. She uses the child's image to remind us that abuse of children has "tremendous ramifications on the society at large because of the damage done to the innocent and the internalized shame that somehow is the child's fault ... the internalized rage ... is stored and manifests itself as inner (self) or overt destructiveness" (*Exhibits* 79).

Pindell questions the definition of a "self" in a number of ways in the painting *In My Lifetime* (1995–96). She is of mixed ancestry: African, Native American, South American, and European — a combination, she says, of "slaver and enslaved" (73).

In her exhibition *Autobiography: In Her Own Image*, she addresses "multiple aspects of [her] being and experience" as she created paintings that represent her own "key life experiences" as an artist with a foot in two worlds, much like Douglas' figure standing with different legs (72).

In the six-foot-square painting *Slavery Memorial* (1993), there is no doubt that Pindell is thinking of the horrors of the generations that preceded her as she has used the image of strong black chains, slashing, cold blue paint, and the listing of the names of slaves as well as the ports that they were taken to by the slave ships. She is giving homage to the ancestors in this work through the tradition of the call and response — the slaves have called to her, and in her work she has responded to their distant call.

Shipler does not specifically discuss art and art history or even the broader topic of creativity, whereas many other occupations are encountered. This omission is a disappointment because an entire world waits in anticipation behind this closed door. There are many secrets waiting to be explored through those avenues. Shipler alludes to, but does not enter them. Perhaps a chapter that addresses the role of creativity and the arts in the lives of blacks and whites in America will redress this unfortunate omission and in this exploration he may find new information and new revelations and enlightenment.

One asks, "How important is the artist and the products that the artist makes and offers to a culture?" According to Minister Louis Farrakhan, speaking in October 1995 at the Million Man March, artists are

> "wonderful, gifted" and he urged artists to "remember that your gifts come from God.... We want to pick you up, so with your rap you can pick up the world, with your song you can pick up the world, with your dance, with your music, you can pick up the world." He ended his speech that day by urging the people in the audience to shout their name so loud that the ancestors would hear it [qtd. in Shipler 341].

Through the visual arts, African-American artists are shouting out the names of the ancestors. Pindell and Douglas have clearly said that they do not see their art and life as separate. Past and present are not separate, but together they form the future. Both artists have found a way to shout the language of two worlds.

References

Clark, Toby. *Art and Propaganda in the Twentieth Century*. New York: Abrams, 1997.

Exhibits USA. *Howardena Pindell Paintings and Drawings: A Retrospective Exhibition*. 1972–1992.

Failing, Patricia. "Black Artists Today: A Case of Exclusion." *ARTnews* March 1989: 124.

Hamilton, Edith. *Mythology*. Boston: Little, 1942.

hooks, bell. *Sisters of the Yam: Black Women and Self-Recovery*. Boston: South End, 1993.

Lucado, Max, ed. *The Inspirational Study Bible*. New King James Version. Dallas: Word, 1995.

Pindell, Howardena. *The Heart of the Question: The Writings and Paintings of Howardena Pindell*. New York: Midmarch Arts, 1997.

Rogerson, John, and Philip Davies. *The Old Testament World*. Englewood Cliffs, NJ: Prentice-Hall, 1989.

Shipler, David K. *A Country of Strangers: Blacks and Whites in America*. New York: Vintage, 1998.

Sims, Lowery Stokes. "Howardena Pindell's Memory Works: Postcards on the Edge." *New Observations #97:* 17.

Who's Who in the Bible. Pleasantville, NY: Reader's Digest, 1994.

6
Musical Style as a Symbol of Black Cultural Identity

Timothy M. Kalil

David Shipler acknowledges the importance of American music to black culture, especially the spiritual and black gospel music as symbols of that identity: "The curriculum and culture of the school [Chicago's Brother Rice High School] were so heavily white that blacks looked to music as a vehicle of pride and identity" (39). C. Eric Lincoln recognizes the importance of black culture to American music: "from spirituals and gospel to blues, ragtime, jazz, rock and roll, soul, and rap; the core of American music has derived from black culture" (Lincoln and Mamiya 380).

During the Second Great Awakening (circa 1780–1830) in the South, African-Americans overwhelmingly belonged to the white historical churches of their masters, mainly Baptist and Methodist. Blacks were many times attracted to these denominations for their music ministry that usually included singing and (portable) organ-playing ministers. Concomitantly, the Baptists and Methodists also actively recruited African-Americans via camp meetings and itinerant preachers. Regarding the former, these segregated meetings featured ministers/song leaders that struck up improvised, inspirational tunes "camp meeting hymns" that were "catchy" and rhythmic. These songs immediately gained new converts and infused the attendees with a sense of enthusiasm and communal participation.

Throughout the early nineteenth century, these camp meetings increased in frequency and it was mainly here that the enslaved African-

Americans in the South created the first large-scale, identifiably African-American religious music genre—camp meetings hymns or spirituals. Asserts Dena Epstein: "What had been seen at camp meetings in 1819 [spirituals] continued to be widely observed throughout the South" (218).

Spirituals were communally composed by the enslaved. The process included adding choruses or refrains to existing hymns or refashioned hymns. Also "conceptually African" elements, such as call-and-response texture, "body percussion" (handclaps and foot-stomps), and the neutral third and seventh (similar to the flattened notes in the blues) notes found in some West African scales were used. Another source for spiritual creation was the nineteenth-century black preacher's sermons/prayers where the spontaneous interaction/call-and-response between the pastor and congregation led to song (see Southern, 176–177; Lincoln, 348–349; Oliver 140–198). Over a period of time, these songs congealed into what we now know as the "African-American folk spiritual" (hereafter spiritual).

Textually, most spirituals also featured "code words" such as "Steal away to Jesus" and "follow the drinking gourd" (i.e., Big Dipper constellation which points to the North Star and the freedom of the North or Canada). These phrases told of plans of imminent escape to freedom via the Underground Railroad.

Spirituals used many characters from the Old Testament — for example, Moses and Daniel, as African-Americans felt a kinship with the Hebrew "children" enslaved in ancient Egypt. The enslaved could relate to these Biblical characters facing overwhelming odds. Titles such as "See Brother Moses Yonder," "Paul and Silas Bound in Jail," and "Didn't My Lord Deliver Daniel" are noteworthy. Also, spirituals "were a principal means of transmission of oral history" (Lincoln 349). States Lena McLin in a 1992 interview with the author in Chicago: "The spiritual is the only documentation of slavery composed by the slaves themselves."

Although African instruments and music-making were eventually viewed by slave captains as necessary to the health and mental state of their African "cargo" during the Middle Passage, once ashore, certain instruments, especially the drum, were confiscated due to their potential utilization as communication tools, perhaps even in the incitement of slave insurrections. Because of this and other factors, pre–Civil War black music (and much of current black music) was vocally oriented or a cappella and used body percussion.

A related genre of the spiritual, the "ring shout/running spiritual," was closely related to the African circle dance. The ring shout was performed during the week or after church services that were usually held in "praise cabins" or also in "praise houses" (Johnson 38). The genre comprised two groups: first, "shouters" who sang and danced in counterclockwise fashion without lifting the feet to ensure that no "secular" dancing was transpiring and, secondly, "basers" who provided the rhythmic texture via body percussion. The shouter's movements consisted of jerks and "hitches," which caused agitation, perspiration, and possession in the shouter (Southern 170–71). The ensuing demonstrative activity (potentially lasting up to eight hours) was eventually brought to a fevered pitch and culminated with the "blessing/possession" of a participant(s) in the Holy Spirit. Such an emotional and demonstrative display was scorned and dismissed by many white Christians as "heathenish" or improper behavior. Eileen Southern notes in *The Music of Black Americans*:

> Nowhere in the history of the black experience in the United States was the clash of cultures— the African versus the European — more obvious than in the differing attitudes taken toward ritual dancing and spirit possession [170–171].

To be sure, spirituals and ring shouts were conceptually African as Lincoln and Mamiya maintain: "Black singing and the performance practices associated with it is [*sic*] perhaps the most characteristic logo of African heritage retentive [*sic*] in the Black Church" (348).

Scholarly opinion, however, continues to be divided between such as E. Franklin Frazier, who believes that "African-Americans lost their African heritage during slavery" and Melville J. Herkovits, who asserts that "the continuity of West African carryovers in African-American culture" is crucial to the understanding of what is meant by "conceptually African" (qtd. in Holloway ix–x). West African culture, and especially the eastern Central African/Bantu culture, many current scholars argue, is inevitably the basis for most black cultural identity (Holloway 1–18; see Simpson 1–20). Portia Maultsby opines:

> The fundamentals of culture established by slaves persist in the twentieth century; they are reinterpreted as social times demand. African retentions in African-American culture, therefore, exist as conceptual approaches— as unique ways of doing and making things happen — rather than as specific cultural elements [qtd. in Holloway 205].

Certainly many musical elements found in genres created by blacks, such as spirituals, gospel, blues, and others, are essentially and ultimately African in conception:

> In spite of such obvious obstacles to the retention and the transmission of the African's cultural heritage in the new context of the American

experience, the evidence [is] that critical elements of that heritage managed to survive and their adaptation in the New World is substantial,
especially in religion [Lincoln 347].

Musically speaking, the African concepts of communal participation
and multimedia effects are both found in African music, of course, and
current black gospel music performances. The Venda people of South
Africa do not acknowledge the notion of "musical talent" and concomitantly believe all human beings are innately musical and thus all should
participate in musical activity (Blacking 36–53). In the Bira (ancestor) cer-
emonies of the Shona peoples of Zimbabwe, all present sing, clap, and
dance to the main accompaniment of the *mbira* or "thumb piano" (Nettl
161–168). At the beginning of a service in most black churches, the gospel
choir "marches" with choreographed steps rather than walks into church.
During the service, most black church congregations clap to a gospel choir
performance and also interject comments when a pastor delivers his or her
sermon. The current gospel concerts of BeBe and CeCe Winans include
multimedia combinations such as voices, sermons, instruments, dance,
costumes, and lighting.

The emotive and graphic singing styles of the *Wolof* and *Mande griot*
or *jalli* ("praise singer") of West Africa are found in the various vocal
effects of the African-American gospel and blues singer — for example,
rasps, growls, whines, screams, and whispers. The vocal music ensemble
Ladysmith Black Mambazo, which originated in the townships of (then
apartheid) South Africa, use an abundance of body percussion and also
link their singing to bodily movements. To digress slightly toward contemporary popular culture, Michael Jackson sings and dances simultaneously in the 1983 video *Thriller*, and Motown's famed Temptations were
known for unifying music and movement throughout the sixties.

The visual nature of African music is also very important. Some Fanté
musicians of southeastern Ghana wear costumes (high collars) and colors
(namely, red) influenced by British colonial military uniforms, which to
many transfers the power and importance of the colonizers to the Fanté
musicians. Today, notes Melonee Burnim in her dissertation, many gospel
choir competitions currently include a special prize for the most colorful
and creative choir robe design. Black culture has never been static because
it continually changes, borrows, and adapts to new situations and contexts within what is conceptually African. Musically speaking, many
African elements remain constant between the spiritual and black gospel
music, in particular the communal participation that is common to both
spiritual and black gospel music performance. However, how communal

participation is musically realized is largely due to the socio-cultural contexts of the genres under consideration. Furthermore, many scholars believe that black gospel music used the often-unaccompanied spiritual and evolved into its current instrumentally accompanied form as a result of socio-cultural conditions in post–Reconstruction America. The spiritual, then, was a product of the enslavement period in American history, whereas black gospel music developed out of the cautiously optimistic conditions following Emancipation (1863) and continuing in the post–Reconstruction South until shortly after the first decade of the twentieth century, asserts Lawrence Levine (5).

A distinction is warranted between the spiritual and black gospel music, however, for both express extraordinary similarities in their resiliency and continuity of African concepts.

Spirituals were communally created out of the inhumane conditions of the enslavement period in the South. It was an oral tradition that was passed down to succeeding generations of African-Americans to the present day. Spirituals became a recognizable and documented genre as early as 1819 and in 1867, *Slave Songs of the United States* became the first large-scale publication of spirituals (Epstein 303–48).

Musically and culturally speaking, the spiritual is a vocal genre that features syncopation and is unaccompanied by instruments but usually accompanied by body percussion with punctuation of beats 2 and 4. Similar to many other black vocal genres, European classical vocal style is not one of its features, for as in Africa, a variety of expressive and graphic vocal timbres and manipulations are used. The genre is communally composed and orally/aurally transmitted and learned.

Spirituals may be sung by a soloist or an ensemble, according to Dena Epstein (161–190). The genre features five, six, and seven-tone scales, neutral thirds and/or sevenths, mainly call-and-response texture, and "extended repetition of short melodic phrases" (Epstein 216; see also Maultsby dissertation for her computer analysis of one hundred spirituals). In addition, the spiritual also includes "rhythmic complexity [and] gapped scales" (Epstein 216). Some of these features are heard in the spiritual "Nobody Knows The Trouble I See."

The spiritual helped the enslaved "get through" the evils of slavery, as it was used to regulate work, signal escape plans, promise a reward in heaven, and in general to cope with everyday life. The spiritual can be "otherworldly"; but in a sense, concentrating on heaven actually enabled one to survive here on this earth. Thus, as in many parts of Africa, the sacred and secular are not separate, but exist in a complementary and symbiotic relationship.

Traditional Black Gospel Music, 1930–1965

Consider traditional black gospel music that flourished between 1930 and 1965. From 1910 to 1920, over 65,000 African-Americans arrived in Chicago from the Deep South (an increase of over 109 percent) during a period known as the Great Migration of African-Americans (*Chicago Commission* 106). Their artistic impact created the genres known today as "traditional Black gospel music" and "traditional Black gospel piano" circa 1930 and the era known as Chicago's Jazz Age during the twenties (Kalil).

Once in Chicago, these migrants brought with them many elements of Southern musical culture and religion to the segregated black South Side of the city. For example, many of the new arrivals were blues and jazz musicians who emigrated from Mississippi, Louisiana (e.g., Louis Armstrong), and Georgia. In addition, Southern Black musicians viewed Chicago as the Promised Land with various positive social, economic, and political attractions. Further, there also existed a professional entertainment district centering on the South Side's the Stroll or "Black Broadway" at the intersection of State and 35th Streets (Haller 725–26).

Chicago's Jazz Age also attracted blues and jazz musician Thomas A. ("Georgia Tom") Dorsey — a Southern migrant turned black gospel composer. Dorsey (1899–1993) arrived in Chicago from Georgia in 1916. His blues and jazz experience facilitated his combining those styles with music of the Sanctified Church and the Baptist hymn to create so-called traditional black gospel music and piano around 1930.

Many of these musical and non-musical migrants attended Baptist or mainly Sanctified (Pentecostal-Holiness) storefront churches (a usually abandoned commercial premises; see Oliver, 175–178; Lincoln, 76–78). It was here in the Sanctified storefronts that musical "Africanisms," including body percussion and chants, were the strongest. To be sure, the American roots of the storefronts inevitably lay in the informal "brush harbors/hush arbors/worship services"— the "Invisible Institution"— of the unassimilated "field" enslaved (not the assimilated "house" enslaved) in the antebellum era in the South, according to Maultsby (qtd. in Holloway 196–99).

It was also in the Sanctified storefront churches that Dorsey, although a Baptist, attended services to observe and learn how blues and jazz could be incorporated into gospel music, thereby developing an identifiable genre in Chicago. In the 1930s and early 1940s, Dorsey performed, composed, and toured with black gospel singer Mahalia Jackson, published black gospel music, and founded a black gospel music school. In 1932, inspired by the death of his wife and baby, he composed the gospel song "Precious

Lord" known the world over. As such, the title the "Father of Traditional Black Gospel Music and Piano" is deservedly his.

The Sanctified Church

In the chaotic aftermath of the Civil War, there emerged on a large scale, the "Institution of the Black Church" — a church controlled by African-Americans. Although most Southern blacks were overwhelmingly Baptist or Methodist, there arose out of Methodism a movement known as "Holiness" that actually began in the 1830s and 1840s (Ayers 398–408). This movement sought, in addition to the conversation experience for salvation, a "second blessing" or "sanctification" (398–408).

The emotional and demonstrative services of the Holiness denomination were replete with handclaps, foot-stomps, and tambourines and created much consternation and conflict within Methodism (398–401). Edward Ayers notes in *The Promise of the New South*: "In 1894, the General Conference of the Methodist Church forced its bishops to choose between Holiness and the church hierarchy"; he further asserts that the "extermination of Holiness failed," yet a

> significant number of Holiness advocates, however, began to accept new, more radical doctrines of divine healing and a third blessing called "the fire." Instead of coming together into a unified Holiness movement, the movement splintered into new churches and new denominations [400].

The third blessing concept as evidenced by "gifts of the Pentecost/Holy Spirit" or "speaking in tongues" (or glossolalia), eventually created the largest and most musically influential black Pentecostal-Holiness denomination in the world, the Church of God in Christ (hereafter Church of God). The sect was founded and led by Charles Harrison Mason, its first Bishop in November of 1907 (Lincoln 77; Oliver 172). The Church of God's emotional, demonstrative, and theatrical activity during services encouraged fast, rhythmic, and expressive music that directly influenced Dorsey and the black gospel music movement of the early twentieth century.

Bishop Mason (1866–1961) attended the lengthy Azusa Street Revival in Los Angeles in 1907 and received the "gifts of the Holy Spirit" there from the founder of Pentecostalism, the black minister, William J. Seymour. Originally a Baptist minister, Mason began preaching the doctrine of Holiness. As a result, Bishop Mason was expelled from the Baptist faith in 1896. Soon after, he began preaching the "doctrine of "sanctification" in an abandoned cotton-gin house in Lexington, Mississippi, on the eastern edge of the Mississippi-Yazoo Delta, an area famous as blues country. Oliver records in *Songsters and Saints* that "in this musically rich area the appeal of a church which encouraged playing instruments in church was considerable, and the new denomination spread rapidly" (172).

Maultsby enthusiastically concurs in an essay:

> Perhaps the greatest single influence on gospel lies in the area of instrumental playing styles. Former blues and jazz musicians were among the first to accompany gospel singers. The instrumental style idiomatic to these genres was slightly modified to create the mood for and complement the style of the vocalists [205].

Gospel and blues authority Horace Boyer adds a footnote in "Gospel Music": "The appearance of black gospel music coincided with the beginnings of ragtime, blues, and jazz, and with the rise of the Pentecostal churches at the end of the 19th century" (254).

In 1897, Bishop Mason established his headquarters in Memphis. This act had important musical consequences for Black gospel music:

> The early days of the Church's life in Memphis was close to Beale Street. On Beale Street, there were blues legends of the time: W. C. Handy, Ma Rainey, Clara Smith, and Bessie Smith. Many of the church's participants had earlier been customers of these blues legends [Boyer and Tolbert 15].

Concomitantly, many Sanctified musicians—for example, blues pianists "Little Brother" Montgomery and Will Ezell—played blues in Saturday night dances and then played in Sunday morning church services. Distinctions between the sacred and secular repertoires began to fade, as the same blues and jazz-oriented styles and songs such as "When The Saints Go Marching In" and "Just a Closer Walk with Thee" could be heard in both venues. As such, many blues songs became religious hymns when one added inspirational lyrics. Further, blues and jazz elements began to enter the music of the Sanctified Church at this point.

These influences were not lost on Sanctified musicians such as evangelist "Sister" Arizona Dranes (c. 1905–1957), whose ragtime and barrelhouse blues-influenced piano and vocal renditions of catchy, rhythmic church songs impacted black gospel music composer Thomas Dorsey.

Arizona Dranes, a missionary and evangelist of the Sanctified Church, directly influenced Dorsey, for she also recorded and performed extensively in Chicago in 1920. Dorsey once professed in an interview: "Yes, I play with them [Sanctified Church members] ... dance with them ... If I can put some of what she [Dranes] does and mix it with the blues, I'll be able to come up with a gospel piano style" (qtd. in Reagon interview).

Dorsey's black gospel piano style, and thus by extension, his black gospel music composition, has its roots in the piano renditions of Arizona Dranes. Horace Boyer believes that [Dranes'] piano style was a model for that of the first gospel songs recorded by Dorsey" (255). Certainly, Dorsey's music departs from Dranes' by his use of an abundance of blues scales, blues harmonies, and "swinging" jazz rhythms.

Dorsey developed the improvisatory black gospel song, not the black gospel hymn, which is sung "as is." In essence, the hymn is used as a point of departure for blues-influenced vocal and piano improvisation. Body percussion is then added to the vocal texture.

The transformation of a gospel hymn into a black gospel song is crucial, for when Dorsey was first contracted to be music director of Ebenezer Baptist and Pilgrim Baptist Churches in 1931 and 1932, he did not publish many gospel songs. His first rehearsals consisted of adding mainly blues and jazz elements and other traditional African-American techniques to what was readily available to and known by the choir — Baptist hymns.

Initially, such "jazz in the church" met with resistance from the large mainline Chicago black churches. Eventually, the popularity of the genre, coupled with congregations literally changing overnight from assimilated Northern blacks to unassimilated Southern blacks, who preferred and related to blues-influenced gospel music, forced most Chicago black ministers to slowly accept the genre.

Vocally, blues techniques and timbres are used including screams, shouts, whispers, moans, and growls, etc. Visual elements include colorful, identifiable choir robes and choreography of the choir. Techniques include the use of call-and-response texture, repeated/lengthened musical phrases or "vamps," and the interaction of the performer(s) with the audience. In the latter example of the "singing preacher," Shirley Ceasar oscillates between sermon and song. Finally, black gospel music enhances and quickens the "calling of the Holy Spirit" in the worship service.

By the 1940s, black gospel music was firmly established in most South Side Chicago black churches. With Dorsey and his Chicago gospel "students" as the focal point, the genre diffused to the rest of the nation via his convention (the National Convention of Gospel Choirs and Choruses, widely known as the "Dorsey Convention"), three publishing companies, a school of music, touring, and teaching. Also, gospel radio stations, recordings, and auditorium or stadium concerts were instrumental in its spreading.

The flipping of white neighborhoods to black throughout America's major cities and the migration of gospel musicians from Chicago to large urban centers, such as Los Angeles after World War II, accelerated gospel's influence — for example, Gwendolyn Cooper Lightner single-handedly brought Dorsey's traditional gospel piano style to Los Angeles when she migrated there from Chicago in the mid–1940s.

Demonstrating the importance of music to black cultural identity and showing its symbolic value enable us to conclude that black music in America is neither a division nor a separation of the races but a bringing together. Today more than ever, it is one bridge across the racial divide as David Shipler asserts: "Although music marks the divide, it can also be a route across the line" (39).

References

Ayers, Edward L. *The Promise of the New South: Life after Reconstruction*. New York: Oxford UP, 1992.

Blacking, John. *How Musical Is Man?* 2nd ed. Seattle: U of Washington P, 1974.

Boyer, Horace. "Gospel Music." *The New Grove Dictionary of American Music*. Vol. 2. 1986 ed. 254.

_____. Interview with Bernice Johnson Reagon [1993]. *Wade in the Water: Afro-American Sacred Music Traditions*. Nat'l Public Radio. Washington, DC. 21 May 1994.

Boyer, James, and Odie Tolbert. "Gospel Music in the COGIC Tradition: A Historical Perspective." *Rejoice* Fall 1989: 15.

Burnim, Melonee. "The Black Gospel Music Tradition: A Symbol of Ethnicity." Diss. Indiana U, 1980.

Chicago Commission on Race Relations: The Negro Church in Chicago: A Study of Race Relations and a Riot. Chicago: U of Chicago P, 1922.

Epstein, Dena J. *Sinful Tunes and Spirituals: Black Folk Music to the Civil War*. Urbana: U of Illinois P, 1977.

Haller, Mark H. "Policy Gambling, Entertainment, and the Emergence of Black Politics: Chicago from 1900–1940." *Journal of Social History* 24 (1991): 725–26.

Harris, Michael W. *The Rise of Gospel Blues: The Music of Thomas A. Dorsey in the Urban Church*. New York: Oxford UP, 1992.

Holloway, Joseph E. Introd. *Africans in American Culture*. Ed. Joseph E. Holloway. Bloomington: Indiana UP, 1960. ix–x.

_____. "The Origins of African-American Culture." *Africanisms in American Culture*. 1–18.

Johnson, Alonzo. "Prayer's House Spirit: The Institutional Structure and Spiritual Care of an African-American Folk Tradition." *Ain't Gonna Lay My 'Ligion Down*. Eds. Alonzo Johnson and Paul Jersild. Columbia: U of South Carolina P, 1996. 8–38.

Kalil, Timothy M. "The Role of the Great Migration of African-Americans to Chicago in the Development of Traditional Black Gospel by Thomas A. Dorsey, circa 1930." Diss. Kent State U, 1993.

Levine, Lawrence W. *Black Culture and Consciousness: Afro-American Thought from Slavery to Freedom* New York: Oxford UP, 1977.

Lincoln, C. Eric, and Lawrence W. Mamiya. *The Black Church in the African-American Experience*. Durham: Duke UP, 1990.

Maultsby, Portia K. "Africanisms in African-American Music." *Africanisms in American Culture*. Ed. Joseph E. Holloway. Bloomington: Indiana UP, 1990. 185–210.

_____. "Afro-American Religious Music 1619–1861: Part II — Computer Analysis of One Hundred Spirituals." Diss. U of Wisconsin — Madison, 1974.

_____. "Influences and Retentions of West African Musical Concepts in U.S. Black Music." *Western Journal of Black Studies* 3.3 (1979): 197–215.

McLin, Lena. Personal interview. 1 March 1992.

Oliver, Paul. *Songsters and Saints: Vocal Traditions on Race Records*. New York: Cambridge UP, 1984.

Shipler, David K. *A Country of Strangers: Blacks and Whites in America*. New York: Vintage, 1997.

Simpson, George Eaton. *Black Religions in the New World*. New York: Columbia UP, 1978.

Southern, Eileen. *The Music of Black Americans: A History*. 2nd ed. New York: Norton, 1983.

7

When Whites and Blacks Met: Performing Artists on Stage and in Film

JAMES R. BIRCH

It was early in the Great Depression. In New York, Cab Calloway and his Cotton Club musical revue was well known. They, as many acts did, toured the country to promote their band and to add to the growing popularity of the jazz music they played. They were playing in Philadelphia, Pennsylvania, when Cab encountered a problem with their next booking. His headlining dance team, Fayard and Harold Nicholas, a.k.a. the Nicholas Brothers, had been given the opportunity to go to Hollywood to audition for a movie. The problem was, they had to go immediately. Cab, being the gentleman that he was, agreed to let them go. But he needed a dance act for his next booking. Somewhat desperate for the next gig, he called the William Morris Agency in New York asking for an act to fill in their next show, and the closest town to their next billing where an agent could be located was the steel town of Pittsburgh, Pennsylvania.

They were scheduled for a booking in Altoona, Pennsylvania. Traditionally, they always had a tap dance act to accompany their performance. The agent had given them two possible leads: both brother acts. In the early 1930s family acts were very much in vogue. This was straight out of the tradition of the Foys in Vaudeville, for example. The Fish Brothers, a local tap act with a comedic flavor and burlesque-type humor, was out of the question for the New York ensemble. Cab Calloway had to have a tap act that showed rhythm, class, and energy to replace the spirited Nicholas

Brothers. The agent described the second brother act and the William Morris agent told the Pittsburgh contact to book the show and have the brothers go to meet Cab the next morning.

The brother act took the Pennsylvania Railroad from Pittsburgh to Altoona to arrive at the theatre where the Cab Calloway Band was rehearsing at 10:00 A.M. the following morning. When the brothers arrived, they went directly to the theatre where Cab Calloway and his famous Cotton Club Band was rehearsing. When they told the stage manager they were the replacement act for the Nicholas Brothers, the stage manager told them he was going to stop the rehearsal. The band director, obviously upset at the interruption of a run-through of the rehearsal, upon seeing the brothers, promptly remarked, "Somebody done made a big mistake."

There was good reason for Cab's skepticism. The tap dancers were both white. Moreover, the dancers were young, too. One of them was still a high school student in Pittsburgh, and the other was a student at the University of Pittsburgh. Nevertheless, Cab Calloway gave them a chance to dance to the song "Stardust." The youngest of the two brothers described the event. Rusty Frank's book *Tap!* (1990) captures the spirit of the encounter of the two brothers auditioning for this musical revue:

> So he asked us, "Did you know this was an all-black show?" And I said, "Yes, but I thought you needed a dance team." He said, "You don't mind working…?" (In those days, there wasn't the freedom, you know, to go back and forth.) "No, we've got your records at home, and you guys really play with a beat. It'd be great to dance to it." So it looked like we were in.
>
> We arrived at the theater for rehearsal and handed the musicians our arrangements. Then one of the guys looks at Cab and he said, "It'll take us a few minutes to dig some of this. But man, these arrangements are wonderful." So Cab said to us, "You kids got nice arrangements. Let's go through it. Now, which of you is the fast dancer?" And I said that I was. He asked what number I dance to, and I replied, "Stardust." Well, "Stardust" isn't a fast number at all. But, I explained, "I start in half-time, and I go into full-time, then I double-time, then I quadruple-time to the finish." He said, "This is something I want to see!" Well, Cab Calloway's band played the thing, and as soon as it was over, they all stood up and clapped and cheered. That was really something. The guys we were nuts about were applauding us!" [177–178].

The brothers were Fred and Gene Kelly. Both went on to have legendary careers in theatre, film, and television. Of significance here is the understanding that a black man, Cab Calloway, had the foresight to recognize the incredible talent of two young dancers, regardless of their skin color. A central premise that is gleaned from this narrative is that performing artists amongst themselves have had respect and admiration for their fellow artists, regardless of race or skin color. This narrative is a look at the mutual respect and admiration of performing artists for the art and craft of their contemporaries regardless of skin color, despite the racial discrimination of the managers, booking agents, executives, and (ultimately) the public who may or may not agree with the convergence of multiple races together in performing artistry.

The history of blacks and whites and racial discrimination in America runs both concurrently and crosscurrently in the performing arts— sadly enough, a history more at odds than in harmony. A look at that phenomenon shows that, when blacks and whites did meet, they oftentimes appreciated the other's art form.

Much has been made of the "Jim Crow" legend in theatre. Many think it condescending to blacks— and rightly so, because much has been made of it as a putdown or a "darky stereotype." Yet, I would like to examine it for what I believe it to be for it's original intentions— a borrowing of a song and dance routine that had innate appeal in its performance and presentation. Much exploitation has certainly come about as a result of the subsequent renditions of this act, but the original intent was a result of a showman's uncanny ability to recognize "drawing power" of an act and characterization.

Thomas D. Rice was a white who made famous the Jim Crow routine. "Before he sang 'Jim Crow,' Rice was considered only a mediocre performer" (Rice 10). According to the Stearnses in *Jazz Dance*, this was "[a]n early example of a professional white dancer 'borrowing' from the Negro folk with phenomenal success.... Rice's borrowed song and dance set the course of minstrelsy" (39). In all likelihood, "Rice was probably a keen observer who merely thought in creating 'Jim Crow' he would have a novel presentation on which he might capitalize. He had no way of knowing that he was setting a precedent that would foster a completely new variety of theatrical entertainment" (Birch 53). There is complete agreement on one point, however: Thomas D. Rice's Jim Crow routine was the rage of the 1830s and set the stage for numerous Negro acts in theatrical performances, not only in America, but in London as well (Wittke 27). Rice got the idea for the Jim Crow routine from a slave in Louisville, Kentucky, during the 1827–1828 theatrical season (Stearns 39). Rice continued to work on the song and dance, and continued to polish the routine. Accounts vary as to when Rice actually gave the first performance of this song and dance, but it is known that the routine appeared in Kentucky in the season of 1828–1829, and subsequently in Cincinnati. He appeared with it in Pittsburgh in the fall of 1832, and in New York City at the Bowery Theatre also that same year (Birch 52–55).

A little known facet of the American theatre is the establishment of the African Theatre, a playhouse for black Americans, that opened on September 21, 1821, with its first performance being Shakespeare's *Richard III.* Wilson notes that this was the "first American performance on record by a Negro company" (69–70). This endeavor was short-lived, however, for "the enterprise was ridiculed and harassed by white racists, many of whom attended the performances to make fun and cause trouble" (Wilson 70–71). Also, the first American play written by an Afro-American playwright, a pseudonymous "Mr. Brown," entitled *The Drama of King Shotaway,* was performed there as well. Two actors, James Hewlett and Ira Aldridge, were in the company, but they could not find lasting employment due to their race. The African Theatre closed for good in 1823. Aldridge, notably, went to England, where he was enthusiastically received as a tragedian in Shakespearean roles (Wilson 71).

This brief theatrical endeavor was at least a start for the emergence of the black performer on the stage. The Stearnses note: "In the 1840s performances by Negro dancers, as contrasted to white dancers in blackface, occurred mostly in low-class dives" (44). The new theatrical entertainment ("minstrelsy") was extremely popular and featured many such white dancers. There was one black dancer, however, who changed the course of theatrical entertainments in this decade. His name was William Henry Lane.

Lane was (again citing the Stearnses) a "free-born Negro," and learned his dancing in and around the Five Points district of lower Manhattan (44). Dancers at this time were held in even lower esteem than actors, and that is one reason why Lane's popularity has not been widely noted by black historians. Furthermore, dance acts were not considered part of the "legitimate" stage at the time, which meant that their performances were normally held on the most tawdry of stages. In spite of all these obstacles, Lane made such a name for himself that in retrospect it remains remarkable.

By 1845 Lane was such an outstanding draw that he was given top billing with four white men in a minstrel show. He had competed with John Diamond (a white dancer) in a series of "challenge" dances beginning in 1844, and had proved the superior dancer in every competition. These dances had occurred at the Bowery and Chatham theatres in New York City and the purse for each night was five hundred dollars, a sizable amount of money in the 1840s. Also by 1845, the handbill for Lane's minstrel company lists him as "Master Juba! The Greatest Dancer in the World!" (Stearns 45). Lane went on to perform abroad in England, where he was received with even more acclaim than in America. This was probably due to the unique and singular freshness of Lane's dancing. Charles Dickens, having toured America and writing in his *American Notes* (1842) about a dancer that he witnessed performing in New York City, describes the fascinating energy, appeal, and spontaneity of the dancer, who undoubtedly was Lane himself:

> Single shuffle, double shuffle, cut and cross-out; snapping his fingers, rolling his eyes, turning in his knees, presenting the backs of his legs in front, spinning about on his toes and heels like nothing but the man's fingers on the tambourine; dancing with two left legs, two right legs, two wooden legs, two wire legs, two spring legs—all sorts of legs and no legs—what is this to him? And in what walk of life, or dance of life, does man ever get such stimulating applause as thunders about him, when, having danced his partner off her feet, and himself too, he finishes by leaping gloriously on the bar-counter, and calling for something to drink, with the chuckle of a million of counterfeit Jim Crows, in one inimitable sound? [82–83].

Minstrelsy contributed to the popularity of Negro dances; unfortunately for black performers, their recognition and acclaim did not achieve similar reciprocation. By the 1870s minstrelsy was dying out, and by 1880 a new theatrical form, vaudeville, was emerging. Vaudeville would remain the entertainment rage for the next five decades. Its end coincided with the start of the Great Depression and the advent of talking pictures as a new form of public entertainment.

However, as had previously been the case in minstrelsy, black performers were not well received in vaudeville either. George Walker and Bert Williams were two such exceptions, earning $40,000 a year just before the turn of the century—an amazing sum of money for anyone at that time. Walker died at age 39. At his death he pondered the status of blacks in the theatre. In 1906 he proclaimed:

> The one hope of the colored performer must be in making a radical departure from the old "darky" style of singing and dancing…. There is an artistic side to the black race, and if it could be properly developed on the stage, I believe the theatergoing public would profit by it…. My idea was always to impersonate my race just as they are. The colored man has never successfully taken off his own humorous characteristics, and the white impersonator often overdoes the matter [qtd. in Gilbert 284].

Negro entertainments continued, nonetheless, in vaudeville. With the development of jazz music in the beginning of the twentieth century an increased interest in black performers emerged on the legitimate stage as well. In 1921 a Negro musical entitled *Shuffle Along* opened at New York's

Sixty-Third Street Theater on May 21, 1921. Note the Stearnses: "When *Shuffle Along* Broke [*sic*] through to Broadway, a new trend was set, a new legend born. Negro musicals were in demand thereafter, and dancing in musical comedy finally took wing" (132). *Shuffle Along* was the first Negro musical to incorporate a literacy of artistry into the show: the performers were skilled in acting, singing, and dancing. This gave the show a realism that previously had not been seen in Negro acts. Not only was the Broadway run a success but when the show went on tour it was equally well received. The show was the brainchild of two authors who had started out as actors and comedians, Flournoy Miller and Aubrey Lyles, and two songwriters named Noble Sissle and Eubie Blake. These four gentlemen gave the show class and professionalism and audiences everywhere loved it. Florence Mills and Josephine Baker became stars from their performances in the show. According to Noble Sissle, "White show people spread the word" (qtd. in Stearns 136).

Shuffle Along was the first Broadway show to use a sixteen-girl chorus line. The jazz music, combined with the spirited dances, merged into an energetic show from start to finish, combined with some excellent acting and comedy routines from the performers. There was even a midnight show on Wednesdays, so that white performers could see the show, too. Marshall and Jean Stearns sum up the many significant contributions of *Shuffle Along*:

> *Shuffle Along* was the first outstanding Negro musical to play white theaters from coast to coast. It also made money. Thereafter, producers and backers were eager to finance another such show, and Negro musicals flourished on Broadway for a decade or so. Attention was focused on the talents of the Negro in vernacular comedy, song, and dance, and jobs opened up for Negro performers. Above all, musical comedy took on a new and rhythmic life, and chorus girls began dancing to jazz [139].

With the advent of talking pictures and sound, the movie industry, after Broadway in the 1920s, provided the next opportunity for Negro performers, although in a slightly different fashion. The 1930s were a time of "teams" of performers—brother and sister, families, or brother acts. Films of the 1930s featured these specialty acts. The motion picture camera had the unique capacity to showcase performers and their abilities in "close ups" which the stage could not do. In the period of the 1930s a dance team combination emerged which captivated audiences everywhere: Shirley Temple and Bill Robinson.

Bill Robinson was born in 1878, came to New York in 1898 and worked a number of places including Coney Island and many theatrical spots in

New York. He worked his way to the top in vaudeville, making an astronomical $6500 week at the height of his popularity. He was a featured performer in the Broadway musical *Blackbirds* in 1928. He performed (what quickly became) his famous stair dance to the tune of "Doin' the New Low Down." He was immediately hailed as the greatest dancer that New York City had to offer, by the likes of drama critics Brooks Atkinson, Alexander Woollcott, and Burns Mantle. Robinson enjoyed this celebrity status, much to the chagrin of other blacks, who felt that he catered to white folks. But one thing is sure: Robinson's tap dancing marked the epitome of clean, clear taps in rhythmic and syncopated precision. Interestingly, Robinson did not perform with taps on his shoes; instead, he preferred working with the older-style wooden soled shoes. He injected his dances with bits of comedy, humor, and quips. He knew how to play an audience. This attribute served him equally well in films, where his appeal was magnified by his onscreen personality.

Shirley Temple and Bill Robinson appeared in a number of memorable films together, and her recollection of their work together has only the highest praise for him. Shirley Temple was the country's number one box office attraction from 1935 to 1938. Films made by her and Robinson during this period were *The Little Colonel* (1935), *Rebecca of Sunnybrook Farm* (1938), and *Just Around the Corner* (1938), among others. She recalled how she and Robinson devised a "communication" system of sorts when they danced together. "We'll have a hand-squeeze system," he proposed. "When I give you three quick squeezes, means we're comin' to a hard part. One long squeeze, really good darlin'! No squeeze at all? Well, let's do it again" (qtd. in Frank 92). Shirley Temple loved her work in the movies, and she maintained a special fondness for Robinson. They got along famously together, both on and off screen. As she says, "Everybody I danced with was wonderful to work with. Buddy and George were certainly two of the finest ones. But Bill Robinson was my favorite. He was the easiest teacher I had, because we could do it by holding hands" (qtd. in Frank 93).

While Shirley Temple and Bill Robinson starred in many films of the 1930s, another equally famous dancer reached critical and public awareness—he, too, with a partner. Fred Astaire and Ginger Rogers became the other celebrated dance team of the 1930s. Astaire had started dancing with his sister Adele in vaudeville, then they had starred on Broadway. When Adele "retired" to marry an English lord, Fred needed to continue working. He was put in a picture entitled *Flying Down to Rio* with a dance partner named Ginger Rogers, and although they were not featured performers, they stole the show. Astaire and Rogers made a series of memorable musicals together in the decade, and *Swing Time* (1936) is perhaps the best of the bunch. In the film, Astaire pays tribute to Bill Robinson in his famous "Bojangles of Harlem" number. In characteristic bowler hat and spats, Astaire puts forth a jazzy, syncopated dance rendition that ends as Robinson characteristically would end a number — by simply walking off the stage.

The other recognized male dance star of the motion picture industry, Gene Kelly, also paid tribute to the Nicholas Brothers by having them appear with him in the 1948 movie *The Pirate*. The Nicholas Brothers were known as a "flash act," putting forth considerable skill in tap and acrobatics in their dance numbers. They had previously appeared to great acclaim in *Down Argentine Way* (1940) and in the all-black musical *Stormy Weather* (1943). Despite the reluctance of the MGM executives to use them (because they thought the film would potentially lose bookings in the South), Kelly decided to cast them in a dance at the close of the film, which shows the considerable and varied talents of the three dancers in an athletic and acrobatic routine. Both Astaire and Kelly recognized the greatness of dancers regardless of their skin color. As Astaire had paid tribute to Bill Robinson, Kelly sought to showcase the Nicholas Brothers with himself in the finale number of *The Pirate*. Dancers appreciate the greatness of the dance, and these two well-known Hollywood stars recognized the greatness of these African-American dancers that had received not enough recognition but had more than enough talent to be considered great dancers in their own right.

We jump to 1985 — and (ironically) to a film that perhaps, shows us how blacks and whites may someday work, play, and live together. *White Nights* (Columbia, 1985) provides us the tandem dancing of a black American and a white Russian portrayed by Mikhail Baryshnikov and Gregory Hines. Simply put, their dance routine remains a metaphor for how blacks and whites can and must put aside differences and dance to the joy of a unified and symbolic brotherhood. As dancers, they show us that despite different styles and orientations, the hermeneutic spirit of celebration can and does exist by which people can live, dance, and share life together. Presented through the artistry of dance, the message that relationships can prosper is quite evident through the unparalleled symmetry of these two men dancing together. That is the message of black and white performers: we can, do, and will work together. As Gene Kelly once remarked in an interview for *Dance Magazine*: "The artist is always ahead of the public." Let us hope so.

References

Ambrosio, Nora. *Learning about Dance: An Introduction to Dance as an Art Form and Entertainment.* Dubuque, IA: Kendall/Hunt, 1997.

Birch, James R. *Tap Dance in the American Theatre: 1828–1880.* Thesis. Kent State U, 1980.

Dickens, Charles. *American Notes.* 1842. New York: St. Martin's, 1985.

Down Argentine Way. Prod. Darryl F. Zanuck. Dir. Irving Cummings. Writ. Karl Tunberg and Darrell Ware. Perf. Don Ameche, Betty Grable, Carmen Miranda, Fayard Nicholas, and Harold Nicholas [uncredited]. Twentieth-Century-Fox, 1940.

Frank, Rusty E. *Tap! The Greatest Tap Dance Stars and Their Stories.* New York: Morrow, 1990.

Gilbert, Douglas. *American Vaudeville: Its Life and Times.* New York: Dover, 1940.

The Pirate. Prod. William LeBaron. Dir. Andrew Stone. Writ. S. N. Berman, Frances, and Albert Hackett. Songs Cole Porter. Perf. Judy Garland, Gene Kelly, Fayard Nicholas, and Harold Nicholas. MGM, 1948.

Rice, Edward Leroy. *Monarchs of Minstrelsy: From "Daddy" Rice to Date.* New York: Kenny, 1911.

Stearns, Marshall, and Jean Stearns. *Jazz Dance: The Story of American Vernacular Dance.* New York: Schirmer, 1968.

Stormy Weather. Prod. William LeBaron. Dir. Andrew Stone. Writ. Jerry Horwin. Perf. Lena Horne, Bill Robinson, Cab Calloway, Fayard Nicholas, and Harold Nicholas. Twentieth-Century-Fox, 1943.

Swing Time. Prod. Pandro S. Berman. Dir. George Stevens. Writ. Howard Lindsay. Songs Jerome Kern and Dorothy Fields. Perf. Ginger Rogers and Fred Astaire. RKO, 1936.

White Nights. Prod. David Watkin. Dir. Taylor Hackford. Writ. James Goldman and Eric Hughes. Choreographer Twyla Tharp. Perf. Mikhail Baryshnikov and Gregory Hines. Columbia, 1985.

Wilson, Garff B. *Three Hundred Years of American Drama and Theatre: From Ye Barre and Ye Club to Hair.* Englewood Cliffs, NJ: Prentice, 1973.

Wittke, Carl. *Tambo and Bones: A History of the American Minstrel Stage.* Durham, NC: Duke UP, 1930.

8
Looking for Jackie and Mike: Race, Sport, and Contemporary American Culture

THABITI LEWIS

> I wish you guys had children so I could kick them in the head or stomp on their testicles so you could feel my pain because that's the pain I wake up with every day.
>
> — Mike Tyson to the media, 18 May 2002

When Jackie Robinson crashed into major league baseball in 1947, he was not chosen because he was the best player the Negro leagues had to offer. This is a fact that does not require explanation. One need only mention the names Josh Gibson and Satchel Paige to make that point. We always hear romantic stories of how Robinson and subsequent black players integrated baseball and America in the process. Although Robinson represented a black face, he was admitted onto the playing field with the express written understanding that he not remind America of his "blackness." Robinson was the player of choice not because he was the best the Negro Leagues had to offer, but because he was college educated, married, had played on the same field as whites in college, was willing to hold his tongue against indignities on and off the field; these components made him the "right" man for the job. It is also well documented that Robinson was outspoken during his career, but during his initial years in the majors he agreed to keep silent for the good of integration. This agreement is what contemporary media lament, a time when blacks accepted their place, were not brash, cocky, self-promoters.

In American sports, the message encoded in modern critiques of African-American athletes resonates in a cry for the early Jackie-like humility, the smile, the affable personality of Willie Mays, or even better, for these African-American youngsters to be more "like Mike." Pioneering black athletes in all sports voiced little resistance to the discrimination they faced for fear of losing their jobs, or being labeled a troublemaker. Despised are the current stars that mirror Jim Brown, Leroy Satchel Paige, Jack Johnson and Ali's cocksure brashness, if not their political focus. Yet the unmistakable irony is that it is flash and showmanship — the very entertaining that media sell and fans purchase without question. The media want athletes molded into images that fit acceptable stereotypes. What writers and producers and programmers lament is a time when there was Babe, DiMaggio, Gehrig, Unitas, Bird — or any other white hero. We are truly, as David Shipler's title expresses, "a country of strangers," and this is a reality that does not deviate in the area of sports. The myth on the American landscape is that sports transcend race, on playing fields the myopia dissipates and for two to four hours fans and players unite in one common cause: victory.

Perhaps this is true, but the truth is that the media deems contemporary athletes, with their tattoos, cornrows, rap albums, black self-expression, dissing, taunting, celebrating achievement in unnecessarily creative manners as egomaniacs, villains—certainly not the heroes sportswriters envision from their boyhoods. The manner in which contemporary athletes (the majority of whom are African-American) are portrayed in sports pages, magazines and on televisions screens suggests that they are hostile foreigners who must be purged from the American imagination, strangers in their own country.

Ralph Waldo Emerson's "Self-Reliance" begins: "Man is his own star." Emerson's mid–nineteenth century transcendental idealism emphasizes self-reliance, self-culture and individual expression. These are cornerstones of contemporary American thought and life, championed by Henry David Thoreau, Walt Whitman, Ralph Ellison and others. Yet when African-American athletes assert similar ideas in their dress, speech and demeanor on and off the playing fields they are received less than favorably. It is impossible to separate self-reliance, self-culture and individual expression in American sports culture. In fact, when these athletes shine as their own stars, the media glare is bright and unfavorable, choosing to confirm predisposed convictions that African-Americans are the culprits behind America's declining moral values. In sports, the mythical contradiction is one of *team* identity, suppressed individualism and *unity*, while the reality is that media heap accolades on individual achievement, eroding the very concept they reverently defend.

An early example of the contradictions associated with African-American self-reliance, culture and individual expression is Satchel Paige who, although a superior player to Robinson, was not the first or even among the first African-Americans selected into the major leagues because he was not what America wanted then or today. Paige was not selected because he was a master showman who was demanding and understood the financial dynamics of the game, as well as his impact on those dynamics, quite well. For example, he knew that when he played people came to the ballparks, which is why he commanded $500 or more per game pitched. Furthermore, Paige's flashy persona was equally problematic for a black pioneer. He drove large, fast, bright cars, he exuded baseball business savvy and self-confidence; these were not desirable, and remain undesirable, character traits for black athletes then and now. The "ideal" player is one that ignores injustice, as Robinson was forced to do during his first two seasons, and resonates the joy and big smile of Willie Mays, the "Say Hey" kid. Like Jack Johnson and Ali, Paige was one of the original what I term "New Jacks." He was then what Deion Sanders, Allen Iverson, Dennis Rodman, Barry Bonds and others are now: "unmanageable" black stars with their own minds and outlook on the world. This makes them hostile as well as strangers.

Media Eyes and the Racial Contract

The media and society not only contradict the ideal of self-reliance, but in doing so their relationships with African-American athletes in modern culture are comparable to one between prisoner and guard. In the sports scenario the sportswriter or commentator assigns himself the role of lawmaker and disciplinarian to the athlete lawbreaker. This power relationship is what Michel Foucault discusses in *Discipline and Punish* with the image of the panopticon as prison (an enclosed defined space observed at every point). The media watch every movement, gesture and thought of modern sports stars, analyzing, judging, critiquing and ultimately attempting to control them — this creates extreme tensions. Over five decades after the first black athletes entered professional sports the scrutiny is equal to that endured by their predecessors. Historically black athletes— in fact, most African-American professionals—find themselves trapped in a panopticon. As incarcerated individuals, their slightest movements supervised and recorded, they are constantly located and examined to ensure they meet white standards. Given the nature of such relationships, it becomes easy to understand why blacks and whites inhabit the same culture as strangers. If judgments and decisions are predetermined the impetus to really "know" the "other" beyond these stereotypes and ideas is nonexistent. David Shipler discusses these very pitfalls in his *A Country of Strangers.*

However, to understand this core of the relationship between media and African-American athletes, I digress to investigate the inner logic of racial domination and how it structures the politics of the US and the world. The relationship between African-American athletes and the media can also be summed up as what Charles Mills calls a *racial contract.* He explains this contract as a racial polity, a racial state and racial judicial system that clearly demarcates the status of whites and non-whites by both law and custom to maintain and reproduce a racial order that secures privileges and advantages of full white citizens and maintains the subordination of nonwhites (14). Thus, the disapproval that the largely white media and society hand down in their daily assessment and moral judgments of African-American athletes stems from implicit or tacit consent of white supremacy. The only star they care to see is one made in their own image.

In America the fallacy we ingest daily is that sports transcend race—that, in fact, the greatest racial strides taken in America have been through sports. "Look," we are told, "at how baseball broke color barriers in 1947, and football and basketball in the 1950s." You cannot talk about race and sport in the same sentence, let alone the same room. However, history corroborates my contention that white misunderstanding, misrepresentation, evasion, and even self-deception regarding matters of race are undeniable. Mills points out that, since the Age of Enlightenment race has "gradually [become] the formal marker of [the] differential status [between white and nonwhite], replacing the religious divide" (23). Our contemporary society remains driven by assumptions of white supremacy as an accepted state of affairs; but as Mills points out, "statements of such frankness are rare or nonexistent in mainstream white opinion today, which generally seeks to rewrite the past so as to deny or minimize the obvious fact of global white domination" (27). So, in the sports world, rather than openly discussing the discomfort with black heroism in American society, color commentators and reporters display, report, regard and present to the world a colonial construct that conveys a hierarchy of races and civilizations, and that whites belong to the superior race and civilization. The implicit and explicit messages are that "these niggers need to change," need to become model sports heroes in the image of Babe Ruth or Larry Bird, but since they cannot, since those white heroes are of a bygone era, African-American athletes must at least comport themselves in terms of these white images or at least in the manner of the pioneer African-American athletes who knew their place and appreciated the opportunity given them. Even better, they should "be like Mike." *Yeah, be like Mike*, America's icon, a man deemed neither black nor white, but just as an apolitical athlete — a statue, or symbol that you place outside an area, or on cereal boxes and sports gear.

Michael Jordan is chocolate-hued vanilla. White media, fans and America identify and adore him. He is not a man, not really a "black" man; his apolitical speech, his frequent smiles, his nattily dressed physique is void of tattoos when unclothed; his pate is devoid of hair, not to mention the dyeing and braiding of some contemporary athletes; in fact, his very absence of hair seems a fact which nullifies the issue. He is an icon, he is just Mike to millions of adoring fans. When people see him, when he presents himself, he is not presenting an "African-American," he is merely a symbol of America, a colorless icon. If the white media journalists, coaches, and David Stern could have their way, they would remake all blacks in Mike's image. Many white fans cry endlessly about what is wrong with the NBA. The argument we never hear, the truth, is that what bugs the retrograde or nostalgic sports fan is that these new black athletes comprise over 80 percent of the league and they ain't actin' like Jackie or tryin' to be like Mike at all.

More Characteristics of the New-Jack Athlete

Sportswriter Gary Pluto wrote a book that was a sorry depiction of the pitfalls of the NBA. He all but said, "The problem with NBA is that it is too black and they don't care about trying to downplay their identity." America, a country notorious for its emphasis on individualism, which concept itself is rooted in capitalism, is the antithesis of the team-work and the socialist, self-sacrificing ideas championed throughout the media regarding sports success. When athletes' behaviors mirror the moral values of the very society that shaped them, athletes are roundly attacked by that very media. There is no "Me Generation" because America is founded on individual expression and concern with self; capitalism is by definition about singular interests taking precedence over those of the whole.

When one compares sports stars of the likes of Jim Brown, Muhammad Ali, Curt Flood and Kareem Abdul-Jabbar to today's athletes, a common critique is that contemporary athletes lack the political edge that

would allow them to overcome constraints and exercise power over institutions and social relations that dominate their lives. The "best" example
of the schism between athletes and the media that try to control them is
the self-destructive "Iron" Mike Tyson, champion of violence and excess.
Before his scheduled June 2002 fight with Lennox Lewis, Tyson told the
media he claims crucifies him: "I wish you guys had children so I could
kick them in the head or stomp on their testicles so you could feel my pain
because that's the pain I wake up with every day" (Jessup). In fairness, I
must also point out that this generation lacks the broad-based movement
that Ali and others had access to. Absent is the political resistance of Ali
who declared himself Muslim and opposed the war.

Still, the undeniable irony is that despite their wealth, contemporary
athletes form a "working class" of sorts, primarily because of their impov-
erished backgrounds and the owner/player dynamics of professional team
sports. Robin Kelly calls such individuals "race rebels"; however I prefer
to regard them as "New Jacks" because, although they are products of
urban decay and capitalist transformation, persistent racism and male
pathos (12), I doubt they consciously struggle for a collective identity that
reflects their race, class, gender and location in the city. Still, their style,
their self-expression, their socio-economic backgrounds inch them toward
resistance on some level, albeit very narrow expressions of resistance.
Nonetheless, New Jacks, with their brandishing of cornrows, tattoos, and
other forms of self-expression, place their personal stamp on contemporary sports, a quasi site of "working-class" politics. Much like their predecessors, the current crop of sports stars have been harvested from a
community influenced by what Kelly terms "the cultural politics of the zoot
suit, bebop, and hipster ethic" (11).

The New Jack and the "Outlaw" Culture

An appropriate discussion of the psychology of "outlaw" culture
attributed to the rap music of today, does not allow for a brief treatment
of Kelly's comparison of the hep cats (as they were called) who donned
zoot suits during the Second World War. These men were indifferent to
the war and defiant towards whites in general and servicemen in particular, but they also placed a premium on the "pursuit of leisure and pleasure; they possessed a laid-back attitude toward work (Kelly 173). The
repercussions for such defiant behavior were "ridicule, severe punishment,
and even beatings ... white soldiers engaged in what amounted to a ritu-
alized stripping of the zoot (172–73). However, this was a popular form of

dress among African-American and Latino youth at the time just as hood-
ies, baggy pants, Raiders caps, braids, gold teeth, cornrows, stocking caps
and boots are the outlaw gear of today. Just as the zoot suit reflected the
style of the 1940s, to a lesser degree the hip-hop gear mirrors the politics
of the current generation. Both styles represent large bodies of the black
working-class youth in urban America "whose social locations have
allowed them to demystify aspects of the hegemonic ideology while reinforcing their ties to it" (181). The New Jacks mostly follow the credo of
hip-hop culture, which is about being "real niggaz," refusing to fake it or
fake it for the public. New Jacks ain't about to smile for "massa." No, for
them playing ball translates into modern hustlers, hipsters who migrate
from the black tops and sandlots of urban working (or not) class black
America, seizing "spaces for leisure, pleasure, and recuperation" (180).
Much like the zoot-suiters, who were hostile to wage labor, and refused
to have a "slave" job, New Jacks display equal resistance allowing "work
to become a primary signifier of identity" (174). Instead of accepting the
posture that they should be happy to have a job as professional athletes,
they flip the script, the teams should be happy to have them playing for
them. The rejection of the traditional work ethic, and privileging leisure
makes the divide between New Jacks, coaches, media and fans erupt. It also
dredges up myths and not so subtle suggestions of blacks as lazy. Professional sports is an escape from alienating wage labor, a way to fully transcend economic boundaries without working; for them it is really a game,
not work, something many would play for free.

New Jacks clearly understand the racial boundaries they cannot leap.
And I would contend that to a limited extent, they understand the oppo-
sitional meanings embedded in their earrings, tattoos, cornrows, style of
dress and other elements that comprise the expressive black youth culture
they represent. However, the world of the modern athlete is much more
complex because of the increasingly corporate nature of the game of sports.
Not only are the current generation void of a movement propelling them
into political action, but the effect of such action is measured in clear dollars and cents. Nonetheless, it is a new age, a time of the New Jack who
demands respect and to meet life on his own terms.

So when Allen Iverson refuses to wear suit and tie, feuding with Larry
Brown without relenting, *he* is the bad guy. Why does Coach Brown fail
to respect and understand his desire to be himself? White coaches fail to
connect with the current crop of young black stars partly because coaches
tend to be nearly all older white males, whose philosophy is that these
"'Negroes' should be happy to be here — look at Jackie, talk to Mike or
Magic." Thus, black players are invisible to them — as invisible as the

stranger Ralph Ellison's nameless narrator meets on the street and nearly beats to death in *Invisible Man*. Latrell Sprewell was invisible to P. J. Carlesimo, Chris Webber was invisible to Don Nelson as is Iverson invisible to Brown. Another huge impediment is the paternal posture these white males take; it is similar to that taken by slave masters. New Jacks resent and resist the paternal relationships these whites attempt to forge, assuming that all come from broken homes and merely need fatherly guidance to straighten them out.

Jordan's apolitical, nonracial persona garners popular approval among white fans, whereas Iverson (a quintessential member of the hip-hop generation) is deemed hoodlum or outlaw for choosing to "keep it real," don sweats, hoods, and sneakers or boots to a job that does not require a suit and tie. Although his performance during the 2001 NBA finals earned him accolades, even the respect from members of the media who previously tried to tar and feather him in their columns and commentary, recasting him as a little giant with a heart of steel, a giant "killer," the truth is that it was a story that never really sold because he failed to change his image, conform in his dress, speech, thought patterns and overall perspective. Nonetheless, Iverson's achievements and season-long response to the media echoe Emerson's "Self-Reliance," which says, "Whoso would be a man must be a nonconformist.... Nothing is at last sacred but the integrity of your own mind. Absolve you to yourself, and you shall have the suffrage of the world" (21). Our society respects Emerson, we teach his ideas, applaud, then emulate him, yet scorned are the New Jacks who practice the same ethics.

The truth is that we live in a country as *strangers*. Whites do not see or want to really know blacks; this compels whites to assume that everyone must comport themselves according to the rules of white supremacy (again, the racial contract). This myopic reality leads spectators and the media to display a disdain for and fear of black athletes that permeates the public transcript. Read any newspaper or magazine, watch any game or sports news program and if you listen long enough you are bound to hear a transcript that suggests the following: blacks are lazy, self-destructive, undisciplined, lack moral character and are prone to criminal behavior. Upheld for all to leer at, proof that "these niggers ain't Jackie or Mike." Listen closely and you will hear that Mike's apolitical, comfortable character is the standard all athletes should aspire to (which is why they brought him out of retirement). If you really pay attention, you will hear the admission that bringing "Negroes" into the popular mainstream sports imagination was an enormous mistake. White columnists, sportswriters and commentators alike are really saying, "Oh, if we could only return to the golden days of white greatness, of the Babe, Rocky [Rocky Marciano], and Larry Bird — hell, we'll even settle for Shoeless Joe Jackson..." (which is why the saccharine-sweet *A Field of Dreams* was such a big hit) and, of course, the more rubbishy Rocky Balboa movies. Bernard Malamud's *The Natural* and its fabled hero Roy Hobbs, a combination of Babe Ruth and Joe Jackson mainly, published in the early 1950s, is a lament for this kind of lore, a yearning for the passing of an era as well as a response to the coming of blacks into the center of America's sports culture.

When modern black athletes decide to express themselves freely, claiming as did Emerson, "What I must do is all that concerns me, not what the people think" (23), they are chided for their independence or solitude. The NJs refuse to live after the world's opinion, thrust as they are in the midst of the crowd. However, the independence of black athletes does not resonate with the same political sting of say Ali whose activism gained focus from the civil rights movement and the war. Today's brand of activism is much different if not more intricate because of the gains of the civil rights movement that make contemporary race issues more covert. As was true in Ali's day, there is no longer a broad-based movement propelling them in a clear direction; however, these New Jacks recognize the disparate treatment of African-Americans. Despite wealth they endure profiling, discrimination and other indignities.

Most of the New Jack athletes in our high profile sports are youth; and as such as they are entitled to partake of the process of discovering the world as they negotiate it. This of course does not sit well with owners, media, league commissioners, and coaches whose jobs it is to wield authority that keeps them from creating new cultures and strategies of resistance.

What is unique about New Jacks is that to some degree they have gained a wider visibility via their associations with corporate products and they tend to avoid many activist causes and concerns. There are few like Ali willing to sacrifice millions in purses and endorsements because of religious or political beliefs. And those like Mahmoud Abdul Rauf, leading-scorer for the Denver Nuggets and budding NBA star, who do risk money, as he did when he refused to stand during the National Anthem prior to each game (on the grounds that it represents hypocrisy and tyranny) wind up like Rauf — traded to the worst team in the league and eventually dismissed from the NBA altogether. Rauf's situation serves as a reminder for NJs that the white sports establishment will deal with them harshly and swiftly, for there will be consequences for controversial political stands.

However, their resistance exists in forms of personal expressions such as braids, tattoos and body piercing; these quieter but obvious political expressions of nonconformity earn New Jacks scorn and displeasure.

As Mills also suggests, nonwhites must function within a society structured around the racial exploitation of nonwhites, and a moral psychology skewed consciously or unconsciously toward privileging whites, "taking status quo of differential racial entitlement as normatively legitimate, and not to be investigated further" (40). These quieter forms of resistance, although not desirable, will be tolerated by media, coaches, owners and fans; but these same people will not endure the politics of athletes like Tommy Smith — who raised his fist to represent Black Power on the Olympic podium — Muhammad Ali, or Abdul Rauf. For these villains the punishment meted out is harsher than for those who fit the stereotype of the mythical "bad nigger" — the reason Mike Tyson will always have an easier time, no matter what new vile behavior hits the headlines. Plagued by what Emerson calls "a foolish consistency [that is] the hobgoblin of little minds, adored by little statesmen and philosophers and divines" (24), power brokers in our society uphold a slave-like reverence for behavior and codes that scare them from self-trust or accepting the self-trust displayed by others. Scorned is the truthfulness, the freedom of self-expression embraced by New Jacks who speak their minds, body and spirits for all to see and enjoy. Because black athletes have supplanted Babe and the boys, the only acceptable models remain Jackie and Mike.

References

Emerson, Ralph Waldo. *Self-Reliance and Other Essays*. New York: Dover, 1993.

Foucault, Michel. *Discipline and Punish [Surveiller et Punir]: The Birth of the Prison*. 2nd ed. Trans. Alan Sheridan. New York: Vintage, 1995.

Jessup, Peter. "Boxing: Welcome to the Weird World of Mike Tyson." *New Zealand Herald*, 18 May 2002. 5 May 2002 <http://www.nzherald.co.nz/storyprint. cfm?storyID=1992670>.

Kelly, Robin D. G. *Race Rebels: Culture, Politics, and the Black Working Class*. New York: Free, 1994.

Mills, Charles. *The Racial Contract*. New York: Cornell UP, 1997.

Shipler, David K. *A Country of Strangers: Blacks and Whites in America*. New York: Vintage, 1998.

9
Southern White Ministers at Mid-Century

ROY LECHTRECK AND ELAINE LECHTRECK

In the middle of the 1900s, three of the major issues in many churches in the South (and to some extent in the North) were whether or not to allow African-Americans to sit in on church services, whether or not to allow them to be become members of the congregation, and what to do with ministers who openly advocated better treatment for African-Americans and obedience to court decisions on racial issues. Several pastors were forced to leave their churches over these issues. Several were never appointed to churches. Others left before they were forced out, or because they could not in good conscience remain in the church where they were. Behind the controversies were different views of the nature of the African-American (based on Scripture or Darwin), different views of the power of the congregation to decide how to interpret Scripture, and different views on the obligation of Christians to obey the civil laws of the country.

Scriptural Interpretations

Many whites had long been taught that the Negro was an inferior human. Scriptural passages were found to substantiate this claim. One such passage concerned Noah and the Ark. Noah was commanded to take his family into the Ark and two of every species of fish, fowl, and animal, and food to sustain them for weeks. Since the flood was supposedly worldwide, whites were all therefore considered to be descended from Noah. Therefore blacks had to be considered part of the animal group, according to the segregationists. Another version of the Noah story was that one of the sons of Noah was punished for being disrespectful to his father, and the punishment was that he was to be the founder of the black race. (Another son was the founder of the red race.) Scriptural scholars, of course, dismiss both interpretations. For example, one scholar "noted that the curse of Ham was placed on his son Canaan, not on Africans" (Alvis 55). St. Paul was also cited to justify slavery. He not only said that slaves were to obey their masters, but when he was given a slave he returned that slave to "its" former owner, even though that owner had told Paul that Paul could release the slave.

Church Governance

Was the black man inferior to the white? In a non-hierarchical church like the Baptists (until the recent takeover of the Southern Baptist Convention by diehard fundamentalists), it was for the congregation to decide. There, the congregation (or its deacons or elders) hired and fired its minister, so they had ultimate control. They determined how the Bible would be taught and applied. One or more ministers had to promise before they were hired that they would not say anything on the race issue that would split the church (Hulan 1963). (Roy S. Hulan was fired from his church in Jackson, Mississippi, when he preached that all should have access to the House of God.) To many, this all sounded like the abdication of ministerial responsibility.

In hierarchical churches, such as the Anglican and the Methodist, the bishop had the authority to decide what doctrines were correct and what ones were not. So the views and behaviors of the clergy in these churches depended to some extent on those of the bishop. Not all bishops, of course, had a "race position" and some left their clergy pretty much alone.

In the Presbyterian churches, when controversies arose, the presbytery — made up of the minister and a layperson from each church in the area — had ultimate supervision of each church. In a case that received national attention in the late 1950s, it was the presbytery, without taking any vote of the congregation, that sacked Robert McNeill from his church in Columbus, Georgia. It was done just after McNeill had given his sermon. The head of the presbytery gave a glowing account of McNeill's ministry, but then at the very end, in a few sentences, without prior warning, fired him — in front of him and his whole family. The reason given, in the words of a *New York Times* reporter who was there, was that "the voice of the pulpit must be the voice of the pew." The pastor had antagonized some members by, among other things, an article on racism in *Look* magazine (McNeill 1965).

Church in Society

Certainly, some White preachers succeeded in turning their congregations around; others did not, and still others (the majority perhaps in the South) did not even try. Besides the theological question of the nature of the black man, there was also the question of "how, when, and where" to integrate. Many who believed blacks and whites should worship together differed among themselves over timing. On one end were those who exclaimed, "Integrate NOW." On the other end were those who believed that the churches should integrate only when society as a whole integrated, for effective integration only occurs when the groups are somewhat equal economically and socially. This is the view of George Yancey. In one of the best articles on this topic, "An Examination of the Effects of Residential and Church Integration on Racial Attitudes of Whites" (1999), he also claims that church members possess more racial prejudice than non-members. He adds that contact, which produces fear and defensiveness, may worsen racial relations rather than improve them. Integration by itself does not alter racial attitudes, until the percentage of blacks in a congregation rises to a certain point.

Some blacks and black preachers actually did not want to worship with whites. They wanted to keep their own traditions of worship. Occasional joint church services or swapping ministers, or an individual black visiting a white church might be acceptable, but nothing more. Among ministers, some felt that even mildly aggressive integration activity might be considered "sheep stealing." At least one white Protestant preacher was disturbed when blacks, refused admission to his church, walked a few blocks and were allowed into the Catholic Church. Refusal of admission for a single service was also considered by some to be poor public relations.

Individual Cases

In our study of the issue, about a score of ministers (or relatives, if the minister had died) were interviewed, and many publications were used.

Archives were consulted. This oral history project began with a few names, but whenever one minister was interviewed we almost always got one or more names of others that had to leave their churches also.

The most widely written about minister who got into trouble for his racial views was William Campbell. He was a chaplain at the University of Mississippi and invited a speaker to campus (during religious emphasis week) who had contributed money to the NAACP. This infuriated the "old guard" and Ole Miss refused to let the man appear, so Campbell just sat mute in front of a large audience during the period when the "guest" would have spoken. Following this, human feces were placed in a punch bowl at a reception Campbell held for new students. He once played table tennis with a black minister, after which he was again called on the carpet by the school authorities. The next morning ping-pong balls were found on his front lawn, one-half white and one-half black. After many obscene phone calls and death threats, he left Mississippi and went to Nashville to work for the National Council of Churches in promoting integration in churches. Very little was accomplished, and he decided to give up working through churches. He always seemed to believe that institutions caused more problems then they solved, and his views intensified and reached the point that he actually thought churches did more harm than good. He then turned his attention to the "rednecks" and members of the KKK whom he considered decent hardworking people who were being exploited and manipulated by the upper classes so they would blame the blacks for their troubles. Campbell feels that we need to be sensitive to the concerns of these people if we are going to change their attitudes towards blacks (Hawkins 1997).

At Little Rock, Dunbar Ogden, Jr., was the only local white minister who answered Daisy Bates' call to accompany the nine black students into the Little Rock High School. He tried to get others to accompany him, but failed. (Campbell came too, but he was not a local preacher.) Ogden was fired from his ministry, and like another interviewed for this project, went to West Virginia.

Another minister, Francis X. Walter, got in trouble with two Episcopal dioceses for advocating the rights of African-Americans, and had to cease normal pastoral duties. He then went to a rural area, and got the women there to make quilts to sell to increase their incomes. This was very successful, and a 30-minute documentary was made about this quilting-bee endeavor. Later he was allowed back into pastoral work when a new bishop took over his home diocese.

Three ministers were interviewed who became embroiled in integrating public schools in Tuskegee, Alabama, and had to leave their churches. One of them was told that the KKK would pay a visit to his home, presumably to burn a cross as a warning to "behave." When he figured out who the cross burners were, he paid a visit to a local tavern where they could usually be found, and said in a loud voice, while conversing with another patron, that he would be waiting with a shotgun. Needless to say, they never showed up; he himself was booted out of his church.

Another minister signed a petition to do away with segregation on the city buses (after such segregation had been ruled unconstitutional in Montgomery). His congregation drastically curtailed their support for the church, and he was about to have his salary cut off, when an unknown woman came to his assistance and weekly donated $200 to $500, in hundred dollar bills, for him to give to the church. He went out of town to a banker friend and had the hundreds exchanged for twenties, and secretly slipped them into the collection plate on Sundays. A black church offered to make up all of his lost income if necessary.

In yet another well-known case, a Methodist minister, W. B. Selah, who had attended one or more Citizens' Council meetings, became disillusioned with them, and later resigned his church after the ushers kept blacks from being admitted. He was not, however, an ardent integrationist. He was a strong advocate of treating blacks justly, and believed strongly that the *Brown* (school integration) decision was the law of the land and ought to be followed without any massive resistance. But he felt that neither blacks nor whites were ready for any large-scale integration. He said, "It is not sinful for white people to prefer to worship with white people." And he said that if a black applied for church membership, he would have to tell him that it was his duty to join a colored church, for these churches were the backbone of the black communities (Crespino 42).

Membership in a Council on Human Relations (CHR) also subjected a minister to reprisals. Robert Hughes of Birmingham in 1960 was ordered to appear before a grand jury, with all records of the Alabama CHR (a demand that the US Supreme Court had held unconstitutional in other cases). He refused to bring the records with him, and the subpoena for the records was withdrawn, but the Methodist Council to which he belonged ordered him to resign his position as executive director and accept a new assignment, or be dismissed from the ministry. Earlier he had had a cross burned on his front lawn, and his wife's life was threatened because he defended a seminarian who opposed the formation of a segregationist Methodist layman's group. His status in the Methodist Church was resolved when he was allowed to be a missionary to Africa (Bryan 134–137).

Clarence Jordan was another white Southern minister who was

harassed because of his integrationist activity. In the 1940s, he and another Southern Baptist minister started an interracial farm community a few miles southwest of Americus, Georgia (and a few miles southeast of Plains), called Koinonia. It grew slowly, and never reached more than a few dozen members. It became a semi-socialistic, but religious, commune. It operated its own farm, and taught literacy classes and modern farming techniques to its neighbors, white and black. In 1950 all Koinonians were ousted from membership in the local church. Their activities, and Jordan's encouraging a visitor from India to attend services at this church, was just too much for the Rehoboth church membership, but the rest of the community more or less left them alone, until the *Brown* decision. In the early 1960s, Koinonia openly supported local civil rights activists and allowed the farm to become a refuge and meeting place for the Student Nonviolent Coordinating Committee (SNCC) and the Congress of Racial Equality. The farm then faced economic boycotts, bombings, destruction of a roadside vegetable-fruit stand, and KKK drive-by shootings (intended to scare but not kill). (In 1968, the farm reorganized as the Koinonia Partners, and is no longer a commune.) The farm almost always needed outside financial help, and lost that help after the civil rights movement died down (K'Meyer; Lee).

An interesting aspect of the all-encompassing racism in some Southern churches and church institutions is that many of them sponsored/supported American missionaries in Africa, to convert the black "heathen," but refused to let these converts attend church services if they came to this country. Mercer U. in Macon, Georgia, after a period of soul searching, began to accept black students in the mid 1960s. Sam Oni, a convert from Nigeria, whose application for admission to Mercer resulted in that school's integration, attempted to attend services at least twice in 1966 at the Tattriall Square Baptist Church (next to the campus), but was rebuffed each time. Pastor Thomas J. Holmes protested his exclusion, and was forced to resign. Mercer's president called this an "act of savagery." The story got much publicity nationally, and Holmes later said that he knew of "at least four other Baptist churches which adopted open door policies" because of what happened at his church (Wills 614–15). Holmes himself wrote a book about the incident and said that two of his deacons were Klansmen and that he got no support at that time from other Baptist ministers (Holmes 73, 102).

Prophecy, in the modern sense, may not be a requirement in a minister, but one minister in Arkansas warned his community that the feeling of the blacks against the White businessmen was so intense that the downtown section of the town was in danger of being burned down. The city fathers, of course, sneered at the warning. A short time afterwards, however, a few buildings were torched.

Some ministers were arrested and sent to jail. Edwin King, a native Mississippian, and a chaplain at Tougaloo College, who had been arrested previously in a demonstration in Montgomery, Alabama, was hauled off to jail when he participated in a ministers' vigil in Jackson, Mississippi, in 1963. A few days later, the Methodist conference voted 89–85 to bar him from all church posts in the state. Like several other ministers, he had been educated in northern seminaries, and this was probably held against him. He was again arrested in Jackson in a dragnet after the funeral of Medgar Evers, field secretary for the NAACP, who was brutally shot on June 12, 1963. After Dr. King was involved in an auto accident, it was discovered that someone had loosened the lug nuts on his tires (Vollers, 12, 143; Branch, 121, 634).

Of course, history repeats itself. The killing of a black in Texas recently by dragging him behind a pickup truck was nothing new. A minister in Georgia decades earlier had faced the same situation. From the pulpit he condemned the act as murder, and for that he himself was forced out.

Demagogues— hiding behind masks or out in the open — many times have said that blood would flow before "niggers" would be allowed in public schools. It was inevitable, then, that one or more ministers would be physically attacked. One such incident occurred in Clinton, Tennessee, in 1956, after the area high school had been integrated. Blacks soon boycotted classes there, after much harassment, for fear of bodily harm. Then a Baptist minister, Paul W. Turner, got word to the Negro children that if they wanted to go back to school, he would walk with them to ensure their safety. Two fellow townsmen accompanied them. They all arrived at school unharmed. The other two townsmen went back to their jobs, but when Turner started to go back to his church, a gang beat him up in broad daylight. It was election day, and after the town heard what had happened, the number of voters increased drastically (instead of falling as they would normally), and the segregationist slate was trounced four to one. Commenting on this beating, an article in *The Nation* stated, "The people of Clinton have learned at first-hand that the high-flown language of nullification [states' rights] is kissing kin to the brutal fist that smacks into a minister's face because he protects law-abiding children" (Dykeman and Stokely 533).

These, of course, are only a few of the stories. They are related here because of their variety. Some ministers have freely told their stories, whereas others do not want to talk about what happened, but no complete understanding of church history or racism can be had without the oral histories of these men.

Discussion

The background of these ministers is varied but most of them seemed to have had a strong moral upbringing. If so, this corresponds to studies of Europeans who helped Jews escape Hitler's camps, but few knew of the many other ministers who ran into trouble with their churches. There was obviously no support group for these brave souls. Isolation was sometimes a problem. Seminaries did not prepare ministers for the backlash that develops when brave souls defy community culture. (Today, one would hope that there would be a web site manned by sociologists, psychologists, and ministers which would improve their morale and give advice on how to handle a particular situation.) One denomination did give financial aid and help with relocation to ministers kicked out of churches due to racism.

Since all or almost all of the major Protestant denominations issued statements approving integration, where did the opposition come from? (We are discussing the area from Arkansas to South Carolina, basically.) Outside of those who sincerely felt the time was not ripe, opposition came from two sources. The obvious one was the white supremacy faction. These were members of (or people who supported) the KKK and the Citizen's Councils, which were created very shortly after *Brown v. Board of Education*. The other was the anti–Catholic faction who saw the Pope as the Antichrist, and supported the Klan because the Klan was anti–Catholic. According to the principle "my enemy's enemy is my friend," many of these people joined the ranks of the Klan and the Citizens' Councils and strengthened their hold on society. The close ties between the Klan and the Protestant Churches are specifically pointed out in Chapter 3 of *Politics, Society, and the Klan in Alabama, 1915–1949* (Feldman 1999).

In spite of denominational statements supporting integration, churches have generally not been active in promoting human rights. Their emphasis has been on personal salvation, not social reform. The Reverend Jerry Falwell, for instance, in a March 21, 1965, sermon condemned activist ministers and said that the Bible does not tell us to reform institutions. The entire sermon can be found in Perry D. Young, *God's Bullies: Native Reflections on Preachers and Politics* (310–317). The majority of mainline Christian churches seem to agree with him. Gary Marx found that civil rights "militancy" (doing several things such as taking part in a demonstration, opposing discrimination in public places, etc.) occurred in only 26 percent of those who attended church more than once a week, and in 45 percent of those who went to church less than once a week. But it occurred in 70 percent of those who claimed to be "not at all religious" (368–9). Ministers who tried to make the country more Christ-like were in a minority or were ignored.

Eventually the churches (or many of them) became integrated. Was this primarily due to the ministers or to the times— the economy, the new civil rights laws, and Black Power? We cannot say. The national press devoted much space to the famous Northern white preachers who came south for marches— and then went home — but the deeds of the real soldiers in the field have been neglected. If some of the ministers failed, at least like the Old Testament prophets, they lived up to their faith.

References

Alvis, Joel L., Jr. *Religion and Race: Southern Presbyterians, 1946–1983.* Tuscaloosa: U of Alabama P, 1994.

Branch, Taylor. *Pillar of Fire: America in the King Years 1963–65.* New York: Simon, 1998.

Bryan, G. MacLeod. *These Few Also Paid a Price: Southern Whites Who Fought for Civil Rights.* Macon, GA: Mercer UP, 2001.

Crespino, Joseph. "The Christian Conscience of Jim Crow: White Ministers and the Mississippi Citizens' Councils." *Mississippi Folklife* Fall 1998: 36–44.

Dykeman, Wilma, and James Stokely. "Courage in Action in Clinton, Tennessee." *Nation* 22 Dec. 1956: 531–33.

Feldman, Glenn. *Politics, Society, and the Klan in Alabama, 1915–1949.* Tuscaloosa: U of Alabama P, 1999.

Hawkins, Merrill M. *Will Campbell: Radical Prophet of the South.* Macon, GA: Mercer UP, 1997.

Holmes, Thomas J. *Ashes for Breakfast: A Diary of Racism in an American Church.* Valley Forge, PA: Judson, 1969.

Hulan, Roy S. "When Men Are at Odds." *Christian* 22 Sept 1963: 4–5.

K'Meyer, Tracy E. *Interracialism and Christian Community in the Postwar South: The Story of Koinonia Farm.* Charlottesville: U P of Virginia, 1997.

Lee, Dallas. *The Cotton Patch Evidence.* Americus, GA: Koinonia, 1971.

Marx, Gary T. "Religion: Opiate or Inspiration of Civil Rights Militancy among Negroes?" *The Black Community in Modern America.* Eds. A. Meier and E. Rudwick. New York: Atheneum, 1964.

McNeill, Robert. *God Wills Us Free.* New York: Hill, 1965.

Vollers, Maryanne. *Ghosts of Mississippi: The Murder of Medgar Evers, the Trials of Byron De La Beckwith, and the Haunting of the New South.* Boston: Little, 1995.

Willis, Ann Scott. "A Baptist's Dilemma: Christianity, Discrimination, and the Desegregation of Mercer University." *Georgia Historical Quarterly* 80 (1996): 595–615.

Yancey, George. "An Examination of the Effects of Residential and Church Integration on Racial Attitudes of Whites." *Sociological Perspectives* 42 (1999): 279–304.

Young, Perry D. *God's Bullies: Native Reflections on Preachers and Politics.* New York: Holt, 1982.

10
The Founding and Early History of Chicago's Newberry Library: Free to Whom?

THOMAS KAUFMAN

The Newberry Library

One of the issues that David K. Shipler addresses in *A Country of Strangers* is that of power in American society. Shipler asserts, "Integration means more than just putting people together — it means sharing power." In some instances, the efforts of the elite to maintain its power and to control the masses have been camouflaged as programs to assist those individuals whom the elite actually desired to control and to restrict. One such example of this is the founding and early history of the Newberry Library in Chicago.

The Newberry Library located at 60 West Walton Street is a quiet presence in the cultural and educational landscape of Chicago. Despite its lack of familiarity to the general public, the Newberry enjoys a highly respected reputation among scholars and researchers in the humanities. The Newberry Library describes itself as an independent research library concentrating in the humanities with an active educational and cultural presence in Chicago. It is privately funded, but free and open to the public. The library's holdings span the history and culture of Western Europe from the Middle Ages to the mid–twentieth century and the Americans from the time of first contact between Europeans and Native Americans (Newberry Gen Info 1). The mission statement of the Newberry Library affirms:

Mission Statement The Newberry Library, open to the public without charge, is an independent research library and educational institution dedicated to the expansion and the dissemination of knowledge in the humanities. As one of the world's leading repositories of a broad range of books and manuscripts relating to the civilizations of western Europe and the Americas, the Library's mission is to acquire and preserve research collections of such materials, and to provide for and promote their effective use by a diverse community of users. As a library, the Newberry is dedicated to the highest standards of collection preservation and bibliographic access; as a research and educational institution, it is committed to facilitation research, teaching, and publication in an atmosphere of full and free intellectual inquiry [N G I].

Through its many activities in the areas of research, book and collection acquisition, educational partnerships, fellowships, and public programs, the Newberry Library accomplishes the goals of its mission statement and acts as a vital, vibrant, and valuable contributor to the culture and society of Chicago.

Although today's Newberry Library is a place that welcomes and encourages amateur and professional scholars in the fields of social history and the humanities, the history of the founding of the library and the actions of its founding board of trustees and its first librarian describe an altogether different kind of institution, one that acted as an agent to promote discrimination and class distinction in late nineteenth-century Chicago.

Walter Loomis Newberry (1804–1868) settled in Chicago in 1833 after making an earlier trip there with Lewis Cass and William Astor. Over the next thirty years, Newberry made a fortune in banking (Newberry and Burch), real estate development (Merchants Loan and Trust), and railroads (Chicago-Northwestern). By 1868, the year of his death, Newberry had an estate of between five and six million dollars. In 1868 he sailed for Paris to meet his wife and two daughters, but he perished at sea four hundred miles out of Le Havre. This was the first in a series of four sad family tragedies that contributed to the giving to Chicago of the Newberry Library. Closely following Newberry's death, the Great Chicago Fire destroyed the Newberry mansion and the substantial gentleman's library of which Newberry was so proud. There then followed the deaths of his two young, unmarried daughters in 1874 and 1876. Finally in 1885, Mrs. Newberry died (Towner 7–9).

Newberry placed a contingent provision in his will stipulating that, should his two daughters die childless, approximately one-half of his estate should be used to establish a "free public library." With the deaths of his two unmarried daughters in the 1870s and Mrs. Newberry's death in 1885, the Newberry trustees held $2,150,000.00 available for the library (Shereikis 10; Towner 9). Due to a unique accident of fate, the trustees assumed the responsibility of deciding what type of library should come into existence without having to adhere to the guidance and direction of its patron.

All of the historical facts concerning the codicil in Newberry's will agree that Newberry desired the library to be a free public library (Finkelman 6; Shereikis 10). However the circumstances described above gave the trustees and the first librarian an opportunity to build whatever type of collection and institution they chose. The will required only that the institution be free, open to the public, and located in Chicago's North Division. Thus the trustees enjoyed a tremendous amount of latitude and flexibility in determining the character and appeal of the institution.

The initial board of trustees consisted of E.W. Blatchford and William Bradley, who were later joined by the Newberry's first librarian, William Frederick Poole. These individuals, like Newberry, were part of Chicago's elite and dedicated to the development of the city. E. W. Blatchford had made his fortune manufacturing lead products during the Civil War and was a partner of Newberry in several business ventures. William Bradley had come to Chicago from Connecticut and served as clerk of the U.S. District Court. William Frederick Poole, the first librarian, was, at the time of his appointment to the Newberry, president of the American Library Association and president-elect of the American Historical Association. He was internationally known as the author of *Poole's Index to Periodical Literature* and was previously the head librarian at the Chicago Public Library (Shereikis 10). Given the backgrounds of the men who laid the foundation for the Newberry Library, it is not surprising that the library projected somewhat of an elitist attitude and intimidated the average Chicagoan.

On July 1, 1887, Blatchford and Bradley announced the establishment of the Newberry Library which was in their words to function as a "library of reference" (Finkelman 7). In his article on the founding of the Newberry Library, Paul Finkelman cites several factors that influenced the decision to create a library of reference. First, Trustee Bradley assumed that Newberry himself would have desired his library to be an equal to the Astor Library because of the relationship and respect Newberry had for William B. Astor and the Astor family. Second, a reference library would be easier to administer than a circulating or general public library. In any event, Chicago already had the Chicago Public Library at the time the Newberry endowment became available. The third and the most important factor identified by Finkelman concerns the backgrounds and the attitudes of Blatchford and Bradley. As aristocrats in Chicago society, the two trustees were inclined toward a scholarly gentleman's library rather than a less genteel institution (Finkelman 9). Finkelman's account poses the question of why the trustees did not place Newberry's bequest in the hands of the Chicago Public Library. This action would have satisfied Newberry's requirements for the disposition of his estate.

The answer to this question can be found by examining the backgrounds, social standing and values of Blatchford, Bradley, and Poole. The three men, like Newberry, belonged to the class of the old gentry — long-standing merchants, small manufacturers, established professional men, civic leaders. According to E. Digby Baltzell, the author of *The Protestant Establishment*, "The old family, college educated class that had deep roots in local communities and often owned family businesses, that had traditions of political leadership, belonged to patriotic societies and the best clubs, staffed the government boards of philanthropic and cultural institutions, and led movements for civic betterment were being edged aside in making basic political and economic decisions by the ostentatious and corruptly rich masters of the newly established corporations" (112). At the same time, the new industrial order that caused the development of cities like Chicago into large, urban, metropolitan areas also created a large working class population that did not adhere to the values of men like Blatchford, Bradley, and Poole.

In defense of their values which represented what George Santayana has called the "genteel tradition" and to eliminate the need to bow to "the tyranny exercised by the taste of the common-schooled millions who have been taught to read, but have never learned to discriminate" (Schlesinger 248), the Newberry trustees established an institution that was nominally public, but by concentrating on certain types of collections and by creating certain institutional rules effectively shut itself off from the masses of Chicago.

As a library, the Newberry was primarily a depository of collected books, but there was also a historic connection between the type of individuals who would be attracted to the library and the types of collecting the library would conduct. William Poole had very explicit ideas about what the Newberry would be about. Before he died, Poole took the lead in determining the areas of disciplinary responsibility of the major libraries in Chicago. Under Poole's direction the Chicago Public Library was to concentrate on research in the social sciences, and the John Crerar Library would focus on science, technology, and medicine. This alignment left the Newberry free to devote its considerable resources to the fields of the humanities and history (Wyly 181–82). This arrangement enhanced the accomplishment of Poole's goal for the Newberry:

> The intention is to make a collection of books that will be complete in all its departments, the purpose being to satisfy the wants of scholars. It will not interfere with Public Library in any way, but will supplement it and relieve the Library Board of the purchase of costly books that they may deem necessary to have. This Library will stand to the Public Library about in the same relation that universities stand to public schools, one being for higher and the other for general education [Finkelman 11].

In the same fashion that universities were almost exclusively the domain of the upper classes, the Newberry would be an institution devoted to and reserved for gentlemen.

Considering Poole's background as a scholar and his close relationship with the American Historical Association, his position on the role of the Newberry Library in the cultural and intellectual life of Chicago is not surprising. Late nineteenth century society was a strikingly undisciplined culture that had thrown off institutional restraints on the individual. "It valued the omnicompetence of the common man above the tutelage of any elite," notes Higham (9). Academic scholars conceived themselves as guides for a democratic society that overestimated material success and undervalued the higher ideals of life. Scholars looked to the cultured patrician class for help in fighting against the rawness of the era. Both groups felt a common mission to maintain "an educated class, to be guardians of the traditions and feelings and aspirations of high culture, and the diffuser of an atmosphere of thought and study" (10). In this regard the Newberry Library guided by its trustees and its librarian would act as barrier against the grossness of the age and be a bastion for the values of Protestant, Anglo-Saxon, Western culture.

Thus during its early years, the Newberry Library in reality functioned as a public gentleman's library. Superficially it was free and available to all citizens of Chicago, but in actuality, because of the emphasis placed on high culture, the library became a device to segment the people of the city. Although anyone could use the library, few of the masses had reason to do so. The *Chicago Times* commented that a "library exclusively for reference is a select affair; it bars out the mob and limits its use to the better and cleaner classes" (n. pag.). Designed to attract a certain class, the early Newberry Library effectively discouraged use by everyone else.

References

Baltzell, E. Digby. *The Protestant Establishment*. New York: Random, 1964.

Chicago Times 17 July 1887: n. pag.

Dain, Phyllis. *The New York Public Library: A History of Its Founding and Early Years*. New York: Macmillan, 1972.

Finkelman, Paul. "The Founding of the Newberry Library." *American Studies* 16.1 (1975): 5–22.

Higham, John. *History: Professional Scholarship in America.* Baltimore: Johns Hopkins UP, 1989.

The Newberry Library. General Information. Chicago: Newberry Library, 2000.

Schlesinger, Arthur Meier. *The Rise of the City, 1878–1898.* New York: Macmillan, 1933.

Shereikis, Richard. "The Newberry Library: An Uncommon Collection of Uncommon People." *Illinois Issues* 8.12 (1987): 10–13.

Towner, Lawrence. *An Uncommon Collection of Uncommon Collections.* Chicago: Newberry Library, 1971.

Wyly, Mary. "Chicago's Newberry Library." *Alexandria* 7.3 (1995): 181–82.

11

From Myrdal to Shipler: The Academy's View of Blacks and Whites in America

ROBERT A. WIDEN

David Shipler is to be commended, first, for the 8 years of effort invested in, and the achievement realized by, the writing of *A Country of Strangers*. I suspect writing a book is a little like raising a child. While one enjoys having their child admired, no one likes having their child either criticized, or falsely praised.

I do not know that I would agree with Shipler's words that "it has been said every American is an expert on race" (16). I would say that too many Americans consider themselves free of racial prejudice, when, in fact, under certain circumstances, the prejudices will surface. I would include myself in this category. David Shipler refers to this as "latent bias ... deeply buried" (562). His study provides a mirror for all of us to examine our own hearts and attitudes in a thoughtful, reflective way. That, in fact, may be the book's greatest strength. He dedicates his book to the purpose of helping our society be "open and truthful about itself," to the end it can be "self-correcting" (19). This is an extremely important idea, that a society can be self-correcting. It is a major tenet of our democracy. Americans, by and large, want to do the right thing. President Johnson once said, "It is not difficult to do the right thing. What is difficult, is knowing what the right thing is." The country has known since its inception that slavery was morally wrong. President Madison, on his deathbed in June of 1835, spoke of slavery as the "Pandora's box of the nation."

An issue as complex as the subject of racial discrimination is multidimensional. One of those dimensions is time. Discrimination, whether of race, gender, sexual orientation, or age, is a matter of perception and attitude. Over time, attitudes can be changed, as a function of modified perceptions.

Shipler has written a book "about the present, not the past" (18). Unfortunately, the present is continually changing, both progressively, and regressively. He recognizes this with his metaphor about the glass being, simultaneously, "half full, and half empty" (16). We have come a long way since the enactment of Amendments Fourteen and Fifteen, passed just a few years after the Civil War. Still, we have a long way to go. The good news is that he describes some very subtle forms of racial discrimination, largely the result of white ignorance, stemming from the cultural, economic, and political gap still separating blacks from whites. If these were all of the negative racial attitudes yet to be overcome, perhaps we could relax a bit. The bad news is that we still have events like the April [2001] riots in Cincinnati. There, the police shooting of an unarmed teenager triggered black community anger because of the supposition of racial profiling. Then there was the trial of Thomas Blanton for the 1963 Church bombing in Birmingham that killed the four little black girls. The black community viewed this trial as an important resolution of a tragic event. The white community seems not so concerned. That Blanton was convicted, brings some closure to the Birmingham event, but does not return the little girls to us.

Precisely because Shipler's book is about the present, it lacks the dimension of time, even though he does some root tracing and wellspring discovery. As compelling as *CS* is, the panorama of racial discrimination is not complete without an overview of what has been printed before, and what has been published since.

The seminal work on race relations in the United States was Gunnar Myrdal's 1944, two volume, 1400 page work, *An American Dilemma.* Professor Myrdal had been commissioned and funded by the Carnegie Foundation in 1937 to do the study. One must remember that between 1868, when the Fourteenth Amendment was passed, and 1944, a period of 76 years, race relations in this country were virtually frozen in time. A caste system had replaced slavery as a social institution. Segregated public restrooms and drinking fountains were ubiquitous throughout the country. While these may have been the most visible and blatant form of racial discrimination, society was shot through with a host of others. Myrdal was assisted in his work by scores of American social scientists, both black and white. The study, funded by the Carnegie Foundation was to cost $300,000,

a considerable sum in the early 1940s, and take four years. It was inter-
rupted, to some extent, by WW II. Myrdal returned to Sweden when Hitler
attacked Poland. When he discovered his American study was likely to be
more important to world history than anything he might accomplish in
Sweden, he returned to the United States to complete the project.

His basic thesis was that the American racial problem was primarily
in the hearts and minds of the white population, because racial discrimination was a contradiction of the American Creed, contained in the Declaration of Independence and the Constitution. Even some Southern
whites, exercising all kinds of mental gymnastics to justify keeping blacks
in a subordinate social, economic, and political position, were prone to
admit it was a contradiction of American political philosophy.

My purpose in bringing attention the Myrdal study is to make the
point that no single book, not Shipler's, not Myrdal's, can paint the complete picture of race relations in the United States as they have evolved,
and are still evolving. Shipler paints a picture that makes it clear we still
have a long way to go. Myrdal's book shows us how far we have come since
1944, just 57 years, as compared to the previous 76. In some respects, *CS*
is a follow-up report on *An American Dilemma*. In so being, it causes a
puzzle, for me, as to why Shipler makes no mention of either Gunnar
Myrdal or his work. Shipler, according to the flyleaf in his book, was, for
a time, a senior associate at the Carnegie Endowment for International
Peace. The Carnegie Foundation, of course, funded the Myrdal study.

There is a multitude of other books enlightening us about the environment of social conflict. Among them is the 1915 work of French sociologist Emile Durkheim, *The Elementary Forms of Religious Life*, which
makes the case that God exists in the collective consciousness. It is the
collective consciousness that works its way into the American Creed and
speaks out about the moral dilemma of Americans caught up in the problem of race. Durkheim wrote another book prior to this in 1893 titled *The
Division of Labor in Society* translated into English in 1933. In this work
he makes a distinction between the solidarity of society based on "sameness" which he terms "mechanical solidarity," and a solidarity based on
diversity of the division of labor, which he terms "organic solidarity."
Mechanical solidarity, based on "sameness," he sees as shallow, and prim-
itive. This can be seen in societies engaged in a variety of racial and religious discriminatory practices. Organic solidarity, based on diversity of
labor, and by expansion, based on diversity of culture and religion, are more
complex and far more productive, both economically and artistically.

When one takes these two themes, God existing in a collective consciousness, and the division of labor within society creating an organic

solidarity of greater productivity, complexity, and richness, one can see the rationale of Myrdal's theme in *American Dilemma*. Its essence is captured in Walter A. Jackson's *Gunnar Myrdal and America's Conscience* (1990). This book not only outlines Myrdal's main thesis concerning the distinction between America's talk and the walk but also details the list of American social scientists, both black and white, who participated with him in the study. It discusses the work's weaknesses as well as its strengths. It provides an excellent picture of race relations in the late thirties and forties in less than 400 pages, as opposed to the 1400 pages of the two-volume work by Myrdal. As a complement to the Jackson work, I recommend the 1945 edition of Charles A. Beard's classic *The Economic Basis of Politics*, which details the relationship between morality, economics, and politics. It reminds us that Aristotle thought the three disciplines inseparable. Beard makes the same point as Myrdal except the former requires a modest 114 pages. If your interests demand a closer look at the issues raised in Richard Hernstein and Charles Murray's 1994 *The Bell Curve: Intelligence and Class Structure in American Life*, and the ensuing arguments pro and con, read Theodosius Dobzhansky's 1973 *Genetic Diversity and Human Equality*. This, again, is a small book in size (116 pages).

Dobzhansky's work makes the following case. Yes, there is a difference in the mean I.Q. scores of whites and blacks of about 15 points. There is also a difference in the mean I.Q. scores across the white population of about 28 points. These differences, however, make no allowances for the environmental differences in the learning situation. We know that environment accounts for about 20 percent of I.Q. scores. Besides, we also know that the real worth of I.Q. scores is in the prediction of the statistical probability of academic success. Other than that, we are not sure of what I.Q. measures. Clearly, a lot of whites are smarter than a lot of blacks. It is also true that a lot of blacks are smarter than a lot of whites. So get over it. We need to make judgments about individuals, not groups.

Orlando Patterson takes us on a different course in his 1997 *The Ordeal of Integration*. Patterson is John Cowles Professor at the Harvard University Department of Afro-American Studies. In his concluding remarks, he makes the point that as of October, 1995, some 67 percent of Afro-Americans said that they still believe in the American Dream, and Afro-Americans were only 2 percent less likely than Euro-Americans to say that they were farther away from attaining the American Dream that they had been 10 years ago. He goes on to make the case, with supporting data from another source, that

> [f]or this two-thirds of the Afro-American population, Martin Luther King, Jr.'s dream has *not* been deferred, as so many Euro-American

liberals and Afro-American advocates insultingly insist, misleading the world. They have, indeed, inherited the fruits of what Anita Patterson refers to as King's "abiding faith in the political efficacy of civil disobedience and love" [172].

Further on, in the conclusion, he highlights the main problem. He states,

> [T]he main problem of the Afro-American poor, especially adults, is not lack of work. The problem, rather, is one they share with their Euro-American counterparts: when they work, they simply do not eat enough to get out of poverty. The problem of the great majority of the Afro-American poor is the problem of income inequality. In a land of extraordinary abundance, the top fifth greedily takes so much that the bottom fifth, even working two jobs, sinks deeper and deeper into poverty [178].

Welcome back, Mr. Aristotle, Mr. Myrdal, and Mr. Beard. Another element of the dark side of things he sees in the "many ironies and contradictions in the long history of Christianity":

> In contrast with the dramatic changes in all other areas in recent decades, 73 percent of Euro-Americans and 71 percent of Afro-Americans still go to churches that are, respectively, almost, or nearly all Euro-American and Afro-American. Surely one of the great ironies of modern America, the most devotedly Christian nation in the West, is that its army, the most powerful instrument of war and destruction, in the history of mankind, is the nation's model of integration while its churches remain the last bastion of 'racial' segregation [198–99].

He has an entire chapter on "Why We Still Need Affirmative Action." His conclusion touches upon the stigma of interracial marriage. He sees ultimate integration as involving greater acceptability of intermarriage, and makes the case for it. He does all of the above in only 200 pages.

A year earlier, in 1996, two of Patterson's colleagues at Harvard came at the issue of racial discrimination from yet another direction in their *The Future of the Race*. They discuss, from different perspectives, their views on what W. E. B. DuBois referred to as the "Talented Tenth." These were the ones, supposedly, who would lead the struggle to overcome white discrimination against blacks. Henry Gates' essay emphasizes that the "Talented Tenth" succumbed, largely, to the attractions of middle class success, and forgot about the less fortunate underclass of poor blacks. Their desertion of the black cause, in a sense, gave the issue of race the dimension of class struggle. Once one, either black or white, reached middle class status, they were inclined to no longer concern themselves with the plight of the less fortunate.

Professor Gates' co-author and colleague, Cornel West, takes a somewhat harsher view of DuBois's advocacy for the "Talented Tenth," and their mission. DuBois, you may recall, born in 1868, was the leading black intellectual of the early twentieth century. He received his doctoral degree from Harvard in 1895 and was a key figure in the formation of the N.A.A.C.P. He saw the "Talented Tenth" as the exceptional man who would lead the way in overcoming the corrosive impact of racial discrimination and elevating African-Americans to an equal status with whites in society.

West asserts that DuBois was himself shaped by "presuppositions and prejudices of Euro-American civilization ... he was a black man of letters, primarily enhanced by 19th century Euro-American traditions" (55). West's greatest intellectual disappointment with DuBois lies with the latter's failure to recognize the similarities between the conditions surrounding the Russian peasantry prior to the 1917 Revolution, and the black community in the U.S. There was also a parallel between the Central European Jewish circumstances a generation before the Holocaust and the black agony in America. Man's inhumanity to man experienced by the Russian peasantry was captured in the literary works of Tolstoy, Chekhov, and Dostoyevsky. Franz Kafka writes about Jews in Prague during the same period. According to West, the plight of blacks in America was captured in the music of Louis Armstrong's *West End Blues*, Duke Ellington's *Mood Indigo*, John Coltrane's *Alabama*, and Sarah Vaughan's *Send in the Clowns* (77). West criticizes DuBois for failure to recognize homo sapiens' basic capacity for evil and suffering as captured in the Russian authors' works, Kafka's writings, and black music in the United States.

All of these creative artists wrote in a mood foretelling of worse things to come, in a sense, predicting the tragedy of revolution and war. In the case of black music, it was the prologue to our most strident times of racial conflict. DuBois failed to articulate any sense of this, and, indeed, seemed to entertain a false optimism, which eventually led to disillusionment, and, in 1963, expatriation to Ghana, where he died in 1965.

Professor West's analysis of the current state of affairs in race relationships is uncomfortably real. Where David Shipler writes of the subtleties of current racial discrimination, West writes of the raw human agony of namelessness and invisibility. He tears away the illusions of being led out of the wilderness of racial discrimination by DuBois' "Talented Tenth," and places the responsibility right in the laps of the black population, themselves.

"The Negro Race, like all races, is going to be saved by its exceptional men." This was the thesis and cornerstone of DuBois's essay about which West has an opposite point of view, for he argues that the

> fundamental role of the public intellectual — distinct from experts, ana-
> lysts, and pundits — is to create and sustain high-quality public discourse
> addressing urgent public problems which enlightens and energizes fel-
> low citizens, prompting them to take public action.... Intellectual and
> political leadership is neither elitist nor populist; rather it is democratic,
> in that each of us stands in public space, without humiliation, to put for-
> ward our best visions and views for the sake of the public interest [Gates
> and West 71].

This theme is exactly that articulated in Derek Bok's recent *The Trouble with Government*. Bok, of course, is the former president of Harvard
University, 1971–91, and currently teaches in the JFK School of Government at Harvard. His concluding remark in his newest book is that democracy "is a collective venture, which falters or flourishes, depending on the
efforts citizens invest in its behalf."

This brings us back to David Shipler's words about the challenge of
becoming a self-correcting society, which is the purpose to which he dedicates *A Country of Strangers*. Both Cornel West and Derek Bok make reference to how this can be done — public engagement. Professor West
concludes his essay with the following words:

> Let us continue to strive with genuine compassion, personal integrity,
> and human decency to fight for radical democracy in the face of the
> frightening abyss — terrifying inferno — of the twenty first century, cling-
> ing to "a hope, not hopeless, but unhopeful" [Gates and West 112].

While West leaves us "clinging to hope, but not hopeful," we need to
reflect upon "why" things are not hopeful from his point of view. Both
West and DuBois perceive Western society as a "Twilight Civilization."
West suggests, in fact, a parallel between late nineteenth century Russia
and early twentieth century Central Europe when 48 percent of the financial wealth was owned by 1 percent of the population, 10 percent owned
86 percent, and 20 percent of the population owned 94 percent of all financial wealth. This same polarization is occurring here in the United States.
In terms of income distribution, between the late 1980s and the late 1990s,
the poorest fifth of the population had an inflation adjusted income
increase of only 1 percent, while the richest fifth had an inflation adjusted
income increase of 15 percent. The richest 5 percent of the population
experienced an inflation adjusted income increase of 27 percent (Bernstein
n. pag.). According to Congressman Martin Sabo, the income gap in America has widened substantially over the past two decades. Since the late
1970s, the average income of the bottom fifth of American families dropped
by 21 percent, while the average income of the wealthiest increased by 30

percent. Now the richest 20 percent of households earn as much as everyone else in America put together. In terms of total financial wealth, as much as 40 percent of total net worth is held by the top 1 percent of the population (Wolf).

The socially destabilizing effect of skewed wealth and income distribution, which leads to "Twilight Civilizations," can also be seen in the history of China. The 4000-year history of China is marked by the rise and decline of at least 14 distinct dynasties. These range from the Xia of pre–1700 B.C., to the Qing, which covered 1644 to 1911. They averaged about 250 to 300 years in length. The first century of a new dynasty is marked by political, economic, and cultural vigor, expansion, efficiency, and confidence. The second century builds and consolidates what the first achieved. The third century is witness to the loss of vigor and efficiency, and the appearance of corruption. The dynasty would ultimately fall (Murphey 19). An early nineteenth-century Chinese scholar who made public comment on these historical propensities in light of the conditions prevailing in his time, and his awareness of the cyclical nature of their development, was Gong Zizhen. He writes in the early 1800s, that when

> the wealthy vie with each other in splendor and display while the poor squeeze each other to death; when the poor do not enjoy a moment's rest while the rich are comfortable; when the poor lose more and more, while the rich keep piling up treasures; when in some, ever more extravagant desires awaken, and in others, an ever more burning hatred; when some become more and more arrogant and overbearing in their conduct, and others ever more miserable and pitiful until gradually the most perverse and curious customs arise, bursting forth as though from a hundred springs and impossible to stop, all of this will finally congeal in an ominous vapor which will fill the space between heaven and earth with its darkness [Spence 145].

The similarities between the Chinese experience and those of Russia and Central Europe are obvious. Perhaps not so obvious are the similarities between all of the former and our own times. West and DuBois, of course, think the similarities are apparent, thus their description of ours as a "Twilight Civilization."

Again, let us return to Shipler's work and particularly his words about the need for us to be a self-correcting society. To accomplish that, he says, "It must first be open and truthful about itself" (19). I bring to your attention the current Washington Administration's efforts to pass an income tax cut and the elimination of the estate tax. Think about it.

Returning to Shipler's words about self-correction, let us also revisit what Beard brings to our attention by quoting Aristotle on how ethics, economics, and politics cannot be separated. Plato felt that the income of the wealthiest members of an ideal society should not exceed that of the poorest by a factor of more than four (qtd. in Mankiw 440). Congressman Sabo points out that in 1970, the average CEO in American business made 41 times what the average manufacturing worker earned. Sabo quotes a 1997 issue of *Business Week* as stating that, in that year, the ratio had risen to 326 to one.

This whole issue of racial discrimination, economic inequity, and political power is spotlighted by Albert Memmi's 1968 work *Dominated Man*. This was followed in 1970 by the far more publicized *Pedagogy of the Oppressed*, by Paulo Freire. Memmi's book takes on the entire array of discrimination and oppression. He writes as a Tunisian Jew, French in political allegiance, but from the French colony of Tunisia. Thus, from personal experience, he can speak of what it means to be Jewish, and what it means to be a second-class citizen, as are all colonial people, vis-à-vis the group that does the colonizing. Colonialism, of course, is economic exploitation. It also contains all the elements of superior (colonizers) versus inferior (colonized). This relationship carries all of the baggage of discrimination and oppression to be found in the treatment of North American blacks by whites, anti–Semitism, and even in the second-class status of women. He articulates what racism is more succinctly than other writers whose works I have reviewed. Thus, racism is the generalized and final assigning to real or imaginary differences, to the accuser's benefit and at his victim's expense, in order to justify the former's own privileges or aggression.

He makes several points on the subject of racism and oppression, just as severe as the observations of Cornel West. Where the latter speaks specifically of the relationship of American blacks and whites, Memmi speaks of the universal nature of racism and its pernicious appeal. He describes a dozen characteristics of racism. I will cite just three: (1) Everyone, or nearly everyone, is an unconscious racist, or a semi-conscious one, or even a conscious one. (2) Racism is one of the most widespread attitudes in the world. Racial prejudice is a social fact. (3) The fight against racism coincides, at least partly, with the fight against oppression (194).

Memmi concludes his essays on racism and oppression by recognizing the difficulty of the fight. In that context, he expresses appreciation for the value of placing oneself in the position of the oppressed person. In a sense, this is one of the values of *CS*. Shipler's collection of vignettes allows us to experience the humiliation and pain vicariously. Memmi says in closing: "While the fight against racism is demanding, and its outcome always uncertain, it is one of the indispensable preliminaries to progress from animality to humanity. We cannot afford not to take up the racist challenge" (207).

Paulo Freire in *Pedagogy of the Oppressed* takes up the battle where Memmi leaves it. Freire writes as a Brazilian concerned about the oppressed Brazilian peasantry in 1970 two years after the publication of Memmi's work.

He pursues the thesis that education of the oppressed is the road to their escape from oppression. However, he makes it clear that the type of education he has in mind is not the standard "bank deposit" kind. He contrasts the latter with what he terms problem solving education. This involves dialogue among the peasants about the conditions that prevail in their lives and lends itself to both an understanding of the basis of those conditions as well as their capacity to change them. Today, we might be inclined to term what Freire called problem solving, as experiential education.

Freire's call for dialogue as a road to transforming society as it pertains to Brazilian peasantry brings to mind Cornel West's plea for the same in changing the status of blacks vis-à-vis whites in society. Whereas Memmi draws a comparison between the circumstances of the colonized, Jews, and American blacks, Freire focuses on Brazilian peasantry and West on American blacks. Curiously, West is the least sanguine, although the group of his concern has made the most progress.

The year 1997 saw not only the publishing of *A Country of Strangers*, but Stephan and Abigail Thernstrom's America in *Black and White: One Nation, Indivisible*. The Thernstroms' book may be the most comprehensive book since Myrdal's *American Dilemma* to view the status of Afro-Americans and ask what progress has been made, how did it happen, and what yet needs to occur. For me, its most enduring value is a table comparing animosity between groups as it still exists in foreign countries (Thernstrom and Thernstrom 531). While only 13 percent of whites admit to negative feelings toward blacks in the US, 21 percent of the English house such negativity toward the Irish. Forty-two percent of the French have negative feeling toward North Africans and, with a range of other nationalities, it is even worse.

I shall conclude this review of works on the subject of discrimination, and its importance to progressively evolving humanity, by recalling Shylock's lines from *The Merchant of Venice*: "If you prick us, do we not bleed? If you tickle us, do we not laugh? If you poison us, do we not die? And if you wrong us, shall we not revenge?" (3.1.66–67). Also, from metaphysical poet John Donne's famous Meditation XVII: "Any man's death diminishes me, because I am involved in mankind." The latter passage ends by admonishing us, "never send to know for whom the Bell Tolls, it Tolls for thee" (qtd. in Raspa 87).

In a more modern vein, here is a poem, about which I know little, except the author's name, R.L. Sharpe. It is titled "A Bag of Tools."

> Isn't it strange how Princes and Kings,
> And clowns who caper in sawdust rings,
> And ordinary folks, like you and me,
> Are Builders of Eternity?
> To each is given a bag of tools,
> A span of time, and a book or rules.
> And each must build, 'ere life has flown,
> A stumbling-block, or a stepping stone.

References

Bernstein, Jared, Lawrence Mishel, and Chauna Brocht. *Briefing Paper*. Washington, DC: Economic Policy Institute/Center on Budget and Policy Priorities. Sept. 2000.

Bok, Derek. *The Trouble with Government*. Cambridge: Harvard UP, 2001.

Craig, Hardin, and David Bevington, eds. *The Complete Works of William Shakespeare*. Rev. ed. Glenview, IL: Scott, 1973.

DuBois, W. E. B. *The Talented Tenth*. Orig. title *The Negro Problem*. 1903. Based on his prospectus *The Study of the Negro Problem* in *The Annals of the American Academy of Political and Social Science*. Jan. 1898. Full text provided on page 133 in the appendix of *The Future of the Race*.

Freire, Paulo. *Pedagogy of the Oppressed*. New York: Continuum, 2000.

Gates, Henry Louis, and Cornel West. *The Future of the Race*. New York: Random, 1997.

Mankiw, Gregory N. *Principles of Economics*. Fort Worth: Dryden-Harcourt, 1998.

Memmi, Albert. *Dominated Man*. Boston: Beacon, 1969.

Murphey, Rhoads. *East Asia: A New History*. 2nd ed. New York: Addison-Wesley, 2001.

Myrdal, Gunnar. *An American Dilemma: The Negro Problem and Modern Democracy*. New York: Harper, 1944.

Patterson, Orlando. *The Ordeal of Integration*. New York: Perseus, 1997.

Raspa, Anthony, ed. *Devotions on Emergent Occasions* by John Donne. New York: Oxford UP, 1936.

Shipler, David K. *A Country of Strangers: Blacks and Whites in America*. New York: Vintage, 1998.

Spence, Jonathan D. *The Search for Modern China*. New York: Norton, 1990.

Thernstrom, Stephen, and Abigail Thernstrom. *America in Black and White: One Nation, Indivisible*. New York: Simon, 1997.

Wolf, E. "Reconciling Alternative Estimates of Wealth Inequality from the Survey of Consumer Finances." A.E.I. Seminar on Economic Inequality. Feb. 9, 2000.

12
What's in a Name? Politically Correct Language On and Off Campus

Todd Sallo

The mascot of the Fighting Whities is a chipper, middle-aged white guy with slicked-back hair who looks a little like Ozzie Nelson, or something out of a 1950s cigarette ad. Grinning broadly, he says, "Every Thang's Gonna Be All White!"

An intramural basketball team at the University of Northern Colorado, the Fighting Whities were organized last February by a group of students who chose the name "to have a little satirical fun and to deliver a simple, sincere, message about ethnic stereotyping," according to the team's Web site, launched as a response to the unexpected maelstrom of national attention they have received.

The team wanted "to make a straightforward statement using humor; to promote cultural awareness through satire," and it generally has been received as intended, as a humorous lark that also delivers a message. Scott Ostler, of the *San Francisco Chronicle*, wondered, "How are the Whities going to be able to win if they can't jump?"

Still, the Fighting Whities really touched a nerve, both on and off campus. Like all good satire, the humor derives from an association with the familiar: We all have seen various groups, especially Native Americans, caricatured in this manner, and used as mascots. It is a sensitive issue, and one that many colleges and universities are addressing, if belatedly and somewhat reluctantly. At the very least, using these mascots gives the appearance of hypocrisy, considering that the higher education community has tended to be at the forefront of progressive racial, ethnic and gender politics—what might be called political correctness—for decades.

The term *politically correct* seems to have originated in leftist circles, who used it to describe modern ways of thought, or to admonish those who adhered too strictly to a dogmatic party line. By the late 1980s, however, the term was being appropriated by conservatives to criticize and attack changes in attitudes and course offerings on college campuses. Curricular revisions, for instance, that were intended to make higher education more inclusive or "multicultural" in orientation were derided as mere "political correctness."

And mixed up in all of it was the hot-button issue of affirmative action, and similar programs, which never have been embraced by the right. Once again, the culture wars were heating up. And the college campus was ground zero. In 1989, Stanford University made a much-publicized revision in its core western civilization courses, placing more emphasis on women and racial minorities. Other major universities, like the University of Michigan and the University of Wisconsin, followed suit. Colleges revised descriptors for minority groups and began instituting speech codes aimed at controlling hate speech.

Conservatives seized the opportunity to engage in a battle over these issues. In 1991 President George Bush delivered a controversial commencement address at the University of Michigan in which he condemned "the dangers of political correctness" (Dowd 1). There was a flurry of articles in *Newsweek, Time, U.S. News and World Report*, the *New York Times*, the *Village Voice* and others about the new political correctness on campuses.

Today, the term "politically correct"—with its vague Soviet overtones bringing to mind a shadowy thought police—is inherently dismissive. Like "tree hugger," it generally is used derisively, and mostly by those who oppose what it represents. Conservatives contend that political correctness—and all of the efforts to broaden curriculum and to make institutions of higher learning more accessible to minorities—is an unnecessary exercise. They argue that it addresses appearances only — and therefore has no real effect — and that it actually is a counterproductive "Balkanizing" force.

"Politically correct," or "PC," is now part of the vernacular outside of academia as well. And everyone is engaged, in some way or another, in the debate.

But is this all just semantics?

At its core, this is simply the age-old debate about the power of language. On the one hand are people who liken modern academia to the

"Royal Academy of Lagado" in Jonathan Swift's *Gulliver's Travels*, with its solemn "projectors" laboring to extract sunbeams from cucumbers and to build houses from the roof down. Their contention is that attempting to achieve social progress by changing the way we use language is mere window dressing, and ultimately futile.

On the other hand are those who are more in sympathy with George Orwell, who wrote: "If thought corrupts language, language also can corrupt thought" (137). They believe that words influence thoughts and actions, and that language is a very powerful force for social change. One thing is undeniable: A great deal of attention has been devoted in recent years to dealing with the complex semantic issues surrounding the delicate politics of race and gender, and to adjusting our use of terminology to suit changing sensibilities.

The Tower of Babel

Humans have demonstrated a special capacity to invent, and use, racial epithets. Some terms that once seemed respectful have, over time, ended up becoming insults instead; and some that were intended as insults ended up being embraced, and used, by those groups.

For instance, "Negro" and "colored" once were considered progressive. In 1841, when John Quincy Adams referred to "negros [*sic*] and persons of color" in a legal brief, these terms were seen as merely descriptive. The same is true of the 1807 Slave Trade Abolition Act, which referred to "any negro, mulatto, or person of colour." During the Civil Rights era, "colored" gave way to "negro," then to "black," which persists to this day. "Colored," though dated, is enshrined as part of the NAACP acronym. "Afro-American" struggles somewhat, linked as it is with big hairdos of the 1960s. But "African-American"—part of a trend in which "American" is added on to the end of just about every group identity—thrives as the current flavor of choice, favored most generally by various published guides on language usage. However, in an interesting twist, "persons of color" seems to be gaining renewed popularity. Has it really taken us more than 200 years to progress from "colored persons" to "persons of color?"

In a similar manner, "Oriental" has been replaced by "Asian," although many institutions have divided that designation into a plethora of subgroups, including Pacific Islander, Native Hawaiian, Samoan, Guamanian, Filipino, Korean, Japanese, Chinese and Vietnamese. "Indians" now refers only to people from India. There are Indian Americans, but American Indians are now "Native Americans," although Native Americans still call each other Indians. And while identifying a Native American by tribal affiliation, such as Cherokee or Sioux, once was considered insulting, many style guides now recommend it as preferable to the more general terms. "Alaska Native" has replaced "Eskimo" and "Aleut," and many guides recommend that it also be accompanied by a tribal affiliation when possible. However, the Association of American University Presses cautions that "native peoples of northern Canada, Alaska, eastern Siberia, and Greenland may prefer 'Inuk' ('Inuit' for plural)."

Meanwhile, whole books have been written about what might be called the "Hispanic–Latino/a–Chicano/a–Mexican American–Puerto Rican–Cuban–Manito–*Raza*" controversy. No one seems to be able to come up with a term that will satisfy this broad constituency.

And, last but not least, there is "white."

Northwestern University's "Ethnic Classification Summary," which is representative of many language usage guides, defines a white as "a person having origins in any of the original peoples of Europe, North Africa, or the Middle East." Some guides allow the use of "Caucasian," "Euro-American" or "European American." The U.S. government now classifies the entire group as "non–Hispanic white." (There is also a "non–Hispanic black" category.) While this may provide more accurate information, it does seem a bit strange to define a majority of the population by what they are not.

The issue of gender in language usage is another area of great concern, particularly on college campuses. The goal has been to use "gender-neutral" or "nonsexist" language, which is intended to purge discourse of any sexual bias. In some languages this challenge is compounded by the assigning of sex to common nouns. Fortunately, English allows for a neutral gender in such cases, but that doesn't get us off the hook.

In addition to now-familiar neutral terms like "fire fighter" (instead of fireman) or "mail carrier" (instead of mail*man*), words like "chairman," "forefathers," and "freshman" must be addressed. (Recommended substitutions: "chairperson" or "chair"; "ancestors"; and "first-year student.") College and government-style guides provide lengthy charts showing the older wording alongside the preferred gender-neutral forms. A tremendous amount of effort has been devoted to gender-neutralizing nouns and pronouns such as "man," "mankind" or even "human" to refer to people, or the classic bias toward the use of "he" and "his."

The University of New Hampshire, in its *Guidelines for the Use of Nonsexist Language*, offers this gem: "Man, like other mammals, breast-feeds his young." It is a beautiful demonstration of a sentence that is constructed correctly, from a strictly grammatical point of view, yet begs for some sort of modernization. The suggested alternative is: "Humans, like other mammals, breastfeed their young." That's the most frequently used escape — switching to plural. For example, instead of "Each student must bring his own supplies," style guides counsel something like "Students must bring their own supplies." Thankfully, "his/her" and "he/she" seem to be falling from favor, although a number of guides still recommend their use.

The guidelines also recommend "parallel structure," thereby avoiding any implied sexism in phrases such as "man and wife." (The preferred phrase is "husband and wife.") For any editor, policy expert, college teacher or media figure, just keeping up-to-date on all of this can be daunting. A radio doctor recently voiced his frustration, and suggested that perhaps we should simplify matters by giving up the words "women" and "men" entirely and refer instead to "persons with ovaries" and "persons with prostates." Of course, since this could draw the ire of people who have had their prostates or ovaries removed, it is an imperfect solution — but an entertaining one.

"Niggardly"

The U.S. Census of 1790 had only five categories: white males 16 years and older; white males younger than 16; white females; other white persons; and slaves. The 2000 Census includes: American Indian or Alaska Native; Asian; Black or African-American; Native Hawaiian or Other Pacific Islander; White; and Some Other Race. In addition, respondents are allowed to select more than one race when they "self-identify," and can choose up to four different categories.

The Office of Management and Budget advises that "Hispanics and Latinos may be of any race," so the census also offers two new "ethnic" categories: Hispanic or Latino, and Not Hispanic or Latino. "In the federal statistical system," the official census Web site explains, "ethnic origin is considered to be a separate concept from race." With all the possible multi-racial permutations, this amounts to government recognition of some 64 different racial/ethnic designations. At last, Tiger Woods, who invented for himself the term "Cablinasian"— meaning Caucasian, black, Indian and Asian—can fully "self-identify," without having to disavow some part of his richly varied racial heritage. Conservative columnist George F. Will decries this trend, and blames "people who make their living by Balkanizing American culture into elbow-throwing grievance groups clamoring for government preferment" (64). In his 1993 *Culture of Complaint*, Robert Hughes, a senior writer for *Time*, wrote that, although "polite white society" has repeatedly changed its mind about what to call black people, "for millions of white Americans, from the time of George Wallace to that of David Duke, they stayed *niggers* [emphasis added], and the shift of names has not altered the facts of racism, any more than the ritual announcement of Five-Year Plans and Great Leaps Forward turned the social disasters of Stalinism and Maoism into triumphs" (20).

Conservatives try to turn the whole matter into farce by concentrating on designations such as "differently abled," and "physically challenged," and even imaginary ones like "vertically challenged" (instead of "short") and "living impaired" (instead of "dead"). Lengthy lists of these can be found all over the Internet.

The PC movement, to the extent that there really is such a thing, has definitely provided fodder for humorists—and ammunition for its opponents. In his book, Hughes chides liberals for their excesses, and wonders, "Where would George Will, P. J. O'Rourke, the editors of the *American Spectator* all be without the inexhaustible flow of PC claptrap from the academic left? Did any nominally radical movement ever supply its foes with such a delicious array of targets for cheap shots?" Mock sympathy aside, Hughes may have a point. Even some on the left think that political correctness, though well-intentioned, may have gone too far.

For example, a quotation from Chaucer that includes the word "niggardly" stirred a controversy at the University of Wisconsin at Madison, when a black student complained about its inclusion in a lecture. Obviously, her confusion resulted from the fact that it sounds like "nigger," but there is no etymological connection between the two words. (*Niggardly* is defined as stingy.) Even so, there were many who insisted that its use was inappropriate, and that it would be best to avoid the word, and any others that might upset people. In a similar vein, many colleges recommend finding alternatives to terms like "black sheep" and "blackmail," and even advise against expressions like "a chink in his armor," or "a nip in the air," because of the possibility that their use might offend sensibilities.

The "One-Drop" Rule

While everyone readily agrees that gender has biological significance, the fact is that race and ethnicity have no real taxonomic meaning. In other words, the idea that the different races are somehow separate kinds of people was discredited long ago. Unlike different species, which cannot produce viable offspring, human races interbreed freely, and frequently. It is literally impossible to tell where one race ends and another begins; such a differentiation would be fundamentally arbitrary.

Who is, and is not, African-American? How much "blood" does one need in order to qualify? The "one drop" rule is one prevailing legal standard. A dubious relic of the slavery era, its original intent is obvious. In 1896 the U.S. Supreme Court, in *Plessy v. Ferguson*, tacitly accepted that a person one-eighth black and seven-eighths white is legally black. But even if this were a rational standard, how could such a thing be determined? How "black" does the relevant great-grandparent have to have been? Cornel West, a professor of Afro-American studies who recently made headlines by moving from Harvard back to Princeton, uses Clarence Thomas as a ready example of this conundrum. In *Race Matters*, he points to Thomas' "undeniably black phenotype." Yet, he notes that the questions "Is Thomas really black? Is he black enough to be defended? Is he just black on the outside?" were "debated throughout black America in barber shops, beauty salons, living rooms, churches, mosques and schoolrooms." Noting that Thomas made much of his African-American heritage, especially by employing racially charged terms like "high-tech lynching," in his Supreme Court confirmation hearings, West argues in his second chapter that "black authenticity" takes the form of "inchoate xenophobia" for many black Americans:

> Hence, only certain kinds of black people deserve high positions, that is those who accept the rules of the game played by white America. In black America, cultural conservatism takes the form of an inchoate xenophobia (e.g., against whites, Jews, and Asians), systemic sexism, and homophobia [27].

Of course, the same question could be asked about any racial category. Insisting that "blackness has no meaning outside of a system of race-conscious people and practices," West advocates "replacing racial reasoning with moral reasoning, to understand the black freedom struggle not as an affair of skin pigmentation and racial phenotype but rather as a matter of ethical principles and wise politics."

Ironically, conservatives are using similar arguments to attack affirmative action programs. They seem to be claiming that racism would disappear if we simply dispensed with all these fine racial distinctions and categories, stopped being so careful about our use of language, and just called ourselves Americans. However, Cornel West — hardly an unflinching supporter of affirmative action — argues that in the absence of such programs, we quickly would see a return to the old patterns of white supremacy in both public and private domains.

We are far from being a colorblind society. It certainly can be a nuisance at times to deal with a barrage of ever-changing racial, ethnic and gender terminology — a steady stream of newer and better names for the myriad sizes, shapes, colors and other variations of humankind. But this may be a price we have to pay for the purposes of social progress, and simple civility. One of the main functions of PC language is to avoid inadvertently slighting or insulting someone by using a term they might find offensive. The easiest, and best, solution is simply to choose alternative words. Language does have power. We use words to convey our thoughts, put intentions into action, and to persuade. While it is true that words have only the power we bestow upon them, we cannot rob them of their power by pretending that they are meaningless.

We should choose, and use, our words very carefully.

References

Dowd, Maureen. "Bush Sees Threat to Flow of Ideas on U.S. Campuses." *New York Times* 5 May 1991, late ed.: 1. (See also Thomas, Evan with Daniel Glick and Eleanor Clift. "Time to Circle the Wagons." *Newsweek* 27 May 1991: 70; and Lewis, Anthony. "Abroad at Home: Liberty and Hypocrisy." *New York Times*, late ed.: 27 May 1991: 19.)

Hughes, Robert. *Culture of Complaint: The Fraying of America*. New York: Oxford UP, 1993.

Orwell, George. "Politics and the English Language." *The Collected Essays, Journalism and Letters of George Orwell*. Vol. 4. Eds. Sonia Orwell and Ian Angus. New York: Harcourt, 1968. 127–40.

Ostler, Scott. "Insensitivity Training in Colorado." *San Francisco Chronicle* 14 Mar 2002. 15 Mar. 2002 <http://www.sfgate.com/cgi-bin/article.cgi?file+/chronicle/archive/2002/03/14/SP193744.DTL>.

Sallo, Todd. *National CrossTalk* 10.2 (2002): 12–13. This essay was first published in *CrossTalk*, a quarterly publication of the National Center for Public Policy and Higher Education.

West, Cornel. *Race Matters*. Boston: Beacon, 1993.

Will, George F. "Dropping the 'One Drop' Rule." *Newsweek* 25 Mar 2002: 64.

13
Organizational Changes Create a New Climate for Racial Equality

EDWARD J. MURRAY

Joseph Campbell (1989) discusses the openness to live a life that responds to and captures the meaningfulness of myth. On September 14, 2001, David K. Shipler reiterated the same theme. This capacity makes one responsive to a metaphor, being "transparent to the transcendence." This vision provides the individual with the strength to share the dangers of another and morally set aside self-protection. The human separateness leaves and you realize that you and the other are one.

A defining moment came on April 16, 1963. Martin sat behind bars in a jail cell in Birmingham, Alabama. He examined his personhood and attempted to define his identity through the written word. He knew the past. In 1957, he left Montgomery and followed the voice of justice and truth. He accepted the call to become transparent to transcendence. However, he sat in jail with fellow advocates criticizing him for sending others to jail but not himself. The Birmingham clergy also castigated him in a public letter. Martin was too racial.

The great "Letter from Birmingham Jail" summarized the clergy's criticism with these meditative thoughts and castigated them in understated tones of distress:

> You deplore the demonstrations that are presently taking place in Birmingham. But I am sorry that your statement did not express a similar concern for conditions that brought the demonstrations into being. I am

145

sure that each of you would want to go beyond the superficial social analyst who looks merely at effects, and does not grapple with underlying
causes [290].

His personal reflections traditionally engage the messages of Paul,
Jesus, and Thomas Aquinas. With Aquinas, he examines the law. Does the
law require obedience? Can a person make moral distinctions about the
law? Dr. King follows Kohlberg's path to higher-order thinking, namely,
post conventional morality. His meditations on Thomas Aquinas gave him
the distinctions between just and unjust law. The unjust law places people in a position of suppression and rejection. The individual becomes an
injured slave to a system of authority which denies equality and freedom.
The just law embodies the spirit of justice and contains the spirit of external and natural law which uplifts the human personality. The unjust law
damages and injures the human personality. To quote King, "We are
caught in an inescapable network of mutuality, tied to a single garment of
destiny. Whatever affects one directly affects all indirectly." These thoughts
caused him to see with Martin Buber that unjust law creates an I-it relationship and this separation of people produces what Paul Tillich defines
as sin.

Furthermore, King embraces the extremist actions of Jesus and peri-
patetic visions of Paul. He saw that, like Paul, he too was beaten and jailed.
Martin and Paul carried the scars of hatred and hostility even while they
attempted to bring to others the message of love, justice and truth.

King contemplated Paul's concept of the body. For him the church
was the mystical body — but a body scarred and blemished through social
neglect. Cahill (1999) describes this concept of the mystical body as a
major theological insight that Paul intertwined in many letters. In Gala-
tians, Paul states, "There is no longer Jew or Greek, slave or free, male and
female, for you are all one...."

The Corinthian passages extend the body metaphor. "And indeed the
body is made up of not one member but of many. If the foot were to say,
'I am not a hand, so I do not belong to the body,' it does not belong to the
body any the less for that...." As it is, there are many parts, but one body.
These visions bridged the separateness for Martin and gave him the courage to carry the prophetic message to all people.

Finally, King describes early Christianity as active and confronta-
tional — a real challenge to the suppression and subjugation of the underclass. Intuitively, King knew the metaphor of the banquet table. When the
dispossessed and poor were brought to the table for a meal, they became
brothers and sisters. At the weekend meal, these outcasts were called to

share with the family. All who ate together became one (Crossan, 1995; Schillebeeckx, 1993). These symbols gave King a sense of personhood and defined his mission. He embraced the meaningfulness of myths which grounded his leadership in the process of bring "transparent to transcendence."

On April 4, 1967, in New York City, Martin applied his vision of justice to all the poor. In "Time To Break Silence," King publicly confronted the Vietnam War. This war brought the black and white poor of United States to the battleground to burn and destroy the villages of poor Vietnamese. He called for a vision of love. A vision set forth for Hindu-Moslem-Christian-Jew-Buddhist. This commitment followed the hope of Arnold Toynbee that "Love is the ultimate force that makes for saving choice of life and good against the damning choice of death and evil. Therefore, the first hope in our inventory must be the hope that love is going to have the last word."

While King spread the concept of the "person-oriented" society with all people sharing in brotherhood and sisterhood, the over-class manipulated the system for their benefits and safety. Between 1962 and 1972, more than 29,700 men graduated from Harvard, MIT and Princeton. However, only 20 died in Vietnam. Fifty-eight thousand United States citizens died in Vietnam and only 12 of these dead were among the elite who had graduated from Harvard (Lind, 1995).

These archetypes provided Martin with a moral framework for change. His mission had a vision. However, Dr. King knew, as well as did Aquinas, that vision without practical implementation was meaningless. Therefore, on his last birthday, January 15, 1968, he attended a coalition meeting of African-Americans, Hispanics, Native Americans and whites from Appalachia to discuss and chart a course for job seeking, income, economic security and economic inclusion for all Americans. The Reverend Jesse Jackson (1999) later commented on this meeting: "We saw then the need to build a vertical bridge from the 'haves' living in the surplus culture, to the 'have nots' living in deficit and debit culture." The archetypes led to the concrete and practical.

In the past 33 years, the United States has experienced massive economic, global and social transformations. These changes demanded flexibility and new attitudes about social conditions. These social changes have radically redefined the market place and demanded that the individual assume greater responsibility for his or her life. The society has become three isolated clusters, the 20 percent who shared the technological wealth, the 60 percent who struggled to get through life and the 20 percent who received the leftovers.

King united people around an ideal. His values gave purpose and directionality to life. The participants built up "social capital." However, the social climate was about to change the concept of social capital as applied to human contact, communications, and a sense of trust and honesty.

In psychology, Gardner (1991) defines these constructs in relationship to interpersonal and intrapersonal intelligence. Goleman (1995) talks about *emotional* intelligence that emphasizes the qualities of altruism and empathy. Stanley Schachter's early study of group affiliation at Stanford (1959) describes these human interactions in relationship to the motivational quality of affiliation. The ability to break the separateness of people generates positive attitudes to develop so-called social capital.

During the period of racial and social justice, social capital showed gains and produced significant positive results. Since the 1960 election, many voting age Americans have decided not to vote. The voting percentages have shrunk from 62.8 to 48.9 (Putnam, 2000). There is also less attendance at political meetings or rallies and fewer people are working for political parties.

These last declines began in 1970. The middle 1970s saw a steady decline in attendance at public and town meetings in conjunction with less attendance at school affairs meetings. Fewer people served as officers of clubs or organizations and they refused to serve on committees. The participation rate in clubs and organizations declined by 50 percent from 1973 to 1995. The decline in participation also applied to active organizational involvement and club meetings. These declines represented a 50 percent decrease in participation. Religious affiliation peaked in the early 1960s and had declined by 10 percent in 1998. Church attendance and involvement had fallen 25 to 50 percent. Since 1970, union membership fell from 30 percent to 14.1 percent.

Memberships in professional organizations also show significant decreases. Medical, dental, nursing and engineering societies, however, have returned to 1945 levels of participation. The act of having friends come into one's home for entertainment has experienced a 40 percent decline since 1975. From 1970 to the present, fast foods and sport bars have replaced restaurants, luncheonettes, bars and taverns. These various changes highlight the lack of social contact and communications.

These various social contacts correlated with volunteering. Club attendance and church attendance related to volunteering. Entertaining friends at home also related to volunteering on a community project. With the decline in social capital, there has been a significant decline in volunteer activities. With the decline in social capital and volunteerism, trust became an issue. Since 1970, trust has significantly decreased! However, during 1985, adolescents displayed less trust than adults. This trend became significantly more apparent during the 1990s. An examination of cohort groups indicated that each age group had less trust than the previous age group. *Business Week* on July 23, 2001, reported data from Costa and Kahn concerning social capital. These findings supported the Putnam research cited in this article and concluded, "People are more likely to volunteer if they can identity with the economic status of those they're helping." These data indicate a critical decline in affiliation motivation and emotional intelligence.

These data strongly also suggest that people from Upper Arlington were unable to identify with the Columbus central city addict. Obviously, people from Plano, Texas empathized with their children's drug problems but not with Houston's problems. The parents of Orange School District worked to improve education for their children, while they ignored the Cleveland school system. On a national level, North Dakota and Montana, which were both high in social capital, had no desire to appreciate the poverty problems of New York and Los Angeles. The decline in social capital suggested that the new United States pattern reflected attitudes of me first and of course, people like me.

With the terrorist crisis so recent, especially in New York and Washington, DC, the social capital climate has undergone some modifications. People throughout the country have responded to the victims' needs and have reached out to one another. The country has experienced a strong sense of unity and patriotism. Have these tragedies created a new environment or have these events just temporarily modified an individualistic nation? The present decade will answer this question. However, social psychology has generated research which provides a caveat about the climate since September 11, 2001. Sherif (1961) asserts the axiom that a common goal unites individuals and nations; the common goal promotes cooperation and minimizes conflict. However, when the common goal is accomplished, the need for social capital declines.

In the early 1980s, the warning signs predicted other major changes or "megatrends" (Naisbitt 1982). The planet was economically changing and the earth had three major economic centers. They were Europe with Germany as the driving force, Asia with Japan leading the growth and the Americas with the United States engineering the change. While people in the States watched the influx of Japanese cars, Singapore, Hong Kong, Taiwan and South Korea changed the global picture in oil, textiles, computer technology and home electronics. With these transformations, China was predicted to become the textile leader in the year 2000. Economic cost had the impact of driving the market place. Japan was moving away from steel and shipbuilding, because South Korea, Brazil and Spain had the capacity to do the job better and cheaper. In 1999, Lester C. Thurow safely stated that the global economy has created a new game. The unskilled worker in a wealthy technological country had the potential to become a third-world person without learning new sets of skills and adapting to a constantly changing knowledge base. His commentary on this global climate indicated that many United States citizens would not join the world team. However, the well-educated United States citizens had the qualifications to join people from India, Europe, and Japan to play in the global experiment. Thurow also hypothesizes that Europe had the qualities for leadership in the 21st century. However, he questioned the European ability to push forward the entrepreneurial spirit. Implicitly, he asks, "Can Europeans take on the role of building global companies which will destroy the national companies?"

At the present time, contrary to Thurow's questionable prediction, the United States has driven the world economy. Cooper and Madigan write on July 9, 2001, in *Business Week*:

> Moreover, it is weakness in the United States that is most responsible for the slowdown in the rest of the world. That's because the United States' global influence goes far beyond its 23 percent share of world gross domestic product. It has significantly greater impact in the areas of tradable goods and financial flows.

Again Cooper and Madigan write in a later issue: "One case in point: Singapore is in recession mostly because its shipments to the United States of semiconductors and other tech components have plunged dramatically" (*Business Week*, Aug 6, 2001, n. pag.).

In 2001, the global economy has impacted the planet and the United States has continued to play the major role. Since the Asian meltdown of 1997, the United States has contributed more to the global economy than any other nation or region.

With the movement toward globalization, new demands were placed on the individual to obtain knowledge and develop skills related to the new economy. In the 1980s, John Naisbitt (1982), and Peter Drucker (1989) discussed the information society and the need for knowledge-based workers. The very nature of knowledge required the knowledge worker to continue learning to remain relevant in the global economy. Drucker (1989) estimated that, without further learning, most professionals were doomed to become obsolete in ten years.

In the 1990s, Thurow (1996) described the multi-national organization which brought together people with first-world talent and skills who worked with third-world unskilled workers. These groups worked together, because the first-world had the technology, leadership, research and development and education, while the third-world group brought cheap labor and the desire to use unskilled abilities. This perception emphasized that people in the first-world countries which possessed third-world skills would receive wages compatible with their skill level. Thurow raised the global economy question. Why would any multinational organization make an investment in an American high-school dropout or a poorly trained high-school graduate, when the organization had the ability to hire a well-educated Chinese or South Korean high-school graduate? Thurow (1999) also raised another global issue. Why educate engineers when high-quality personnel can be encouraged to come to the United States for employment? Obviously, many of these people had the potential for a significantly cheaper education in another country.

In the Cleveland *Plain Dealer*, a columnist pointed out on July 29, 2001, that Ohio had a knowledge drain (Frolik, n. pag.). The state attracted and produced fewer college graduates than the national average, which fact resulted in below-average economic compensation for Ohioans. A recent article appeared in *Inside Kent State* which supports these findings (Kirksey, 2001). Research performed by Cassell and Hanauer showed that the median income for Ohioans was below the 1979 level. These data also pointed out that Ohio had only 13.8 percent of the population with a college degree and less than 7 percent attained a graduate degree. These data reflected the impact of the global economy and the knowledge based society on the individual. The individual had to attain intellectual growth or remain left behind.

The result from the global economy and knowledge based society showed up in a National Association of Manufacturers Study. The findings indicated that 25 percent of manufacturing firms rejected 75 percent of the applicants (Kurlantzick, 2001). The article specified that unskilled cheap Southeast Asian and Latin American laborers had great attractiveness, while skilled and semiskilled Chinese brought in manufacturing. Thurow (1999) added to this picture with two sets of data: "Sixty-six percent of American employers do not think high-school students have the skills to succeed in the world of work.... At age 18 the bright American high school graduates are behind their contemporaries in the rest of the world. Not even the smartest among them could pass the high school exit examination set in any of the world's developed countries.

In a recent visit to Philadelphia, this author examined the trademark tags at Christopher and Banks. Most of the clothes in this clothing store for women had been made in the Asian Rim with knitting work coming from China. These data replicated anecdotal findings from a Winkleman Study this author performed a few years ago. These data strongly suggested that without strong skills the individual lacked the potential for success in the global economy. In the twenty-first century, the global economy and the multi-national organization have become an integral part of life. These resources generated cheaper and better products. However, they also created a highly competitive environment which rewarded the creative and knowledge-driven person.

During the 1980s, social capital and trust declined, the market place and work force became global and each individual was expected to increase knowledge and skills. While these changes produced some social turmoil, quietly the economic base had changed. Actually, the base changed in the 70s for both sexes. Independent of the educational level, males and females experienced economic declines. The female aged 45 to 54 with more than a four-year college degree represented the exception with an economic increase of 13 percent (Phillips, 1989). The 1980s produced a divide. College graduates and people with post-graduate studies achieved very positive economic growth. Independent of age, females received a 31.33 percent increase in wages, while males received on average a 14 percent increase. When people with a high school diploma or some college were examined, males' salaries declined 4.33 percent and females' salaries increased 14.33 percent (Phillips, 1989). From 1954 to 1986, a major shift in wealth happened. The bottom 40 percent of workers saw no economic growth and the 3rd and 4th quintiles experienced only a 33 percent increase in real wages. However, the top 20 percent had a 102 percent increase in salary. These data controlled for inflation through the process of using a constant dollar which adjusted for inflation and other economic changes.

In the late 1990s, Thurow (1999) pointed out that the top 5 percent of the nation had the market wealth of the bottom 60 percent of the nation. The middle 20 percent of families saw their inflation adjusted wealth decline by 3 percent from 1989 to 1997. Thurow went on to discuss the national transformation from the stagnant mid 1980s. The renewal factor produced downsizing, restructuring and offshore manufacturing and during these 15 years, ⅔ of the work force received a 20 percent cut in real wages. These various data strongly indicated that the top 20 percent of the United States increased in wealth from 1954 to 1997, while other quintiles remained economically stagnant or declined in wealth. In July, 2001, The *Washington Post* examined this issue of the economic divide by reporting the Pew Research findings. The sample consisted of 1200 adults. When they were asked about the divide between the "haves" and "have-nots," 44 percent stated that this difference existed, while 53 percent stated that it did not exist (Williams 2001). The article also sighted the Congressional Budget Office Study which showed that the gap between groups widened in the 1980s and 1990s with the widest point in 1997.

The divide between attitudes and reality appeared at a recent gathering of the Democratic Leadership Council. In The *Washington Post*, David Broder (2001) stated that many DLC members quoted a poll which showed that Gore lost to Bush because he presented the issue of "the people versus the powerful." Al From, political strategist, says, "We need to promote growth and opportunity, not redistribution."

The 1980s and 1990s accentuated the wealth shift in the United States. This change accompanied another transference of burdens. From 1977 to 1990, the tax base of this country was modified. Obviously, this pattern continued into the 21st century with George "W." During the late 70s and into the 80s, the taxes for the lowest 80 percent of the nation increased by 0.2 of 1 percent. These increases represented a small burden; however, the top 20 percent experienced a 5.8 percent decline in taxes. These declines became more pronounced when the top economic brackets were examined (Phillips 1993). The top 10 percent of the nation had a 9 percent decline in taxes, while the top 5 percent paid 13.5 percent less in taxes and the top 1 percent contributed 24.7 percent less in taxes. What did this tax shift produce? An examination of federal taxes showed that in 1970 the median income family paid 16.06 percent in taxes, while the top 1 percent of families paid 68.6 percent in taxes. By 1990, the median income family contributed 24. 65 percent in taxes, while the top 1 percent gave 26.7 percent in taxes.

With the shift in the tax burden, the lowest 80 percent of the nation felt a 3.5 percent decline in wages from 1977 to 1990, whereas the top 10 percent increased their wages by 19.9 percent with the top 5 percent generating a 25.4 percent increase. The big winners were the "overclass," or the top 1 percent who increased their wages by 45.5 percent (Phillips, 1993).

This last trend demonstrated that the United States has changed its wealth base. Obviously, the global economy, the knowledge based society and educational levels have related to these shifts. Another factor appeared to be the inability to identify with people who were different or who were poorer. The loss of social capital has had a drastic impact on the tax code. The importance of social capital on economics is shown in a *Business Week* article reflecting the Costa and Kahn research (Koretz, Feb. 2001, n. pag). These findings indicate that economic inequality correlates with the decline of social capital outside the home. In other words, the wealthy 20 percent have no ability to identify with the lower 80 percent of the United States population.

After the 1979 to 1981 depression, another unnoticed trend slowly transpired. The economists became critical of the United States and began to hypothesize that the twentieth century left the United States in the rubble of a destroyed mechanical complex. Thurow (1999) discussed his participation in this analysis and justified his criticism of worn out United States industries. The decline of industry was evident in all areas and especially in the Rust Belt. However, another silent change began in the late 1970s and extended into 1995. The visionaries, the creative and the achievers marched to their own cadence and created an unprecedented entrepreneurial climate. A silent new achievement-oriented, climate-changed United States' society and existing organizations (Farrell 2000).

In the middle of the 1980s, Drucker (1985) discussed the need for innovation and entrepreneurship. He described the sources for purposeful innovation, which included demographics, new knowledge and changes in the industrial structure or the market place. For Drucker, the innovative person systematically searches for changes to produce economic and social innovations. These changes help the individual approach problem-solving from a new and different vision. However, these principles for change apply not only to individuals but also to organizations and businesses.

During the 1980s and 1990s Waterman (1987) and Peters (1992) emphasized the importance of innovation and change. These authors recognized the need for renewal. The principles of entrepreneurship were relevant for the individual but they were also necessary for organizational change. Naisbitt (1982) pointed out that the spirit of renewal and entrepreneurship began in the late '70s. The depressed job market from 1979 to l981 caused individuals to examine new opportunities and set up their own businesses. The new spirit required self-reliance and demanded that the individual cut the chains of institutionalization and ignite the fires of ambition. A new climate had risen from the dust of decaying industries.

In the mid–'90s, Bridges (1994) described the shift in jobs. He commented on a society which had come full circle in that each individual worked for himself or herself. The knowledge-based society demanded that the individual define his or her talent base and recognized the contributions which these skills made to society. This environment expected the person to act as a vendor selling his or her skills to other people or businesses. The talent-based society created careers for people who moved from one project to another. The individual called "Company You" contributed to an organization for a week or for a year and moved on to the next-highest bidder.

With this new climate, Reich (2001) reinforced Bridges' concept that each individual worked for Company You. Reich called the change "The end of employment as we knew it." He stated, "All institutions are flattening into entrepreneurial groups, temporary projects, electronic communities and coalitions, linked to various brands and portals." The individual came to the realization that responsibility was delegated to him or her. The strong emphasis on individualism has contributed to the decline in social capital, since these variables represented counter valences. The entrepreneurial spirit which has permeated the whole of American society created new, unique organizations—for example, Microsoft. These new structures own nothing of value except knowledge (Thurow, 1999).

These entrepreneurial and knowledge based changes have also influenced the wealth factor. Since 1980, the top 20 percent of the population increased their share of the total income from 40 percent to almost 50 percent, while the next 60 percent of the population declined from 54 percent of the total income to 48.6 percent (Reich, 2001).

In the past 33 years, the United States moved from an institutionalized manufacturing society to an entrepreneurial knowledge based society. Educational demands intensified. The economy lost a national emphasis and expanded reciprocally throughout the planet. Individual creativity and responsibility replaced social capital and institutional supports. The innovative knowledgeable individual walked away with the societal wealth and the talented few were rewarded with lower taxes. These historical patterns showed significant changes. However, major questions remain? What do these patterns mean? Are these patterns accidentally converging in time, and space? Are these patterns a systematic plan to control society?

Michael Lind (1995) analyzes these changes and calls these patterns the "Brazilianization" of the United States. He describes a country with the white elite, the overclass, at the top and most of the browns and blacks at the bottom, forever. For Lind, the Brazilianization results from racial separation by class. These racial class division flow from taxation policies. His ideas presents this interesting story. Since the late '70s and early '80s, the overclass and the upper middle class have paid lower state and federal taxes. The 21st century potentially will further reduce these responsibilities. Obviously, these groups do not want to pay taxes. A depletion in the tax base generates fewer dollars for educational programs and these groups do not care about the educational decline in the United States. They have privilege and they exercise it for the secondary educational experience. These groups follow one of 2 patterns. They send their sons and daughters to private schools or they buy a $300,000 house in Wexford, Pennsylvania, and the taxes secure a good educational experience. In the global picture, the sons and daughters generally leave the secondary educational experience with a knowledge base below the planet's expectations. This picture is somewhat more positive than Thurow's (1999) evaluation in that Naperville, Illinois, students compete effectively with the rest of the planet. A few other young people from private schools and elite public schools also perform at an international level. Lind's argumentation continues on an educational level with the pattern of skewed admissions to colleges. The overclass have connections to the elite universities and their sons or daughters receive acceptances, because a family member previously attended the school. The upper middle class have the powerful contacts which open the doors for a premier education. With these educational experiences, the children of the 10 percent can compete in the international game. If many of these young people complete graduate school they are at a superior level. Lind finishes the picture by stating that these young people are now ready to become wealthy.

This author finds Lind's hypothesis fascinating and disturbing. Do the overclass and upper middle class plan these trends or do they just happen? The real answer suggests that a planned attack or an unplanned attack have the same effect. U.S. wealth is unevenly distributed and the present national entrepreneurial spirit suggests that this trend will continue with the support of differential educational opportunities and experiences.

This problem is graphically exposed by a recent 2000 United States Census Bureau survey which indicates that 29 percent of young people between the ages of 25 and 29 have bachelor's degrees. These data represent a 6 percent increase in 10 years (Koretz, 2001). The breakdown shows that 30 percent of females have a 4-year degree and 28 percent of males have bachelor's degrees. Asians and Pacific Islanders have 51 percent of young people who receive a 4-year degree while, whites have 34 percent with a college degree. African-Americans have only 15 percent who graduate with a bachelor's degree.

Obviously, the educational level affects economies. The United States Department of Labor reports that the average salary of a high-school graduate is $26,312, while the average salary of a college graduate is $43,316 (Torabi, 2001).

Thurow (1999) adds data to these differences, when he points out that in the United States, the lowest 66 percent of the work force have skills and education below world standards. These data suggest that ⅓ of the U.S. workforce is ready to reap the economic benefits. However, the actual historical data show that only 20 percent of the population economically benefits with the upper end of this group collecting the real wealth. This picture has one more variable, namely productivity. The U.S. GDP showed

1 percent growth for the '70s with a slight increase in the '80s. From 1990 to 1995, GDP growth was 1.5 percent with a 3 percent increase from 1996 to 2000. These data suggest that productivity is a limited resource.

These data complement the previously described social changes and reflect "conflict theory" in action (LeVine, 1972). Group theory hypothesizes that hostility, prejudice and discrimination result from group competition over limited resources. The data indicates that for the past 30 years productivity has experienced limits. The economic and educational data show that education creates stratification and the taxation code reflects the attitude of the wealthy to be non-supporters of education. A traditional pattern of discrimination comes from substandard education. The uneducated group has limits on their capacity to problem solve which creates limits on employment. With limits on education and employment, they have a decrease in economic rewards. Unfortunately, these experiences become self-perpetuating. Do these experiences lead to hostility? The Pew Research shows that 44 percent of a large sample see a divide between the haves and the have-nots and this finding represents a 5 percent increase from previous research. However, in one of his editorials, political commentator David Gergen supports the "hostility" model. A society where winners take all and losers take the hindmost is one that will become "divisive, rancorous, and morally blind." A recently spotted decorative decal on a car window highlights the casual vitriol seen everywhere in society—"Your University Sucks."

The present social climate places great emphasis upon personal responsibility and self-reliance. Health benefits are an excellent example of the responsibility shift. Twenty percent of former employers pay health-care costs for early retirees, while 40 percent share the cost and another 40 percent transfer the cost to the retiree (Nicholson, 2001). Today, current workers find that health-care benefits are not always part of the organizational commitment. In 1979, 66 percent of workers had healthcare coverage, while today only 54 percent have coverage. This 12 percent decline shows up in all wage groups and these changes are blamed upon the rising health care costs. The individual is responsible for himself or herself. Up to the 1970s, corporations set up "defined benefit" plans for retirement. With the uneven investment returns of the '80s responsibility is transferred to the individual and the 401K plan becomes the norm (Farrell, 2000). The individual invests his or her money in some program with the possibility of matching funds from the organization. Mary Farrell (2000) calls this change the entrepreneurial retirement in which the individual is in control of his or her money and the individual is responsible for the profit and loss. These principles can potentially apply to Social Security with partial privatization.

With the emphasis on personal responsibility, are people controlling their destiny? Recent research indicates that 39 percent of workers have a plan for economic needs in retirement. Approximately 54 percent of workers between the ages of 45 and 64 have no retirement account. The average worker between the ages of 55 and 64 has a retirement account, which totals $57,331 (Duffy, 2001). These data support a Pain Webber and Gallup Survey (Farrell, 2000). The findings show that in general most people intend to work in retirement. Of the 986 investors, only 15 percent plan to travel and "enjoy life." The group have 566 people with investments between $10,000 and $100,000, while 420 people have investments of over $100,000. This study concludes that many of these somewhat knowledgeable investors are unrealistic about retirement, because they lack the economic resources for retirement. An examination of money sources in retirement shows that 42 percent of income comes from Social Security, while 23 percent results from 401K plans and 21 percent from savings. These three sources account for 86 percent of retirement income. Only 1 percent is generated by employment (Lim, 2001).

Some other data about retirement suggest that the general society needs greater frugality. In retirement, a person needs 70 to 90 percent of his or her present family income. The person who reaches 65 years of age can expect to live 20 more years. In the general population, 75 percent of households save for retirement with African-Americans and Hispanics at approximately a 50 percent level (Jackson and Jackson,1999). These various data indicated that people in the United States do not plan for retirement, do not evaluate the sources of income in retirement and do not invest enough money for retirement.

In this entrepreneurial individualistic environment, the individual receives encouragement to take up his or her mantle and survive the challenge of life. Responsibility is in the hands of the individual and the path to success has two lanes. Thurow (1999), Jackson and Jackson (1999), Stanley and Danko (1996), and Brown (1995) encourage the individual to become an entrepreneur. The risks are high in that one-half of all new businesses fail within 4 years (Jackson and Jackson, 1999). On the optimistic side, 18 percent of household heads are self-employed or own a business and these self-employed people have a 4 times greater chance to become millionaires than those who work for others. According to Thurow (1999), the contemporary entrepreneur builds the global organization, which helps to destroy the national organization. Through this process, the entrepreneur creates chaos, which generates wealth for the individual and provides growth for the economy.

The other path which these various authors reinforce follows the road to investments. Since 1926, the stock market has provided an annual return of 11 percent (Farrell, 2000). John Bogle (2000) set up the rules for investments in his senior thesis at Princeton University 50 years ago. He wants everyone invested in a stock fund which reflects a stock index — for instance, the S and P 500 or Wilshire 5000. His advice encourages the investment of pretax dollars, when this strategy is possible. He also expects each individual to find a low cost fund, since a 2 percent annual fee can eat up significant dollars over 20 years. His final admonition points out the rewards for compounding money. At an annual return of 11 percent, money will double in 6.5 years. Bogle (2000) supplies another example of compounding investments. A $10,000 investment in stock at a 10 percent annual return in 40 years produces $450,000, while the same investment in bonds at a 5 percent annual return generates $70,000 in 40 years.

The economic climate in this country has changed in recent decades and the individual now faces the demand for education and the responsibility to build wealth. The choices are made by the individual and the consequences of his or her choices are lived out by the individual. Each person is working alone, and personal decisions determine the quality of life.

These visions for building wealth are the practical gospel of Salem Baptist Church in Chicago, Illinois (Marcus, 2001). The Reverend James Meeks recognizes the importance of the message of Martin Luther King, for he asserts, "Political power without economic power is not enough." The church members receive instruction on debt reduction and strategies for investments. The parable of the talents encourages people not only to multiply their natural gifts but to build wealth.

References

"The Big Picture." Editorial. *Business Week* Jan. 22, 2001: n. pag.

Bogle, John C. *John Bogle on Investing: The First 50 Years.* New York: McGraw, 2000.

Bridges, William. *Job Shift: How to Prosper in a Workplace without Jobs.* Reading, MA: Addison, 1994.

Broder, David S. "A New Democrat Revival. Washington, D.C." *Washington Post* July 30 — Aug. 12, 2001, nat'l weekly ed.: n. pag.

Brown, Tony. *Black Lies, White Lies.* New York: Morrow, 1995.

Cahill, Thomas. *Desire of the Everlasting Hills: The World before and after Jesus.* New York: Random House, 1999.

Campbell, Joseph. *The Hero's Journey.* San Francisco: Harper, 1989.

Cooper, J. C., and K. Madigan. "Business Outlook." *Business Week* Aug. 6, 2001: n. pag.

Crossan, John Dominic. *Jesus: A Revolutionary Biography.* San Francisco: Harper, 1995.

Drucker, Peter F. *Innovation and Entrepreneurship: Practice and Principle.* New York: Harper, 1985.

_____. *The New Realities.* New York: Harper, 1989.

Duffy, R. "Vital Statistics." *U.S. News and World Report* June 25, 2001: n. pag.

Farrell, M. *Beyond the Basics.* New York: Simon, 2000.

Frolik, J. "A Quiet Crisis." *Plain Dealer* [Cleveland, OH] July 20, 2001: n. pag.

Gardner, H. "Beyond a Modular View of Mind." *Child Development Today and Tomorrow.* Eds. William Damon. San Francisco: Jossey, 1989.

Gardner, Howard with Emma Laskin. *Leading Minds: An Anatomy of Leadership.* New York: Basic, 1996.

Gergen, David. "Listen, Learn — Change." *U.S. News and World Report* May 15, 2001: n. pag.

Goleman, D. *Emotional Intelligence.* New York: Bantam, 1995.

Jackson, Jesse L., Sr., and Jesse L. Jackson, Jr. with Mary Gotshall. *It's about the Money!: The Fourth Movement of the Freedom Symphony: How to Build Wealth, Get Access to Capital, and Achieve Your Financial Dreams.* New York: Three Rivers, 1999.

King, Martin Luther, Jr. "Letter from Birmingham Jail." *The Essential Writings of Martin Luther King, Jr.* Ed. James Melvin Washington. San Francisco: Harper, 1986. 289–303.

_____. "A Time to Break Silence." *A Testament of Hope.* 231–45.

Kirksey, R. "Kent State Professor Co-Authors Report Detailing Ohio Workers Gains and Loss through U.S. Economic Recovery." *Inside Kent State* [Kent, OH]: Sept. 17, 2001: n. pag.

Koretz, G. "Economic Trends." *Business Week* Feb. 5, 2001: n. pag.

_____. "Economic Trends." *Business Week* July 23, 2001: n. pag.

Kurlantzick, J. "Not Made in America." *U.S. News and World Report* July 2, 2001: n. pag.

LeVine, Robert A., and Donald T. Campbell. *Ethnocentrism: Theories of Conflict, Ethnic Attitudes and Group Behavior.* New York: Wiley, 1972.

Lim, P. L. "Making Your Money Last As Long As You Do." *U.S. News and World Report* June 4, 2001: n. pag.

Lind, Michael. *The Next American Nation: The New Nationalism and the Fourth American Revolution.* New York: Free, 1995.

Marcus, A. D. "The Gospel of Money." *Money* n. d. 2001: n. pag.

Naisbitt, John. *Megatrends: Ten New Directions Transforming Our Lives.* New York. Warner, 1982.

Nicholson, T. "Long Goodbye to Benefits?" *A. A. R. P.— Modern Maturity* July–Aug 2001: n. pag.

Peters, Tom. *Liberation Management: Necessary Disorganization for the Nanosecond Nineties.* New York: Knopf, 1992.

Phillips, Kevin P. *Boiling Point: Republicans, Democrats, and the Decline of Middle-Class Prosperity.* New York: Random House, 1993.

_____. *The Politics of Rich and Poor: Wealth and the American Electorate in the Reagan Aftermath.* New York: Random House, 1990.

Putnam, Robert D. *Bowling Alone: The Collapse and Revival of American Community.* New York: Simon, 2000.

Reich, Robert B. *The Future of Success.* New York: Knopf, 2000.

Schachter, Stanley. *The Psychology of Affiliation: Experimental Studies of the Sources of Gregariousness.* Stanford: Stanford U P, 1959.

Schillebeeckx, Edward C. F. A. *Church: The Human Story of God.* Trans. John Bowden. New York: Crossroads, 1990.

Sherif, Muzafer, et al. *Intergroup Conflict and Cooperation: The Robbers Cave Experiment.* Institute of Group Relations. Norman: U of Oklahoma P, 1961.

Stanley, Thomas J., and William D. Danko. *The Millionaire Next Door: The Surprising Secrets of America's Wealthy.* Atlanta: Longstreet, 1996.

Thurow, Lester C. *Building Wealth: The New Rules for Individuals, Companies, and Nations in Knowledge-Based Economy.* New York: HarperCollins, 1999.

_____. *The Future of Capitalism: How Today's Economic Forces Shape Tomorrow's World.* New York: Morrow, 1996.

Torabi, F. "Price Pony." *Money* Sept. 2001: n. pag.

Waterman, R. H. *The Renewal Factor.* New York Bantam, 1987.

Wills, Garry. *Certain Trumpets: The Call of Leaders.* New York: Simon, 1994.

Williams, K. "Rich Poor and Making Ends Meet." *The Washington Post* July 9 — 15, 2001, nat'l weekly ed.: n. pag.

14
Dreaming Beyond the Number Two: Race, Work, and Wholeness

Eileen Sheryl Hammer

The dream, then, is to get beyond not only the number one — the number that determines unity, of body or self — but also beyond the number two — which determines difference, antagonism, and exchange conceived merely as the coming together of opposites.
— Donna Haraway "Incalculable Choreographies" in *Simian, Cyborgs, and Women* (Routledge, 1991)

The American Dream Business

Following World War II and most memorably in the 1950s and early '60s, many Americans shared a uniform, even stereotyped image of the businessperson as that instantly recognizable figure dubbed "the organization man" by sociologist William Whyte. Icon of suburban stability, mythologized on television and immortalized in movies and magazines, he would kiss his wife (his emotional life) goodbye each morning as he picked up his briefcase for another day of poker-faced gamesmanship until he could pull into the driveway and say, "Hi, honey; I'm home."

Recent corporate restructurings, the graying of America, new medical knowledge on lifestyle and health, the stress-management industry, the men's movement, and increased awareness as to the correlates of alcoholism and other addictions— including "workaholism"— have accelerated a growing segment of society's generalized discontent with the model of making money as the meaning of life. This section explores the price of the American dream, and whether it is worth it. It looks at what has been sacrificed, and what might be redeemable.

The Up Side of Downsizing

Since the 1990s more ensconced (i.e., white, male, middle-class) managers, successful and less so, have come increasingly to share some of the dissatisfactions of workplace newcomers. Like white women and minority women and men who express disillusionment after brushes with the glass ceiling and velvet ghetto, many from the ranks of the so-called "old-boy-network" have been coming to question some previously taken-for-granted beliefs about what is reasonably required to "make it," and how we define "success." Aimed at a post-downsizing, post-dotcom audience, books like psychologist Stan Katz's *Success Trap*, which offer guidance to "rethink your ambitions to achieve greater ... personal fulfillment," have begun to be featured in the same in-flight catalogues that had always showcased motivational mementos, totems and talismans such as pencil-holders and paperweights inscribed with inspirational sayings like, "whatever it takes." As we grow to understand what qualities— and which members of the talent pool — are left out of the reductive equation in which we can only see "the pursuit of happiness" as a single-minded swim toward socioeconomic "success," can we start to imagine a more humane American myth?

Faced with both obvious and invisible barriers, black businesspeople have explicitly addressed the ambition/fulfillment issue for a lot longer. Well before the ascendance of mainstream gurus like Steven Covey and "discoveries" like "emotional intelligence," African-Americans had to muster the spiritual and psychological resources to offset the onslaught of assaults and insults to one's sense of self-worth at work. Lay citizens as well as religious/political leaders have often sought to soften the slings and arrows of the workaday world by reflecting on a sense of archetypal struggle and themes that are larger, more enduring, more meaningful. As Audrey Edwards and Craig Polite write in *Children of the Dream*, "Success has always been a relative phenomenon in black America ... measured as much by what has been overcome as what has been achieved...." What do minority members of the workforce have to tell about being at odds as they try to get even? How are minorities' experiences of what social scientists call "role strain" and "role conflict" instructive for all of us with emergent or resurgent (or insurgent) interest in humanizing a workplace which, for an unacceptable number of Americans, is no place like home?

Same/Difference

In our current (anti-affirmative action) political context, many white Americans seem still to act from an assumption that to take note (explicitly) of racial-ethnic distinctions is embarrassing (except in the realm of broad sitcom caricatures, in which pent-up censored send-ups escape like cultural flatulence). Reverence for the value of universal quality is mistaken for an injunction about sameness. Too many well-meaning whites imagine that it is most tactful to espouse and strive for this rose-colored distortion, as if to admit that to notice another's ethnicity is to say that one has automatically made some sort of negative valuation. According to this scheme, a successful person of color can only be seen as having surpassed the "limitations" of her or his heritage. In lieu of appreciating that such a person's success might in fact "stand on the shoulders" of a community that gave social and spiritual sustenance, perhaps financial support, white Americans often unconsciously look at nonwhiteness as a "cultural" deficit, a lack, occasionally overcome by an exceptional individual. Such a superstar (e.g., Oprah Winfrey) then becomes the exception-who-proves-the-rule that group-level discrimination is neither overwhelming nor insurmountable for a sufficiently motivated individual. As San Francisco diversity expert Ron Brown says, some things "need knowing" by white people.

In my work as a clinical sociologist consulting for groups and organizations, I have focused for fifteen years in the area known as managing diversity. As a result of a long-term research commitment in collaboration with a minority nonprofit, and with technical assistance from a corporate sponsor, I was able to compile a uniquely extensive survey of 210 African-American employees in 17 United States cities, mostly around the Midwest. The results comprise a clear set of statistical snapshots: pictures of people's job mobility and their self-reports on career satisfaction. With these data as a backdrop, I went on to conduct in-depth, open-ended life-history interviews with those survey participants who gave the richest responses to qualitative questions on work and life-stress, strategies for dealing with prejudice and discrimination, and the role and shape of community, politics, and spirituality in their lives. When I bring workshops to corporate, classroom, and civic settings, I am always updating, amending, and amplifying my information. This hands-on experience with groups teaches me how people live in/live out the tension between the reality of racism and the American Dream.

This section shares stories about survival strategies in an insecure and unfair job market. It examines avenues of self-empowerment against what has been called "second-stage" or "soft" racism, "When the words are right but the music's wrong," as put by one workshop participant. This is the subtler, subterranean undermining that can in certain circumstances be more insidious and unsettling than blatant bigotry. The peer group that populates this piece shares an ethos that translates the American Dream into a more grounded, "real" myth of "making it" that isn't impossible. In a variety of vignettes, their observations accent key themes of integrity and authenticity that are coming up with increasing frequency at this point in the American story.

Comments come from a series of interviews with 44 individuals in their 30s and 40s. They were recruited during high school and college, through what economists call a "third-party helper" organization. Following the social-science convention of protecting participants' anonymity, I refer to this helper-agency here as MAINSTREAM. A nonprofit group, MAINSTREAM's goal is to divert some of the flow of minority talent that traditionally has remained "occupationally segregated" within a restricted range of professions. The idea is to increase the numbers of minorities throughout American business life, starting with those companies that agree to try out candidates "brokered" through the third-party helper. Social psychologists have a phrase for this sort of strategy: "the contact hypothesis." Simply, becoming acquainted with more people from different backgrounds helps dispel the prejudice that flourishes in the ignorance of "racial isolation."

The Role of Work, Role at Work

Many of the MAINSTREAMers I met are part of a hinge-generation, the children of civil-rights-era parents. They tend to describe themselves as concentrating on their careers, with a self-searing but sincere belief and hope that they are widening the horizons of possibility for younger people of color to come. The phrase "paving the way," and the terms "frontrunner," "pioneer" and "role model" recurred frequently in the interviews.

MAINSTREAM members express a sense of immediacy about needing to demonstrate to the public at large that African-Americans are just like anyone: "It kind of bothers me that the people who are setting the image of blacks have to be on television and not in the business world.

Until we get more blacks coming up through the ranks and staying in these cities, I think it's going to be that way." In contrast to television, the business world signifies real life. It is partly because of television and advertising, however, that a well-known company is quickly considered a bona fide playing field. A job at a famous firm represents respectability, and full participation in the good things of American life.

Throughout my attendance at dinners, awards presentations and other formal occasions, I heard as refrains the phrases, "giving back to the community," and "remembering where you came from." During informal discussions, MAINSTREAMers often invoked this premise: that the development of a cadre of African-American corporate leaders ultimately brings benefits back to the broader black community. In this worldview, getting ahead doesn't have to mean leaving others behind. Yet at the same time, MAINSTREAMers cite numerous examples of conflict, between one's identity as a developing professional and one's identifications of and with the black community. They characterize common tensions in their stories of social interaction at work, and talk about what can be felt as a tug of war, between corporate-cultural norms and community values.

Workplace Personae

To an overwhelming extent, MAINSTREAMers report that being in corporate America means "acting white." As one accountant states, "If I'm going to advance in the organization, I've got to get in there and blend." Operating both as a part of and apart from the established (white) corporate culture, the MAINSTREAM members I met spoke in some detail about how they are mindful to keep an internal continuity, while shifting between their work personas and their "community" [home, friends, family, (old) neighborhood] selves, and throughout all the gradations and combinations of public-professional personal-private. For instance, a telecommunications marketing manager described a kind of inner-clock-radio consciousness, that prompts her to play particular tapes on her car stereo. She gets geared up on her way to work with classical brass, relaxes and releases emotions on the way home with Teddy Pendergrass. The same process many non–African-Americans obviously follow, but with a chiaroscuro-like heightening in the sense of disjunction.

In the same way that many managers make an effort to dress for success, MAINSTREAMers at work self-consciously "speak for success." Because Black English is a stigmatized dialect associated with negative stereotypes, these role-models-in-training keep a sharp focus on "the right way to speak." An electrical engineer explains, demonstrating his knowledge of linguistics terms:

> You code switch. The black people walking around here still talking like they are on the street corner, these are not viewed as the type of persons who are promotable.

MAINSTREAMers reserve Black English — which they refer to as "slang"— for home, for family and friends. On the job they are strict about the usage of what many call "clear and good English."

> When I first started I was really black. I would talk very black. You know, use a lot of slang and also I was not used to being around a lot of white people so I would talk loud. My mentor would always soften things up for me with my boss. I owe her a lot.

Strategic Optimism

MAINSTREAM grooms its alumni according to a culture of common understandings, involving a purposeful affirmation of the meritocratic American Dream, deferred or not. In just about every interview, MAIN-STREAMers brought up the classic image of "climbing the ladder" as the metaphor for career advancement. MAINSTREAMers strive to make it so, that determined talent triumphs. A typical assessment:

> In terms of the racism, it's not necessarily something that has to hold you down. Just fight it.

It is not that many of these newcomers are naive about racism, although in fact many in the younger generation feel quite differently than their parents do— they believe things are better, and can be quite critical of their parents' "obsession with black and white," as some people put it. More to the point, they are trained to use a positive outlook as a heuristic tool, to "act as if" they can overcome the odds. This means that the focus stays on the precise particulars of any presenting problem; it is not characteristic of most MAINSTREAMers to reside in the realm of radical critique. In fact, the majority define themselves politically as "moderates." The emphasis is on being practical, on what works; mental energy goes into strategies for circumventing the obstacles, not on venting about what is wrong with the system as it is, or inventing ways in which it could be fairer. In the pragmatist American spirit, MAINSTREAMers are experts on alternative routes.

MAINSTREAMers voice definite opinions about what they variously call the old-boy network, "the buddy-buddy system," and "pulling strings." MAINSTREAMers may question whether meritocracy is a myth, but nonetheless express determination to "make it" through hard working as well as networking. The remark "I almost believe it's a 50/50 split," between luck — which includes "connections" — and achievement, reflects a pervasive sentiment. But MAINSTREAMers are no defeatists. They speak with sophistication about self-presentation, about "politics" and "the way things really work." What I intend to do is work hard, and, hopefully, work smarter.

> Q: What does "work smarter" mean?
> A: Make the right contacts, impress the right people. It's more perception than anything else.

Work and Interaction: The Interpretive Dance

MAINSTREAMers often find themselves having to make quick decisions, on a moment-by-moment basis, about what to make of or how to construe white co-workers' or clients' words, actions, and omissions. A MAINSTREAM salesman smoothly insists, with both "presumptuous" and "superliberal" white clients who "try to grab my thumb," on "doing a regular handshake," "the correct way." With each of these encounters he keeps the continuity of the transaction yet communicates his clear preference for the same ritual handshake one would offer a non-African-American rep. He manages to overrule inappropriate attempts at over-familiarity, interrupting the stereotyping without interrupting the business at hand.

"You always ask yourself, 'Is a comment racially-motivated or is it just normal?'" a chemist explains. MAINSTREAMers frequently mention "giving people the benefit of the doubt." Throughout the interview sessions, locutions like "I try not to think it's race," "I don't want to think it's race," or "I'd rather not look at it as race," were the norm. In addition, many spoke of having implicit interpretive frameworks that inform their personal policies for anticipating and averting potential run-ins, so the can "stay in the game":

> You have to define the difference between racism and favoritism. But you cannot jump to conclusions. Because as soon as you jump to conclusions, you've already put yourself in a different ball game. If you come out and say it's racism, then you have people around you hostile.

Vigilant about avoiding "playing the victim" or "using race as an alibi," MAINSTREAMers tend to be very thorough in allowing for the possibility of other possibilities. People cited gender, age, even marital status as alternative explanations. The best strategy is to keep interpretations open. But this leaves the door ajar for ambiguity and self-doubt. And in a number of anecdotes, this cultivation of equanimity by stressing self-determination and steering clear of us/them judgments, did shift into moments of self-questioning, even self-blame.

The Down Side of Moving Up

How surprising is it, then, that this brand of self-consciousness in some instances will shade off into a snobbish or "forgetful" comment, like: "If you come from like, say, a ghetto, whatever, you might not know how to eat. Well, hopefully by then you know how to eat. But you might not know how to socialize with people." As their peers put it, once people take on the veneer of the *arriviste*, it seems to slip their minds "how much support comes from the community where they came from." For those few who "get brainwashed, or just completely caught up in their own personal growth," immigrating into the middle-American middle-class means losing sight of the positive qualities of people they once played with. Once these exemplary "mentors" get ensconced in the ranks of successful suburbanites, those still in their socioeconomic status of origin seem to have "no class" at all. As a trainee complained, after watching some older MAINSTREAMers' metamorphoses: "It's almost like they change races or something."

"Color-Blind" Double-Blind

In *American Theater* magazine (May-June 2000), Greg Tate refers to the fear of being "embraced to death by white America" as the main reason for anxiety among African-Americans in the post civil rights era. The majority of MAINSTREAMers have plenty of trepidation about avoiding what Tate terms "assimilation into annihilation." There are ways in which they are willing and not willing to exhibit the prescribed and eliminate the proscribed from their behavioral repertoires.

Re-creation in/of Black and White

Despite a focus on equal opportunity and gray areas during working hours, a polarized image of fun in black and white develops after hours.

Many MAINSTREAMers made a point of mentioning the salience of "different interests" based on "different backgrounds" with reference to preferences in recreation. Several examples had to do with tastes in music, but by far the most elaborated lists of "black ways of doing things" and "white ways of doing things"; "things blacks like to do" and "things whites like to do," involved sports. At the most alienated of the spectrum a sales manager says,

> Like, their children might be into gymnastics or horseback riding. "My daughter is equestrian," they'll say, and you're sitting there. "What on earth are they talking about?"

A computer programmer offered a more common comment: "Black folks get out on the basketball court, play football. But the older white males, they golf. That's all they do, you know? Play golf."

Dinner Roles

For the most part, MAINSTREAMers emphasize taking responsibility for one's own discontent, instead of being "cliquey," or having what some spoke of as a "minority syndrome"—a certain insularity, a reluctance to mix much with whites. "Blacks who don't feel comfortable around a lot of white people…. They might use that as an excuse to not attend the company picnic. Instead of trying to open up, try something new, test the waters."

This willingness to test the waters implies all kinds of "homework." For instance, various MAINSTREAMers said they did a lot of reading, so that they could feel more familiar with foreign conversation topics at lunch. Moreover, even the physical task of lunch-eating becomes an "identity prop":

> When I eat, I tell people I have a Mellon Bank eat, and a home eat. The way I eat at home is the way I feel like eating. If I am going out [for work], then I have to eat the way they expect me to at Mellon Bank. It's more than proper, because you're showing off for other people; you want to show your good manners, above and beyond being good. Not saying I am sloppy at home, because I do my best to eat neat at home also. But at the same time, when you're out with the company you want them to see you above and beyond anything you might do at home.

Tight and Loose

Many spoke in terms of a tightness-looseness axis: "You don't what I call "get loose" at work…. Even if I've just finished a project, I don't get loose in my attitude." Reasons for staying "tight" had to do with an awareness of being "in the limelight," given "the once-over and twice-over as blacks." "I have to be blue-chip all the way around" was a steady refrain. There is no margin for the interpersonal error that could come from relaxing these perfectionistic standards. Being a role model means you must always look the part; you can't be caught looking like your whole self. Or, in the words of one alumnus, "There is a time and a place for being the businessperson, and a time and a place for being yourself."

Job Performances

For MAINSTREAMers, impression-management at work is a full-time job. To effectively navigate the work environment, first you make yourself over in the corporate image, and leave complicating complexities out in the car. Considering the corporate custom of "dressing for success," a senior manager compared his morning routine to that of an athlete putting on a uniform: "You have to consider it as part of the job. As opposed to, 'That's not me and I don't want to look like that.' You can't look at it like, 'My clothes are me.'" His peer points out, "I think I've done well, because people at work tell me they can't imagine me wearing blue jeans, or they think I am an accountant all the time."

Americans do not yet have a whole lot of complexity tolerance. We get confused when faced with mufti-facetedness, the way kindergarteners are shocked to see their schoolteacher at the mall with kids of his or her own. We haven't yet learned to be multidimensional with our categories. On a recent episode of the sitcom *Girlfriends*, the character Lynn calls herself "a complex woman." Toni, who usually talks in textbook standard English, answers: "I hate to break it to you, complex woman, but in America, you black."

So if you want to be seen as more than just your race, being yourself is not something you do at work. Many people put it in terms of appropriateness; you figure out which "white" or "black" identity features or emblems you want to display and how prominently, depending on the situation. As a customer relations specialist tells it,

> When you are around white people on the phone your voice changes. It's just, it's hard to explain. You become more formal with a more white kind of voice. When you are on the phone at home you have a more casual tone of voice.

Work is white; family and friends are black. At work you are the "professional"; at home or with friends in the community you can be casual, you can be yourself. As you get to know work friends or work associates, it can be excruciatingly problematic, because you are somewhere in between:

> Say, for instance, if I come home and throw on the tackiest of clothes, jeans with holes in them — you try not to let your friends at work see you like — if they want to meet with you, you say okay, I'll wear slacks, when that may not be your normal attire after work.

In Between

MAINSTREAMers' stories of transitional times, like commuting hours, and interstitial situations, such as company outings, are especially instructive. The nuances of variation between "real leisure" and "role leisure," "friend" and "associate," predominantly African-American settings and predominantly white ones, speak volumes about what is experienced as performance, and what is felt as relaxed, authentic, spontaneous.

When it comes to socializing with people from the office, defining the separation between work and leisure becomes crucial. Well-instructed as to the dimensions of organizational politics, MAINSTREAMers by and large express the view that participation in company gatherings is a kind of unofficial overtime that comes with the territory. A technical trainee stressed the need to draw clear and crisp boundaries (the fact that she is female factors too in her firm commitment to always maintain her workplace persona): "Occasionally I will go out with them. But it's like that's part of work, too. When I go out with them, I say that's part of work, and those are the confines in which I stand."

However, where processes of information-sharing and decision-making often go on after hours and in social settings, absolute adherence to a work/leisure dichotomy is recognized as an impediment to success. MAINSTREAMers know that if you want to be "visible" in the company, attendance at social functions is vital. But it is clear that the socializing is not fun. A financial analyst summed it up: "You know a dance of that nature, a dance at the white country clubs— I've been to a few and it's not really even a dance — it's politics. If you go there and dance as black people do, you're looked at as, well — you're dancing, the dancing that blacks do as opposed to the majority of whites and it's different."

It's politics, because it's not a "real" dance. You're being looked at, looked over. Sociability becomes social control. And as soon as you "let your guard down" and dance unselfconsciously, you're presenting a self that is "not in context," in one MAINSTREAMer's phrase. Performance, in the sense of display, counts for more than performance in the sense of work competence. In general, MAINSTREAMers find these informal company events to be problematic and stressful.

Professional Reserve

While MAINSTREAM alumni often speak with pride about their "versatility," "adaptability," "being a people-person," they will also say that you can be only just so friendly with co-workers. "I'm cordial, but I do not like all my business in the office" is a common kind of comment. There exists an apparent consensus that because corporate waters can be treacherous, too much familiarity will "come back to haunt you." Several mentioned the concern that "some people are just looking for things to use against you." With this sharp division between "work associates" and friends, only the latter are people you would not mind inviting home or introducing to your family. The prohibition against mixing the two seems virtually universal.

When alumni talk about "real friends," they are usually, although not always, referring to other African-Americans. "I think I might relax a bit more when I'm around black people; you don't need to mind your p's and q's." The adjective "natural" was often used in this context. MAINSTREAMers consider "friends" to be people who provide support and share ideas and information, particularly with respect to career-related concerns. They are usually referring to other middle-class African-Americans, often fellow MAINSTREAM graduates. Fellow alumni provide a kind of bridge, a respite from all the ambivalence, a sense of belonging and identity — a community.

"Real leisure" for MAINSTREAMers means not only the often-cited picnics and shopping with family and friends, but also organized activities at church and other voluntary associations. It is at neighborhood events, such as school career days, or when serving as Big Brothers and Big Sisters, where MAINSTREAMers most often merge their corporate-cultural selves and their community selves.

Paradoxically, by playing the role of role model for a hometown audience, MAINSTREAMers can finally relax.

15

The Strangest of Kin: Blacks and Whites in America Viewed from the Borderlands

GREGORY K. STEPHENS

It took me almost a year to read David Shipler's *A Country of Strangers: Blacks and Whites in America*. My reactions to the book alternated between irritation, what has been called "race fatigue," and an admiration for Shipler's accomplishment. There is much to admire: Shipler seems to aspire to give us a modern-day journalistic equivalent of Gunner Myrdal's *An American Dilemma*. And within that black-and-white framework, he often succeeds. But I want to engage in what I hope is some constructive criticism of Shipler's myopia, which renders invisible the America in which I live.

"Everywhere I have looked, I have seen a country where blacks and whites are strangers to each other," Shipler writes in his preface. The social landscape Shipler describes is not hard to find; in fact the evidence is everywhere. And yet, at the same time, Shipler clearly found what he looked for. What he did not look for he did not see; what he could not imagine he could not find. Yet there is another America beyond the black-and-white binary, which is also easy to find, for those who do not wear the blinders of binary racial mythology. In this other America, "our America," many people think and live in terms other than black and white. They are bilingual or multi-ethnic or in other tangible ways multi-centered. For me, the people of "our America" are a deafening absence in Shipler's book.

I know the world Shipler describes all too well, and I still move through it at times. It is that world, in which "race" is such an over-determining obsession, that evokes in me a sense of "racial fatigue." It fatigues me because I have heard all these arguments rehearsed too often, and I see them going in circles. I know that there will be no resolution of "the American dilemma" as long as people think in black-and-white. Racism is a "diseased imagination," as Frederick Douglass once said. One cannot cure or contain the disease without presenting a more attractive alternative, a different sort of imagination. And the great unlearned lesson of North American race relations, voiced by some of our most visionary leaders (but understood by few) is that one can never solve the problems of racism with the language of race. Clearly, it is important that people who do see the world racially, who do define themselves as black and white, learn to talk to each other, even if indirectly, through mediums such as this book. But the black-and-white America is a hall of mirrors. My fatigue comes from a restless certainty that there is no escape from that hall of mirrors unless we begin to widen the discussion, to include other Americans who do not see the world in black and white.

My irritation with David Shipler's book is in part simply based on the fact that he does not describe the America I live in most of the time. In my America ("our America") Spanish is a language I speak daily. Latinos or Hispanics are now in fact the largest "minority" in the United States. Even within the black-and-white America of *A Country of Strangers*, I have a variety of interracial relationships with people for whom "race" is not the great tragic divide that Shipler takes as normative. This America of borderlands or racial frontiers is far more common than the dominant black-and-white racial mythology can allow us to recognize. As Guillermo Gomez-Peña insists, "The dominant culture is no longer dominant," and if there is a dominant culture, it is border culture: that of people with their feet in more than one culture, language, or nation.

Invisibility is often painful. In this era of rapid demographic changes, when many of us are hungry for more accurate representations of ourselves in all our diversity, we tend to tune out stories and institutions that exclude us. My natural impulse would have been to table Shipler's book, which seemed anchored in another era. At the same time I felt duty bound to read and comment on the book, because it is often impressive and carries the weight of authority, and because it describes (narrowly, but exhaustively) a domain that has long been my specialty, as a journalist and scholar: "race relations."

Yet I am part of a tradition that puts more emphasis on the "relations" part of the race-relations equation, as someone once said about Robert Park. Being able to imagine relations that are not over-determined by "race" means we have to be able to de-center race, to understand that it is in fact a social fiction. This does not mean that we diminish the legacy of racial oppression or the continuing problems of racism. It does require us to recognize that the root cause of racism is *racialism*, the "insidious confusion of race with culture," as Ralph Ellison wrote, and that this is a problem perpetuated by people of all colors. Our shared complicity in perpetuating racialism is implicit in the concept of racial formations. This means that although "race" is a fictional construct, institutions, language, and culture continue to racialize us, in often pernicious ways. David Hollinger has referred to this deep institutional investment in racialism as an "ethno-racial pentagon." Thinking outside the racialized box would require us to recognize "the true inter-relatedness of blackness and white-ness," as Ellison put it. Recognition of this inter-relatedness leads to an understanding that we are not just a nation of strangers, we are the strangest of kin, even if racial mythologies have rendered our kinship invisible.

For me the most exasperating weakness of the book was something beyond the author's control. In hundreds of minor and major ways, Shipler reveals himself as a case study of a psycho-social phenomenon I call "the white liberal guilt complex" (WLGC).

The project that became *A Country of Strangers* was Shipler's "way of coming home," he explained to one skeptical subject. He had spent much of the last quarter of the twentieth century living in and writing about other countries: Vietnam, Russia, and Israel, as a *New York Times* reporter. He had received a Pulitzer Prize for his book about intractable inter-eth-nic problems in another country, *Arab and Jew: Wounded Spirits in a Promised Land*. But Shipler's homecoming reveals a longing for the sim-plicity of another era, when heroes and villains were clear, and could be identified primarily as black or white.

Shipler returned to America with a worldview shaped by the "awful, indelible images" of his boyhood in the 1950s. He is still "haunted" by "cute little white girls who twisted their faces into screams of hatred as black children were escorted into schools." Shipler's conclusion was clear: "Here was the enemy" (4). His view of the heroes who would champion the solution was equally clear: he remembers interviewing Martin Luther King Jr., whose "perfect righteousness ... summoned the conscience of America."

Like many good liberals, Shipler felt deeply betrayed that "we did not get the revolution we anticipated." His return to America confronted him with a changed nation, with few of the moral certainties of the earlier era. This led to a crisis of faith. Early in the book, he recounts a dialogue with

Bill Lawson, an Afro-American Baptist pastor in Houston, Texas. Shipler wonders if he and other Americans were naïve to believe that white Americans, once their conscience had been awakened, would "give" Afro-Americans equal opportunity. Lawson agrees that a central assumption of the Civil Rights movement was the belief "that there's a national conscience" (5). And although many Americans are now cynical about such an ideal, Lawson tells Shipler that he is not naïve to believe that this American conscience can still be awakened.

This becomes the central framing device of Shipler's book. He seeks to awaken the national conscience, which he bifurcates along racial lines. Like most good white liberals, he idealized the conscience of "black America" as a *moral center*. His mission becomes to awaken the dormant conscience of "white America" to the "debilitating bigotry" Afro-Americans suffer, (86) which has left them "powerless" (401, 436) and indeed "impotent" (412) in the face of "the racism inside white people" which is portrayed as arising from unconscious sources (348). This means that of course the burden of change is on whites, if they can free themselves from "white lies," through the moral agency of black people. As one of Shipler's Afro-American subjects says: "If the whites can liberate themselves through our knowledge and information, then we can come together and develop a oneness as a human race and as a people" (159). This point of view is an article of faith for many with a WLGC.

The primary focus of *A Country of Strangers* is not in fact race relations, it is a portrait of "black America" by a white liberal who looks at the present through the prism of the King years. And the dominant theme is the burden of "being black in America" (399). The strength of the book is that Shipler lets his subjects express this burden in their own words, in countless ways. The weakness is that the assumptions of Shipler's WLGC seem largely unexamined. When he speaks from the heart, the song he sings makes it clear that he worships in the church of black victimization.

This leads to several forms of myopia. Sometimes he projects the image of racist whites from the past into the present. Euro-Americans who do not agree with party lines on affirmative action, sensitivity training, etc., are portrayed as the "enemy"—the kin of those "cute white girls" whose visible hatred left such an indelible impression on Shipler. There is an incident in a Boy Scout troop involving Shipler's own son Michael, a "flash of racism" which sets off Shipler's complex. He calls a meeting with the other parents, and tries to awaken their conscience. Shipler was "expecting compassion, indignation, a resolve to make amends," but encounters what he interprets as passivity. His language takes on the flavor of Leonard Jeffries' racial typology: "their faces are frozen, expressionless, almost lifeless. *They don't care*," Shipler intones, twice. Perhaps these "white faces" really were "bland and uncaring," as he wrote (458–59). Perhaps they were also weary of the moralizing of white liberals with a guilt complex. In any case, such passages of racialized commentary do not inspire confidence in Shipler's objectivity.

For the do-the-right-thing white liberal with a guilt complex, few things get under the skin so much as other people of European descent who claim some knowledge about race, or worse, portray themselves as victims of racism. Because the good white liberal of course defers all authority in things "racial" to Afro-Americans. Thus Shipler can barely conceal his contempt for "unsolicited comments by whites about race" (459). The worst offenders, of course, are those who "told unsolicited stories in which whites were often the victims" (11, 411). The key word that gives away Shipler's bias, it seems to me, is "*unsolicited.*" He certainly would never disparage comments from Afro-Americans as unsolicited. In numerous ways, he reinforces the conventional wisdom that only blacks are the victims or racism, and that therefore only they have the right to speak about race. Thus he passes on the dubious racial mythology that in interracial marriages, the black partners inevitably take responsibility for teaching their offspring about race.

Occasionally, Shipler allows a few voices of counterpoint to introduce a problematic note into the neat racial binary that dominates the book. Many of these share his white liberal perspective but are shocked or troubled by intolerance or demonization they have experienced around Afro-Americans. Jessica Prentice, the only Euro-American at Tougaloo, recalled how his classmates routinely described whites as evil, saying, "[W]hite people are just pure greed, and black people love the earth and love everybody else" (349). Shipler also has a chapter on race-mixing, which provides some nuances without seeming to change Shipler's worldview. A biracial informant tells him, in an observation I have heard many times, that "I felt more racism from blacks than from whites" (251; 129–30).

One of the most memorable quotes by a Euro-American in the book comes from a police chief in Teaneck, New Jersey, Donald Giannone, who expresses his unvarnished cynicism about diversity training in this way: "If we go to a scene and somebody says that they screwed with my mother and she's the best piece of ass they ever got and stuff, or I'm a dirty [motherfucker] or whatever it happened to be, and I haven't used any derogatory terms, if their answer to that is to send me to sensitivity training, well, so be it. That's the political answer" (522). Yet as Shipler notes, Giannone was actively recruiting black cops, and some diversity training had been employed in his department.

Although there are plenty of quotes by the subjects in this book that are not "political," Shipler's commentary often attempts a Procrustean fit of the evidence into his ideological preconceptions. Along with the evidence of continuing racism or ignorance in "white America," we also get some glimpses of problems in "black America," but almost always rationalized. Thus, in a chapter on morality, Shipler reviews the shocking statistics on the rise of births to Afro-American women in the U.S. outside marriage, from 16.8 percent in 1950 to 70.4 percent in 1994, with one-third of those single mothers being teenagers. Shipler then employs that archetypal example of the white liberal guilt complex, Andrew Hacker, to argue that since Euro-American single motherhood has risen from 1.7 percent to 25.4 percent in the same period, whites are actually closing the gap in this dire trend (331–2). Shipler briefly considers a cultural explanation, but his stance is in line with a perspective I heard voiced in January 2002 by William Darrity of the University of North Carolina, that there is *no* cultural explanation for the problems plaguing "black America." Shipler elsewhere repeats the party line of this school of thought, that black women are "twice condemned" by racism and sexism (417).

To his credit, Shipler tries to continue to struggle with some of the troubling evidence of his primary subject, "the burden of being black in America." For instance, he acknowledges that "by every available index … blacks are more heavily involved in violent street crime than whites." But his conclusion reveals a typical WLGC myopia: "The question is what whites make of that truth" (376).

This was one of many points in the book where I wished I could bring Shipler into "our America," into my classes, for instance, and let him hear the comments about black crime or black bigotry by some of my Asian students. Those who are recent immigrants don't know yet what is politically correct to say. Their voices are needed here, as are the voices of Latinos, especially immigrants, whose relationships with Afro-Americans are often tense, and who freely express opinions about American race relations that should be a revelation to both sides in Shipler's black-and-white America.

At a very few moments, Shipler allows himself to briefly look outside the WLGC script (black victimization/white guilt) and briefly address topics such as black racism. He considers the blacks-can't-be-racist-because-they-have-no-power argument; then he concedes: "Many blacks have used it to confer a kind of immunity on themselves, a permission to be racist without admitting to it" (460). He observes that many "think their persecuted status cloaks them in permanent absolution for the sin of racial bigotry" (447). But then he quickly reverts to form, repeating the book's dominant motif that "[i]f you are black in America, [dealing with whites is] an exhausting effort." Having quickly skirted the troublesome subject of the black racism, he returns to the WLGC pulpit, endorsing a subject who believes that "blacks possessed X-ray vision about this society," and arguing that "whites could learn a great deal about themselves and their country if they would only listen to what blacks have to say" (448–49).

In "Memory: The Echoes of History," the book's best chapter, Shipler does move beyond WLGC platitudes long enough to engage in a critique of racialist attitudes on both sides of the racial divide. His discussion of the debate about the significance of Thomas Jefferson's mixed-race legacy is excellent. And his critique of the blind spots into which Afrocentrists have been led by their racial romanticism is sometimes dead-on. More importantly, he observes that "because of the virtual segregation of black history into its own niche in the curriculum, blacks and whites are learning different stories, even within the same institution" (195). Learning different stories is less the problem than the often unchallenged belief that there is no point of intersection between those stories. Resolving this would require an integrative, rather than an assimilative, imagination: "the re-integration of American history." Shipler closes this chapter on the power of racialized memory by musing: "Somewhere in American life, there must be room for the multiple truths of a complex past, for the blend of many honest melodies" (226).

Shipler does make some room for these "multiple truths" in another compelling chapter, "Mixing: The Stranger Within." It is here, predictably, that some of the cracks in the racial divide appear. There is a fascinating section about Reggie Daniel and his aspirations for a "multiracial Zionism" (131). There is an all-too-brief encounter with a woman named Angela Alvarez, who is of mixed Cuban, Mexican, African-American, and Irish ancestry. Still looking through his black-and-white lens, Shipler says that she appears black. But "culturally and linguistically, she calls herself 'Latina'" (139). Alvarez is just a blip on the screen in this book, the barest tip of an iceberg that would completely disrupt our attitudes about race, were we aware of its depth. Many, perhaps most Dominicans, Puerto Ricans, Cubans and Panamanians "appear black" to North American eyes, yet culturally and linguistically they exist outside the black-white binary. In fact, most people of African descent in "our America" speak Spanish, not English, a continental reality of which most North Americans remain blissfully unaware. Yet our own census says that "Hispanics can be of any race," which ought to be a wake-up call to Americans of all colors who want to update their view of "race relations."

Yet the only other time Latinos make even a fleeting, indirect appearance in *A Country of Strangers* is within the context of a discussion of

Latinos supposedly seeking white privilege, or expressions by Afro-Americans of the pervasive (but misguided) point of view that Latinos are trying to be white, or only want to ally themselves with whites (492, 461). (Shipler frequently discusses the "unearned advantages" of whiteness, yet also includes a statistic that troubles easy assumptions about "white privilege," that 2/3 of the people below the poverty line in the U.S. are of European descent) (302, 438). A Houston sheriff named Perry Wooten expressed a form of ethnocentric bigotry I have heard far too often when he told Shipler that Mexicans "didn't pay no dues, no price, no nothing. They don't try to fight for their rights ... they're too busy trying to play like they're white."

The fact is that most Latinos are trying just as hard as Afro-Americans to claim their rights, and hang on to their culture. They just don't usually define himself as black, even when they look phenotypically like what we are accustomed to calling "black." And from the perspective of many Afro-Americans, anyone who doesn't define themselves as black must be, by default, white. This is of course a perpetuation of the old "one-drop" racial ideology, rooted in white supremacist thought, but whose strongest advocates today tend in fact to be Afro-Americans.

While reading *A Country of Strangers*, I often thought about it in counterpoint with another massive book on "race" published in 1997, Werner Sollors' masterwork *Neither Black nor White Yet Both*. Sollors provides an encyclopedic survey of the myriad places in American culture where people have expressed their longing for or their conflicted experience of the "multiple truths" of American race relations. These truths have emerged through a long historical experience of what Ralph Ellison has characterized as "antagonistic cooperation" between people of African and European descent. In my own book *On Racial Frontiers*, I have followed the path cleared by pioneers like Ellison and Sollors, and have argued that whether one chooses to focus on the antagonism or the cooperation of this relationship, the end result is still co-creation, to which all of us can lay claim, and for which all of us must take responsibility.

Shipler, like most North Americans, does not seem to grasp the historical reality that what we are accustomed to call "race" in fact emerged out of a collective "denial of ... 'interracial' and 'biracial' realms," as Sollors insists. That means that, despite our many differences, we really are at least as much kin as we are strangers (10). Sollors believes that recent scholarly and popular interest in interraciality (our "true inter-relatedness") signals "a turning point in the racial symbolism of the United States, which may be moving in the direction of the Latin American models" (10).

I hope so. The concept of *mestizaje* is certainly an improvement on the "one-drop rule." As well-intentioned and thorough as Shipler's book is, I found it impossible to forget that these "Latin American models" were entirely absent from Shipler's project. This seems to me inexcusable in any major discussion of intercultural relations in our era. I understand that this would have had to be a very different book, were Shipler to have included Latinos. But I think that all of us would have profited from the attempt. We have no choice but to make that attempt, or those who define themselves as black and white risk confining themselves to a corner, in a museum perhaps, while the rest of "our America" looks at their squabbling with a mixture of amusement and contempt.

In a strange way, Shipler's narrative is both my story, and the story of a self-referential social world from which I have made a declaration of independence. During the year in which I read his book, off and on, the following noteworthy events took place. News reports made it official that Latinos have now surpassed Afro-Americans as the largest "minority" in the U.S. After 11 years of an interracial marriage, I got a divorce. The mother of my children, who is Afro-American, intensely racialized the experience. Yet I continue to speak Spanish with my children, as I have from the beginning, and I continue to maintain personal and professional relations with people who define themselves as "black," "white," and "Latino," among other things. I got a grant from the University of North Carolina to do ethnographic research among Spanish-speaking immigrants, which I have undertaken even as my "antagonistic cooperation" and coalition-building with Afro-Americans has continued.

At the end of this year, thinking about Shipler's America through these personal and social prisms, I am drawn back to his discussion of Thomas Jefferson and his mixed legacy. One of Shipler's informants, an Afro-American descendant of Jefferson named Robert Cooley, draws a Biblical parallel. "In my family, when you talk about the black Jeffersons and the white Jeffersons, we all attribute our parentage to Thomas Jefferson, which is similar to what Abraham did to the Arabs and the Jews" (174). Abraham had an illicit son Ishmael, born to the slave girl Hagar, who was taken by Arabs as their connection to the patriarch. Abraham's son by Sarah, Isaac, is seen as the forefather of the Jews. And of course Abraham is also a patriarch for Christians.

Musing on this parallel suggested by Cooley, Shipler remarks that, with all his contradictions, "If there is any patriarch of the American idea, it is Thomas Jefferson" (175). If we truly understood the meaning of this troubled inter-connectedness, we could recognize our kinship, however strange its form.

References

Darity, William Jr. "Racial and Ethnic Economic Inequality: Why Culture Is Irrelevant." *Race, Ethnicity and Culture in Research and Service*. Chapel Hill: U of North Carolina, 2002.

Esteva-Fabregat, Claudio. *Mestizaje in Ibero-America*. Tucson: U of Arizona P, 1995.

Freehling, William. *The Reintegration of American History: Slavery and the Civil War*. New York: Oxford UP, 1994.

Gomez-Peña, Guillermo. "The Multicultural Paradigm." *Warrior for Gringostroika*. St. Paul, MN: Graywolf, 1993.

Martí, José. "Our America." ["Gestaci?n de Nuestra América"] *Obras Completas*. Vol. 2. La Habana: Editorial Lex, 1946. 95–113. For recent explorations of this concept in English, see *José Martí's "Our America": From National to Hemispheric Cultural Studies*. Eds. Jeffrey Belknap and Raul Fernandez. Durham: Duke UP, 1998; *José Martí: Revolutionary Democrat*. Eds. Christopher Abel and Nissa Torrents. Duke UP, 1986. See also José David Saldívar, *The Dialectics of Our America*. Duke UP, 1991.

Sollors, Werner. *Neither Black Nor White Yet Both: Thematic Explorations in Interracial Literature*. New York: Oxford UP, 1997. ("Denial of interracial realms" 62.)

Steele, Shelby. *The Content of Our Character : A New Vision of Race in America*. New York: St. Martin's, 1990. "Racial fatigue"— Shelby Steele; "Diseased Imagination"— Frederick Douglass from "The Races." *Douglass Monthly* August 1859. Qtd. in David Blight, "W. E. B. DuBois and the Struggle for American Historical Memory." *History & Memory in African-American Culture*. Ed. Genevieve Fabre and Robert O'Meally. New York: Oxford UP, 1994. 52. Michael Banton writes that it is "of particular importance that [Robert Park] moved the emphasis in the expression 'race relations' from the first word to the second." Qtd. in *Racial Theories* Cambridge UP, 1987. 88–89. "Insidious confusion"— Ralph Ellison's "Going to the Territory." *The Collected Essays of Ralph Ellison*. Ed. John F. Callahan. New York: Modern Library, 1995. 606 and "True inter-relatedness"— from his "Change the Joke and Slip the Yoke." *Collected Essays*. 107. "Ethno-racial Pentagon"— David Hollinger, *Postethnic America: Beyond Multiculturalism*. New York: Basic, 1995. "Moral center"— Jesse Jackson's comment of occupying a "moral center" of American politics in William Freedly's 1988 biography.

Stephens, Gregory K. *On Racial Frontiers: The New Culture of Frederick Douglass, Ralph Ellison, and Bob Marley*. Cambridge: Cambridge UP, 1999.

16
Let the Dialogue Begin

CAROL PUTHOFF-MURRAY

Onward and Upward. This is the title of a 1999 statistical findings report about African-Americans in the United States, a redaction of which appeared in *U.S. News & World Report* in the March 5th issue of 2001. These statistics disclose that only 24 percent of African-Americans in the U.S. currently live below the poverty line. It highlights the fact that the median income for black households rose by $6,200.00 between 1980, in which the median income level was $21,790.00, to $27,910 in 1999. The article further states that in 1999 17 percent of African-Americans had completed a four-year college or professional degree. It also points out that the black middle class is "swelling" and they are moving into suburban areas.

White Americans believe that most of the United States African-American population is achieving an onward-and-upward status and that actual equality is commonplace. However, this is a huge and incorrect misconception. Whether these beliefs arise from ignorance, indifference or hatred, such misinformed perceptions foster stereotyping and only serve to plant deeper seeds of prejudice, hatred, hostility and discrimination. However, white America's mistaken perception is challenged by a national survey conducted by The *Washington Post*, the Henry I. Kaiser Family Foundation and Harvard University. This survey, reported by Richard Morin in the July 16–22 issues of The *Post*, is entitled "It's Not As It Seems."

The survey reveals that between 40 percent and 60 percent of the United States' white (i.e., "European") population think that the average black American is faring about as well and even better that the average white American. They also feel that black Americans are not disadvantaged.

In fact, these misinformed individuals believe that white Americans and black Americans are equal and that no disparity exists in relationship to social factors, health care, employment, education and economic opportunities. Indeed, 61 percent of the whites surveyed state that they feel the average African-American possesses equal or better access to health care services. The truth is that African-Americans are twice as likely to be without health insurance and live in neighborhoods where health care services are limited. When the survey subjects are questioned about job status, 50 percent of the whites in this survey perceive that the average African-American is as well off as the average white American.

However, current government data indicates that one-third of white Americans are employed in managerial or professional positions, while one-fifth of black Americans have these positions. The data also reveal that twice as many blacks are employed in lower paying, less prestigious and dead-ended jobs which do not receive benefits. In the 1990s, the black American unemployment rate was 2.5 times the rate for whites. Currently, black citizens are twice as likely to be underemployed or unemployed and twice as likely to live at or below the poverty level. The figures from the May 2001 jobless rate rank unemployment for blacks at 8 percent compared to 3.8 percent unemployment rate for whites. One contributing factor is that people with less training and less education are more vulnerable. They are the last hired and the first to be downsized. This rationale explains the January 2001 data, when black female unemployment leapt from 5.7 percent to 7.3 percent. The 1999 median black household income of $27,910 reported in "Onward and Upward" is correct. However, when this income is compared to the 1999 household median income of $44,366 for United States whites, there exists almost a $16,500 disparity. Only three out of ten white Americans earn less than $25,000, while nearly 50 percent of black Americans earn less than $25,000 and are overly represented in service level positions, according to Westbrooks and Starks (2001).

When those surveyed are questioned about black versus white Americans' educational experiences, 49 percent of whites respond that there are no educational differences. In other words, the educational experiences of white America and black America are viewed as equal. However, demographics indicate the opposite. Seventeen percent of African-Americans complete a college degree, while 28 percent of whites complete a college degree.

Some blacks have progressed and narrow the gap in the areas of education and income. For example, a higher percentage of black students are graduating from high school than previous experience demonstrates (Westbrook and Starks, 2001). The data show that more African-American students are obtaining college and professional degrees. However, most of the African-American people are not on equal footing or equal status with the U.S.' "European" whites. Today, only 8.2 percent of African-Americans males are employed in executive positions and African-American women are only employed at a rate of 1.3 percent in senior level positions (Finnigan, 2001).

As the United States enters deeper into the twenty-first century, a huge gap still exists. Restricted opportunities, inequities and discrimination result in limited choices and disparities with regard to socioeconomics, education, employment, adequate health care, affordable housing, welfare, safety and security needs. "Institutionalized racism helps to maintain the disproportionate number of African-Americans in the criminal justice systems" (Aquirre and Turner, 1995). The compilers of data from the National Institute of Mental Health have been iterating a gloomy statistic since 1987: "African-Americans were more frequently diagnosed with severe mental illness than were other ethnic or racial populations" (Manderscheid and Sonnenshein, 1996). White America refuses to focus on, look at, or listen to the overwhelming evidence that demonstrates a racial divide. This separation is still besieged with even greater disparities, barriers, inequities and disadvantages. For example, *The State of Working Ohio* discloses "distressing news about declining minority wages and growing racial wage disparities." It reveals that the median wage in 2000 for white males is $15.00 per hour which is a wage decline of 8 percent between 1979 and 2000. However, the 2000 median black male wage is $11.44 for an hour of work. This change represents a 23 percent difference between groups and further real declines in black male wages. These data highlight the growth disparity and the racial divide in that black males receive 23 percent less than white males. This report also points out that Ohio's black female workers earn less than their white female counterparts.

In a July 16, 2001, *Washington Post* article, Morin states that "42 percent of whites believe that the typical black earned as much or more than the typical white." He adds that 70 percent of the surveyed whites hold at least one misperception about blacks and that 56 percent of the white population surveyed held two or more distorted or faulty views. It is sad that today many Caucasian Americans still refuse to recognize or acknowledge that equal opportunity and equality are not reality. Historically, a huge vertical racial divide stretched across this country beginning with the agricultural society which encouraged slavery and this divide continued after the emancipation, reconstruction period and industrial revolution. For many years, African-Americans were segregated according to neighborhoods and schools and denied access to political, economic, corporate, educational and social systems. They were dismissed and dishonored.

Justice came slowly in that African-Americans attained limited rights. In 1869 with the passage of the Fifteenth Amendment, blacks received the right to vote with the caveat that they pass a reading test. During the 1960s and 1970s, the War on Poverty, the Civil Rights movement and the Economic Opportunity Act opened the doors to increased opportunities and through these processes African-Americans have experienced some positive gains in the political and economic arenas. More blacks now are graduating from high school than previous generations and many are obtaining degrees in higher education. No doubt, the African-American middle class is increasing. However, many still remain stuck within the trenches of poverty and deprivation. They too are devalued and dismissed.

Today, the racial divide is expanded to include the economic divide and the digital divide. The new century encompasses transformations such as the information age, the technological climate, globalization, cyberspace, cyber-highways and cyber-symbolism. With this crucial knowledge base so adversely divided, it means that the top 20 percent of our nation, the "haves," control and manipulate the destiny of the remaining 80 percent of the "have-nots." Today, there exists another phenomenon: the new wave of immigration. According to Hernández, the 1998 demographic data reflect that over a million new immigrants entered the United States each year in the 1990s.

The landscape of the United States is rapidly changing due to the increase of immigrants, multi-ethnic and interracial marriages and biracial children. Today, newcomers arrive from Latin American nations and from the Asian Pacific Rim. The former chief-of-staff of the Senate Foreign Relations Committee, Pat Holt, states in The *Christian Science Monitor* of December 20, 2000, that immigration is responsible for changing the American people into a heterogeneous mix of Europeans, Hispanics, Asians, and Africans with Europeans slipping into a minority status. Gerry Khermouch underscores this radical demographic shift in his commentary in *Business Week* (June 22, 2001); according to the U.S. Census 2000, African-Americans, Latinos and Asians now account for 79 million out of 281 million Americans and collectively they possess a $1 trillion annual spending power in a $6 trillion United States economy. The census statistics for 2000 also reveal that the American landscape is constantly reshaping itself. Today, the largest minority group comprises Latinos. David B. Woods, writing in the April 9, 2001, issue of The *Christian Science Monitor*, states that in the diversity of Los Angeles, whites are now the official minority group, while in California the white population has spiraled down from 57.2 percent of the population in 1990 to 46.8 percent in 2000.

The foundation of our country was established and developed by immigrants with the exception of our Native Americans or First National People. During the nineteenth century, most waves of immigrants arrived voluntarily on our eastern shores from European nations. The majority of the English, Germans, Irish, Italians, Scandinavians, Jewish, and Slavs came freely with hopes and the goal to achieve for the American Dream. However, centuries earlier African-American migrants came involuntarily and were forced to enter America, where they were marginalized, segregated and granted no rights or choices. They were viewed differently and dismissed. Peter Rose perfectly describes the issues in his 1997 *They and We*: "Rarely were 'colored people' ever seriously considered on a par with white immigrants."

Many white Americans feel threatened and are fearful of losing their power, prestige and privileged status. They feel and taste the rippling effects from increases in minority groups, diverse population changes, the arrival of the information technology age and the climate of globalization. All of these factors generate change. Many white conservative American workers are experiencing difficulties in adjusting to and adapting to these changes and with these evolutionary experiences their image of obtaining the American Dream is slipping and fading. It is now but a fantasy. Someone or some group must be held accountable, a scapegoat is needed to blame, a scapegoat on which they can project and transfer their resentments, fears, hostilities, anger and disappointments. Therefore, the targeted group is the group necessarily viewed as different and inferior. The targeted group (Rose's They) is selected and the racial divide is deeper and racism once again is on an upswing. Annie Finnigan, writing in the April 2001 *Working Women*, discloses that over the past 10 years the Equal Employment Opportunity Commission reports dramatic increases in charges concerning racial harassment in the workplace. People of color complain of being denied promotions and raises.

On September 10, 2001 National Public Radio featured a piece about minority attorneys. It related that even after many years of loyal service and successful performance black and Latino/a attorneys across the United States are consistently passed over for promotion to partnerships within law firms. Most partners in law firms are white European males and the message is clear, "If You're Black, Stay Back" (qtd. in Harrington).

A *Washington Post* article on racial profiling by Morin and Cottman entitled "The Invisible Slap" reports: "More than 8 out of 10 blacks and two thirds of all Latinos and Asians say that they encounter invisible discriminatory acts of prejudice delivered by white Americans." Some of the invisible acts poor service or lesser treatment in stores and restaurants, racial slurs, name-calling and demeaning put-downs. These minorities also describe their experiences, which generate racial or cultural harassment. Author Lena Williams describes these behaviors in "It's the Little Things: The Everyday Interactions That Get Under the Skin of Blacks and Whites"; blacks receive what she calls the "white eye treatment."

Similarly, Lillian B. Rubin's *Families on the Fault Line* argues that most white Americans have a national historical obsession with race which begins with the arrival of the first slave. Today, the racial divide in our society is pronounced and ugly:

> Race is one of the most enduring categories of American social thought, an idea buried deep in our social consciousness.... Race as, but difference we measure as in inferior and superior, difference that says people of color don't match up to those who are white.

Examples of blatant racial discrimination, prejudice, hate crimes and social injustice are found throughout the United States in the behaviors of the Ku Klux Klan, white-supremacy hate groups, and of course racial profiling. DWB (driving while black) is the acronym coined by Patrik Jonsson in his racial-profiling article; Kit Roane's "Policing the Police Is a Dicey Business" avidly concurs. Jonsson reports data about police department investigations about racial profiling in Buffalo, New York City, Charleston, WV, Detroit, Washington, DC, New Orleans, Cleveland, Tulsa, Riverside, California, and Orange County, Florida — and most recently from Cincinnati, Ohio. Two local incidents, reported in the *Star Beacon* [Ashtabula, OH], affirm the national problem locally: in June 2001, a cross was burned on the front lawn of an biracial couple's home, and four months later, a Caucasian adult male stood up at a local school-board meeting and said, "We don't want our kids mixing with them blacks. We white people have no rights anymore."

Social psychologists generate scientific explanations and theories which describe why individuals deny and darken factual information and cling to their narrow-tunneled, isolated and twisted beliefs about race and racial issues. Psychologists think that the person's mental cognitive structures or schemata are used to select, organize and categorize knowledge and this knowledge serves to process how people think, perceive and interpret themselves, others, life and the world (Aronson, 2000). Culture, race and ethnicity are very important elements which influence schemata and social cognitions. White Americans do not perceive themselves, life, others and their social world in the same way that blacks do. Blacks see their world and self as distinctly different from those of whites or other ethnic and multi-cultural groups. "First Nation People" see their world and self as different from those of Latinos or Asians (Atkinson et al., 1998).

Schemata become more complex and more cumbersome, when they include all the variations between groups, for example, multi-culturalism and ethnicity differences coupled with the generational differences and socioeconomic stratification.

Lillian Rubin relates a conversation with a friend who was a black woman. They were discussing racial and cultural similarities and differences. Finally, out of desperation Lillian's friend asked her this question: "When you look in the mirror, what do you see?" Lillian replied, "I see a woman." Her friend countered by saying, Lillian, "When I look into the mirror I see a black woman." People's perceptions, interpretations and their visions of reality are all grounded and shaped by the thickness, tint, angle and shape of their ecological holistic racial and ethnic lenses.

Social cognitions and schemata give birth to beliefs, attitudes, prejudice and stereotypes which are learned and reinforced by environmental forces. Petty, Weagener, and Fabrigar (1997) define attitudes as "a mixture of belief and emotion that predisposes a person to respond to other people, objects or institutions in a positive or negative way." Attitudes have the potential to direct or predict future behavioral outcomes and these attitudes reflect the individual's impressions about self, life, the world and others. People like to make inferences about causality and the behaviors which lead to the attribution theory. Fritz Heider, the father of the "attribution theory," reminds society that attributions may be positive or negative and all people engage in attributions. The mental detective game of attribution theory applies to an internal or dispositional attributional inference. Causality in this case is attributed to the person or something about them, e.g., personality, attitudes, character traits, skin color or facial features. Situational attributes are based upon inferences using situations or the environment. Heider also states, "There is a tendency to pin the cause of the behavior as residing in the person, because we focus upon the person and not the situation." He also says that many times people are inaccurate in that they are only guessing at the causation of a certain behavior. Attributions, especially negative attributions, contribute to and reinforce prejudice and stereotypes. To extrapolate from the many examples within Shipler's book, there is a tendency to overestimate or excessively attribute the behavior to an internal cause or disposition and underestimate the role of situational or external factors. Social psychologists call this phenomenon the Fundamental Attribution Error (Tavris, 2001; Aronson, 1999). People are prone to distort their view of behavior due to their attributional biases. For these reasons, Heider states that most attributions are incorrect and distorted. Attitudes, attributions, prejudices and stereotypes are learned, nurtured and reinforced by strong influences from the environment and through role models.

Prejudice is a strong negative emotional and cognitive attitude directed toward a specific group or individual (Coon, 2002). Prejudice is defined as possessing three components. The first component consists of faulty, unjust negative social cognitions and beliefs. Affect or feelings like fear, hostility and anger comprise the second component. The third component of prejudice is discriminatory behavior. These thoughts and feelings provide the predisposition to act out in a negative, unjustified, harmful and aggressive manner toward another, because they have membership in a particular group. Prejudice is a two-edge sword. On the one hand, prejudice blames the victim and targets the group for their own plight. "It's their own fault." And this attitude fosters scapegoating which justifies unhappy frustrated people in the displacement of their aggression on a specific disliked group because of visible differences, such as, clothes, different customs or norms, the expression of foreign languages or skin pigmentation. People with strong deep-seated prejudicial attitudes do not experience conflict and they possess little or no guilt. The emotional component of prejudice makes them rigid, resistant and immune from wrestling with truthful factual evidence or data. Gordon Allport's famous 1954 definition of prejudice is worth repeating; he states, "Defeated intellectually, prejudice lingers emotionally." Social psychologists argue that prejudice is learned or at least the components and factors which make up prejudice are learned. This process is powerfully illustrated by Jane Elliot's famous 1977 Blue Eye/Brown Eye experiment with third-grade students from rural white Riceville, Iowa. Within hours, Jane Elliot produced degrading schemata, negative attributions, prejudicial attitudes, stereotypes, ethnocentrism and discrimination. At first, Elliot verbally and behaviorally treated the blue-eyed children as superior and special. They were granted privileges, while the brown-eyed children were given negative attributions, and stereotypes and denied privileges; later she reversed the method and the brown eyed children became the superior ones, while the blue eyed children were inferior. The same prejudicial thinking and stereotypical behavior occurred. *A Class Divided* is still a powerful presentation of Elliot's work on prejudice and stereotypes.

Stereotyping is the cognitive component of prejudice. Aronson (1999) describes the stereotype pattern as a "generalization about a group of individuals with identical characteristics which are assigned to virtually all of the members of the group, regardless of actual variation about the members." Stereotypes are based on selective perceptions and reflect cultural beliefs which usually are demeaning and degrading with negative oversimplifications and distortions. These attitudes accentuate differences and overlook similarities and commonalities. When David Shipler assigns a simple stereotyping exercise to university students exploring the attitudes white people hold about blacks and what blacks hold concerning whites, the following labels appeared: "Poor, violent, lazy, athletic, ignorant, inferior, like to complain, bigots, selfish, powerful, leech off society, church-going, homeless, undereducated, all look alike, dirty, party animals, dope dealer, fatherless, wanting sex, untrustworthy, comedians, poor English-speaking, money hungry, back stabbers, arrogant, manipulative, superior race, cold, scared, confused, can dance and can't dance." Walter Lippmann's 1992 description of stereotypes summarizes prejudice as "the little pictures we carry around inside our head which rob people of their individuality and cause exclusion surrounded by hostilities, hatred and prejudice" (qtd. in Aronson, 1999). Once they are formed, stereotypes are resistant to change and serve to intensify ethnocentrism, discrimination and hatred (Tavris, 2001).

Why do people preserve and cling steadfastly to their distorted, filtered and tinted schemata and attributions, although factual data and abundant information based on solid scientific evidence disproves their faulty views and behaviors? A partial answer is found in Thibaut and Kelly's 1959 cost-versus-reward (or "exchange") theory. When a person believes that the value is high and the cost outweighs the benefits, a person will change. However, when the benefits or rewards outnumber the cost, the person will not change. The perceived benefit rewards them and allows them to remain within their emotional comfort zone and this benefit further permits them to maintain and preserve their need for positive self-esteem and a strong self-image. The prejudiced person then continues to feel that he/she is good, decent, privileged, competent and superior. To sustain this perseverance effect, an individual must invest lots of energy, time and effort into filtering and discounting evidence that contradicts his or her schemata. In other words, he/she distorts the facts. Therefore, this process serves to reinforce the negative attributions, prejudicial attitudes and stereotypical behavior. Heider states that the perseverance effect reinforces ethnocentric thinking.

William Graham Sumner defined the term *ethnocentrism* in 1906 as that which "leads a people to exaggerate and intensify everything in their own folkways which is peculiar and which differentiates them from others." Rose (1997) states that the superior group, the WE or the US, is given positive attributions and the out-group or the targeted group is viewed as different, inferior and fearful. They are always THEY and THEM. Ethnocentrism is the cognition that one's own group, race, ethnic culture or religion, the US, is far superior to all other groups, the THEM.

Although our nation was conceived in the spirit of "liberty and justice for all" and dedicated to the Jeffersonian principle that all men are created equal, endowed by their Creator with inalienable rights, ethnocentrism supplies individuals with ample ammunition to reinforce and fuel their negative schemata and stereotypes. These choices heat up discriminatory behaviors and ignite the flames of hatred.

An excellent example of ethnocentrism appears in an article entitled "Interest in Hate Groups Worries Ohio Authorities" in the July 16, 2001, issue of the *Toledo Blade*. The author states that in Ohio, the heart of it all, "white supremacy hate groups are recruiting more young people [in the central part of the state] through direct mailings, internet, music and other sources." Persuasive messages with the presence of persuasive cues reinforce prejudices against certain groups which in turn enhances security and certain personal needs. The white Americans, who are more misinformed about black circumstances, are less likely to vote for governmental intervention and human service programs, and less likely to render support for social justice.

Thomas Edsall, writing in The *Washington Post*, states, "Racial issues such as busing and affirmative action have pushed blue collar voters into the GOP." A survey headed by Stanley Greenberg of the Institute for America's Future discloses that our nation's white high-school graduates and GEDs display more positive regard better feelings for, and align themselves more with, the Republican Party than the Democratic Party. These findings are further reflected by these facts. In the 2000 presidential election, the majority of persons with college or advanced college degrees in, 17 of the 25 most affluent counties in America, cast their vote for Al Gore, in contrast to nine out of ten of Kentucky's poorest counties, which saw the majority of these folks voting for "W."

Individuals are not born possessing negative ideations, attitudes and feelings about a certain object, person or group of people. These attitudes appear for many individuals within early childhood and continue to development throughout life. Psychologists explain that prejudice, stereotypes, discrimination and ethnocentrism are all learned through socialization and environmental landscapes.

Bronfenbrenner's model about the ecology of human development states that the development of all human beings is shaped and molded by a series of complex environmental interactive systems. He refers to family, peers, school, church, workplace and media as microsystems. These microsystems supply direct influences on the individual's immediate environment and subsequently interrelate with one another (he refers to these interrelationships between microsystems as "mesosytems"). The settings in which the person does not immediately participate but which indirectly affect the individual, such as school board, local community or govern-ment, are called the "exosystem." The last ecological level is the "macrosys-tem," which comprises the "blueprint for defining the institutional life of society or social policy" (Bronfenbrenner, 1979).

The Ecological Model focuses upon human development which receives important input from family, genetic background, socialization, environmental exposures and social interactions. The impact and influences from family, culture, religion, ethnicity, gender, peers, com-munity, educational level and experience, socioeconomic status and age, along with one's abilities in the cognitive, physical, social and emotional domains, serve to play vital roles in forming, nurturing and developing social cognitions, schemata, attitudes, attributions, prejudice and stereo-types. Recently, George Appleby published *Diversity, Oppression and Social Functioning*, which places importance on life transitions, environmental pressures and interpersonal processes in contributing toward the forma-tion of attitudes and attributions.

Hacker's 1992 *Two Nations* reminds society that America has "always been the most competitive of societies. It poises its citizens against one another, with the warning that they must make it on their own. Hence the stress on moving past others, driven by a fear of falling behind. No other nation so rates its residents as winners or losers."

Today, the United States of America possesses a diverse and unique culture with different environmental experiences. We need to celebrate our sameness, stop our stereotyping and begin to challenge our preju-dices. Emphasis should be on the experiences and themes which unite us and which bind us together. We are all diverse, we are all unique and we all share commonalities and similarities. For instances, all infants require the union of the egg and the sperm which contributes to the individual pairs of chromosomes, genotypes and phenotypes. All these people have affiliation and physiological needs regardless of race, creed, religion or ethnicity. This journey through the life developmental cycles has to meet Maslow's (1954) vision of needs, namely, food, shelter, safety, security, belong-ing, love and self-esteem. While many people engage themselves with reaching to achieve security, success, power, happiness and a piece of the American Dream, most parents and caretakers desire that their children receive a challenging education, experience good health and create freedom absent from danger and harm. These parental units wish to equip and sup-ply their children with opportunities for a great variety of choices in life. These aspirations emphasize the oneness of society and universal needs.

The ethnocentrism and prejudice of society divides and isolates peo-ple. The negative attributions continue the oppressive climate and these experiences leave a void and emptiness, while the society sinks into the waters of despair. Society has a responsibility to confront and examine these issues.

I conclude by asking you to *look at* and *listen to* yourself, really look and listen. Look at and listen to people of color. Look at and listen to what our competitive society is saying to us.

Let the dialogue begin.

References

Allport, Gordon W. *The Nature of Prejudice*. Rev. 1979. Cambridge, MA: Addison, 1954.

Appleby George A., Edgar Colon, and Julia Hamilton, eds. *Diversity, Oppression and Social Functioning: Person-in-Environment Assessment and Intervention*. Boston: Allyn, 2001.

Aquirre, A., and J. Turner. *American Ethnicity: The Dynamics and Consequences of Discrimination*. New York: McGraw, 1995.

Aronson, Elliot, et al. *Social Psychology*. 3rd ed. New York: Longman, 1999.

Asante, Molefi K., and Mark T. Mattson. *Historical and Cultural Atlas of African-Americans*. New York: Macmillan, 1991.

Atkinson, Donald R., et al. *Counseling American Minorities: A Cross-Cultural Perspective*. 5th ed. New York: McGraw, 1998.

"Attorneys of Diversity and U.S. Law Firms." National Public Radio. Washington, DC. Sept. 10, 2001.

Blight, David W. *Race and Reunion: The Civil War in American Memory*. Cambridge, MA: Harvard UP, 2001.

Bronfenbrenner, Urie. "Ecological Systems Theory." *Development in Context*. R. H. Wozniak and K. W. Fischer, eds. Hillsdale, NJ: Erlbaum, 1993: n. pag.

A Class Divided. Prod. of Yale Univ. Films for *Frontline*. Prod. for Documentary Consortium by WGBH, Boston. Prod. and dir. William Peters. Writ. William Peters and Charlie Cobb. Videocassette. PBS. 1992.

Coon, Dennis. *Essentials of Psychology: Exploration and Application*. 7th ed. Pacific Grove, CA: Brooks, 1997.

_____. *Psychology: A Journey*. Pacific Grove, CA: Wadsworth, 2000.

Cottin, M. H. "The Invisible Slap." *Washington Post* July 2–8, 2001, nat'l weekly ed.: n. pag.

Davis, L. "FBI Joins Efforts: Flowers Planted Where Cross Burned into Lawn." *Star Beacon* [Ashtabula, OH]: June 22, 2001: n. pag.

Edsall, T. B. "The Shifting Sands of American's Political Parties." *Washington Post* April 9–15, 2001, nat'l weekly ed.: n. pag.

Finnigan, A. "Different Strokes." *Working Woman*. April 2001: n. pag.

Fletcher, M. A. "Linquist Assailed for Blaming Blacks for Low Status." *Sun Sentinel* Jan. 6, 2001: n. pag.

Fong, Rowena, and Sharlene B. C. L. Furuto, eds. *Culturally Competent Practice Skills, Interventions, and Evaluation*. Boston: Allyn, 2001.

Francis, D. R. "Pink Slips Hit the White Collar Set." *Christian Science Monitor* Aug. 7, 2001: 1+.

Gerow, Joshua R. *Psychology: An Introduction.* 5th ed. New York: Longman, 1997.
Hacker, Andrew. *Two Nations: Black and White, Separate, Hostile, Unequal.* Expand. ed. New York: Ballantine, 1992
Hanauer, A., and M. Cassell. "Policy Matters Ohio." *The State of Working Ohio.* Cleveland: n. pub., 2001. Harrington, Michael. *The Other America: Poverty in the United States.* New York: Penguin, 1981.
Heider, Fritz. *The Psychology of Interpersonal Relations.* New York. Wiley, 1958.
Hernández, Hilda. *Multicultural Education: A Teacher's Guide to Content and Process.* Columbus, OH: Merrill, 1989.
Holt, P. "Rich versus Poor, Old versus Young; Heed the Cries." *Christian Science Monitor* July 5, 2001: n. pag.
"Interest in Hate Groups Worries Ohio Authorities." *Toledo Blade* [Toledo, OH]. June 16, 2001: n. pag.
Jonsson, P. "Courts Balk at Limiting Racial Profiling." *Christian Science Monitor* July 6, 2001: n. pag.
Kelley, Harold. H. "The Process of Causal Attribution." *American Psychologist* 28 (1973): n. pag.
Khermouch, Gerry. "An Almost-Invisible $1 Trillion Market." *Business Week* June 11, 2001: n. pag.
Manderscheid, Ronald W., and Mary Anne Sonnenshein, eds. *Mental Health, United States, 1996.* US Department of Health and human Services. Washington, DC: USGPO, 1996.
Maslow, Abraham H. *Motivation and Personality.* 2nd ed. New York: Harper, 1970.
Morin, R. "It's Not As It Seems." *Washington Post* July 16–22, 2001, nat'l weekly ed. : n. pag.
"New Economy's Help Wanted." *Christian Science Monitor* July 2000: n. pag.
Obernyer, F. "Race Issue Rises at Hearing." *Star Beacon* [Ashtabula, OH] Sept. 28, 2000: n. pag.
"Onward and Upward." *U.S. World & News Report* Mar. 5, 2001: n. pag.
Petty, R. E., et al. "Attitudes and Attitude Change." *Annual Review of Psychology* 48 (1997): n. pag.
Roane, Kip R. "Policing the Police Is a Dicey Business." *U.S. News & World Report* Apr. 30, 2001: n. pag.
Rose, Peter I. *THEY and WE: Racial and Ethnic Relations in the United States.* 5th ed., New York: McGraw, 1997.
Rubin, Lillian B. *Families on the Fault Line: America's Working Class Speaks about the Family, the Economy, Race, and Ethnicity.* New York: HarperCollins, 1994.
Shipler, David K. *A Country of Strangers: Blacks and Whites in America.* New York: Vintage, 1998.
Shute, N. "Where We Come From." *U.S. News & World Report* Jan. 29, 2001: n. pag.
Smith, R. L., and M. Bernstein. "Gender Gap Shows Up in Paycheck." *Plain Dealer* [Cleveland, OH] Aug. 12, 2001: n. pag.
Sumner, William Graham. *Folkways: A Study in the Sociological Importance of Usages Manners, Customs, Mores, and Morals.* Boston: Ginn, 1906.
Tavris, Carol, and Carole Wade. *Psychology in Perspective.* Upper Saddle River, NJ: Prentice, 2001.
Thibaut, John W., and Harold H. Kelley. *The Social Psychology of Groups.* New York: Wiley, 1995.

United States Bureau of Census 2000. *United States Census of Population.* Washington, DC: GPO, 2000.

Westbrooks, Karen L., and Saundra H. Starks. "Strengths Perspective Inherent in Cultural Empowerment: A Tool for Assessment with African-American Individuals and Families." Eds. Rowena Fong and Sharlene B. C. L. Furuto. *Culturally Competent Practice: Skills, Interventions, and Evaluations.* Boston: Allyn, 2001: 101–18.

Williams, L. "It's the Little Things: The Everyday Interactions That Get under the Skin of Blacks and Whites." Editorial. *U.S. News & World Report* May 28, 2001: n. pag.

"Woman Not Scared That Cross Was Burned into Family Yard." *Star Beacon* [Ashtabula, OH] June 22, 2001: n. pag.

Wood, D. B. "New Diversity Meets First Big Political Test." *Christian Science Monitor* Apr. 9, 2001.

Racial Profiling: Good Policing or Discriminatory Policy? A Look at the Existing Literature

IRENE JUNG FIALA

David Shipler's book talks about racial profiling in terms of shoplifting. But my focus will be on traffic stops in the context of racial profiling as the current literature regards this recent phenomenon in race relations. For this purpose I reviewed over 250 articles from reputable academic journals and various agencies responsible for collecting in-house service data.

In conducting my review, I concentrated on key words such as "racial profiling," "profiling in law enforcement and/or policing" and "racial discrimination in law enforcement and/or policing." My intent is to objectively report what I have found to be consistent themes in these articles and studies, not to make any political statements or to support any particular theory.

"Profiling," "stereotyping," "attribution"—whatever you call it—we all do it. Human beings make initial assumptions about others based on a number of variables. If we meet someone for the first time at a party, for instance, we categorize them according to their perceived race or ethnicity, sex, age, dress, mannerisms and physical attributes. When I presented this as a paper at the colloquium, the audience saw a petite, blonde female of a particular age and professional dress—and made some judgments.

When they heard that I am a professor at a major state university, they made some attributions as to who I am, what I might be like, where I might live and how I might spend my time. In other words, they were involved in a complex of judgments.

I might have proved some of those assumptions to be wrong and I might have surprised them by others made in the wake of revised assumptions as my talk proceeded. I might have forced some or many to revisit their earlier ideas. But those assumptions, that stereotyping, represented a starting point for interaction. They used a mental shortcut, a heuristic, to quickly sum up a new situation. Is this kind of rationalization or conceptualization problematic? It is when assumptions are used to intentionally harm someone.

Speak of "criminal profiling" and you will find that everyone has some familiarity with this investigative tool. Whether because of television shows, such as *The Profiler*, movies such as *Silence of the Lambs* or books such as *The Monster Within*," criminal profiling has gained a reputation as a law-enforcement tool first used systematically by the F.B.I. and now associated with their Behavioral Sciences Unit. Among students in criminology and psychology, many are jumping on the bandwagon and are looking to study "profiling." Schools have responded by adding criminal profiling classes to their curriculum. Mention "racial profiling," however, and the tone immediately changes. Instead of an investigative tool, racial profiling has become synonymous with "driving while black." So what is racial profiling anyway?

Unfortunately, the media, researchers and legislatures alike have been using a term that has been poorly defined and have oftentimes made recommendations based on emotion and public outrage. That is to say, when racial profiling is mentioned, people see "red" and the real issues remain hidden from view. To date, there is no universal agreement as to the definition of "racial profiling." In general, the literature suggests that most writers define racial profiling as the practice by police of searching minorities for drugs during a traffic stop. An alternative definition has been offered which differentiates the role that race plays relative to a "profile." In this alternative definition, "hard racial profiling" refers to the use of race as an exclusive criterion, whereas in "soft racial profiling" race is only one of several other criteria used in an investigation. It is important to have an agreed upon definition of racial profiling as legislation banning racial profiling has been passed in 11 states and is being considered in 13 other states. Similarly, the House of Representatives has passed the End of Racial Profiling Act of 2001 (sponsored by Conyers D-MI), although the Senate has not acted on this particular bill which would outlaw racial profiling. The Senate, however, has its own bills on the floor.

The concept of "hard racial profiling," whereby a person's race is the sole reason for a traffic stop and subsequent search, is largely viewed as unacceptable. Nonetheless, one can find examples throughout American history in which hard racial profiling was practiced — for example, in the so-called "Operation Wetback" or in the internment of Japanese and Italians during World War II. Also, during the Civil Rights Movement, civil rights activists, particularly African-Americans, were repeatedly stopped in traffic stops as part of a harassment technique employed by law enforcement. One irony of the September 11 tragedy is that racial profiling had been extensively used to gauge suspiciousness relative to potential hijackers as a result of the spate of airline hijackings twenty years ago. No question, this profile is being returned to service immediately. And, reportedly, most recently, forest rangers in the U.S. Forest Service in California's Mendocino National Forest were instructed to "question all Hispanics whose cars were stopped" (i.e., a field interrogation) and, moreover, "to develop probable cause for stop." A *Resource Guide on Racial Profiling Data Collection Systems*, published by the U.S. Department of Justice, defines racial profiling as

> any police-initiated action that relies on the race, ethnicity or national origin rather than the behavior of an individual or information that leads the police to a particular individual that has been identified as being, or having been, engaged in criminal activity [3].

This definition is similar to the concept of "hard racial profiling." It would appear that in the current literature, few would condone hard racial profiling.

In contrast, "soft racial profiling" has engendered heated debate. On the one hand are those who maintain that racial profiling is inherently discriminatory and that the practice should be abolished. On the other hand are proponents such as the police who argue that racial profiling is an investigative tool necessary to more efficiently fight the War on Drugs.

The legality of the traffic stops has been questioned in the literature. Some maintain that police, when cause is absent, look for a reason to stop a vehicle. Moreover, a majority of writers maintain that, because minorities are over-represented in traffic stops, that fact in itself strongly suggests discriminatory practice on the part of law enforcement.

Accordingly, I shall examine the various sides of the issue by looking at racial profiling from the perspective of law enforcement as well as from the perspective of minority groups who experience being profiled. Unless stated otherwise, the definition employed when referring to racial profiling is that of "soft racial profiling."

Perspective of Proponents for Banning Racial Profiling

Those who maintain that racial profiling is racist and should be banned base their arguments on several facts. These arguments surround the fact that minorities are over-represented in traffic stops based on their numbers in the population, anecdotal evidence by individuals who have been wrongly detained because of their race, and the debate of police bias in the surveillance and arrest of minorities, all of which are believed to exaggerate minority involvement in crime.

The first argument is that because minorities are over-represented in traffic stops that this suggests discriminatory practices. Chad Thevenot reported in *Crises of the Anti-Drug Effort* that "76 percent of the motorists stopped along a 50-mile stretch of I-95 by Maryland's Special Traffic Interdiction Force were black.... Blacks constitute 25 percent of Maryland's population and 20 percent of Marylanders with driver's licenses." A San Diego study found that Hispanics comprise 29 percent of traffic stops and blacks represented 12 percent. The racial composition of San Diego is 20 percent Hispanic while 8 percent are black. Videotape from Volusia County, Florida, showed that minorities represented 70 percent of motorists pulled over on one stretch of highway yet minorities constituted only 5 percent of the drivers.

The second argument is based on experiences that minorities have encountered. In a poll co-conducted by The *Washington Post*, Harvard University and the Henry J. Kaiser Family Foundation, 52 percent of black men said that they had been stopped by the police because of racial profiling. A 1999 Gallup poll reported that 42 percent of African-Americans felt they were the victims of racial profiling, having been stopped by the police because of their race. The Gallup organization found that 59 percent of U.S. adults feel that racial profiling is widespread and 89 percent disapprove of the practice. Fifty-six percent of whites surveyed said that racial profiling was widespread, whereas 77 percent of blacks believed this to be the case.

Finally, the third argument is one in which sociologists from the conflict theory school have long argued, and that is that minorities are targeted more often for surveillance and, as a result, have higher rates of detection for participating in criminal activities. Basically, this is an "if you look for it, you'll find it" argument. Differential surveillance practices compounded with differential arrest, prosecution and conviction will lead to the types of profiles that were created by agencies such as the Drug Enforcement Agency. Moreover, as I have argued in papers on medicolegal death investigation, statistics are socially created. They are a social construct and, rather than measuring the existence of a particular phenomenon, they represent a myriad of social factors that are generally not recognized as having any influence on the production of statistics.

Law Enforcement's Perspective

Those in law enforcement have made several arguments that racial profiling is not discriminatory and that it should not be banned. Essentially, the arguments surround the issues of police being viewed as "racist" and the consequences of further damaging police-minority relations, of "de-policing," which may follow from the fear of lawsuits, resulting in higher crime rates, and of "profiling" being arguably inherent in law enforcement as profiling represents the recognition of existing patterns.

The first argument is that of police and others in law enforcement being identified as "racist." Steve Young, the national vice president of the Fraternal Order of Police, stated that a bill proposed by Corzine (D-NJ) "will widen the gap between law enforcement and minorities" because the bill "is written with the presumption that racist tactics are common tools in our nation's police departments." In an article by *U.S. News & World Report*, a Seattle police officer offered the following: "Parking under a shady tree to work on a crossword puzzle is a great alternative to being labeled a racist and being dragged through an inquest, a review board, an F. B. I. and U.S. Attorney's investigation and a lawsuit" (qtd. in Leo 10). If police believe they will be labeled as racist and potentially get fired because they are doing what they consider to be their job, then law enforcement activities will decline. This outcome has already been demonstrated in Cincinnati as a result of the shooting of an unarmed black youth in the Summer of 2001 and the subsequent three-day riot.

The second argument is related to the first. Police argue that the only impact that state mandates such as requiring police to maintain logs of traffic stops for the purpose of statistical analysis would have is that it would result in their scaling back on their law-enforcement activities, a practice referred to in-house as de-policing. In de-policing, "police overlook much suspicious behavior. For example, they stop trying to prevent low-level crime and simply react to 911 calls. Crime soars."

In the third argument, law enforcement maintains that racial profiling is an investigative tool to gauge criminal suspiciousness in modern-day crime fighting. Because police have limited resources, the practice of racial profiling is justified on the basis of "laws of probability." John Derbyshire states, "A policeman who concentrates a disproportionate amount of his limited time and resources on young black men is going to uncover far more crimes— and therefore be far more successful in his career — than one who biases his attention toward, say, middle-aged Asian women."

Where Did It All Start?

Gene Callahan and William Anderson suggest that racial profiling is tied to the War on Drugs. Specifically, Callahan and Anderson state, "The sources include the difficulty in policing victimless crimes in general and the resulting need for intrusive police techniques; the greater relevancy of this difficulty given the intensification of the drug war since the 1980s; and the additional incentive that asset forfeiture laws give police forces to seize money and property from suspects" (36).

The authors further argue that investigators who wish to uncover so-called "victimless crimes" such as drug use must use intrusive techniques. As was noted in the literature review, the focus of almost all racial profiling cases is the belief that a drug crime has been committed. A document entitled *Occupant Identifiers for a Possible Drug Courier*, obtained by a New Jersey newspaper, and later picked up by the *New York Times*, instructs troopers to look for "Colombian males, Hispanic males, Hispanic and a Black male together, Hispanic male and female posing as a couple" (Ruderman n. pag.; Kocienewski 53). The document also states that, if someone fitting the above profile was observed on the highway, the officer should engage in a traffic stop, even if that means under a pretext such as "speeding" or "failure to drive within a single lane" (40). In *Whren v. United States*, the U.S. Supreme Court in 1996 ruled that pretextual traffic stops— that is, using a minor traffic infraction, real or alleged, as a reason to stop and search a vehicle — is constitutional.

Furthermore, argue Callahan and Anderson, police, though motivated to maximize drug arrests, are also profiting from such arrests. During the 1980s, Congress and state legislatures passed "forfeiture laws," which gave "police forces [the power] to seize money and property of suspects" (37). Just in 1992 alone, the DEA reported that the total value of such seizures reached nearly $1 billion. In 1997, taken together, local police departments received $490 million in forfeitures.

Minority Over-Representation: "Fact" or Fiction?

One argument that is often heard is that minorities are disproportionately over-represented in engaging in criminal behavior. This has been demonstrated in the empirical literature to be a sociological and criminological "fact." The explanations offered for this "fact" vary. Conflict theorists and those on the political left assert that minorities are targeted by the dominant group and, as a result, are more likely to have contact with the criminal justice system. Others may assert that, because minorities have encountered prejudice and discrimination, legitimate opportunities to achieve financial and occupational success have been denied to them; therefore, illegitimate activities have been viewed as a viable alternative. Those on the political right suggest that the increase in single-parent families, high drug use and the like among minority groups have resulted in a tearing of the social fabric and have led to delinquent or criminal behavior. Whether the explanation focuses on the over-policing of minorities, or because of higher levels of impoverishment or because of poor neighborhoods, deviant peer groups or so forth, the empirical evidence does demonstrate that minorities are more likely to engage in criminal activities. Moreover, the evidence indicates that biases in policing practices cannot account for all of the variation in these differences.

Even if minorities engage in more criminal behavior, as measured by the data from the Bureau of Justice Statistics, much of this criminal behavior would not be addressed during a traffic stop. It has been shown that blacks account for 66 percent of all robbery convictions, 38 percent of fraud and embezzlement convictions and 27 percent of sexual-assault convictions. Irrespective of the variation in criminal behavior, vehicle searches by police are oriented toward drug interdiction. It is extremely unlikely that an embezzler would be apprehended in the course of a traffic stop. And, although possible, it is not very probable that a murderer or rapist would likewise be apprehended. Moreover, the above figures refer solely to convictions. There is ample empirical evidence in the criminological literature that blacks are more likely to be convicted following an arrest than are whites, even for comparable crimes.

The intent of drug interdictions, such as "Operation Pipeline," represents a tactic in the War on Drugs. Nonetheless, some ask, against whom are we waging war? A University of Toledo professor of law, David A. Harris, law professor at the University of Toledo, maintains, "Today, blacks constitute 13 percent of the country's drug users; 37 percent of those arrested on drug charges; 55 percent of those convicted and 74 percent of all drug offenders sentenced to prison." These facts suggest a self-fulfilling prophecy, a powerful dynamic, on the part of law enforcement. That is, agents of law enforcement expect to find minority motorists carrying drugs, officers then stop minorities in traffic stops and, in the course of a search, find drugs, which then reinforces the perception that minorities are more likely to engage in drug trafficking than whites. However, because whites are not expected to be engaged in drug trafficking, they are not drawing the attention of police which means that whites are less likely to be pulled over and searched for drugs. This again reinforces the perception that whites are less likely to engage in drug trafficking than minority groups such as blacks and Hispanics.

Current and Pending Legislation

President George W. Bush told Congress he had ordered AG John Ashcroft "to develop specific recommendations to end racial profiling: "It's wrong, and we will end it in America" (qtd. in Callahan 37). In a "Memorandum for the Attorney General," dated February 27, 2001, and released by the Office of the Press Secretary on February 28, President Bush wrote:

> I hereby direct you to review the use by Federal law enforcement authorities of race as a factor in conducting stops, searches, and other investigative procedures. In particular, I ask that you work with the Congress to develop methods or mechanisms to collect any relevant data from Federal law enforcement agencies and work in cooperation with State and local law enforcement in order to assess the extent and nature of any such practices.

A report by the Institute on Race and Poverty outlined key components of effective racial profiling legislation. These components include: mandatory collection of traffic-stop data; necessary data categories, which include location of stop, date/time, race, age and gender of the driver, reason for the stop, disposition of the stop and data relating to searches; ongoing data collection; officer identification and other accountability measures, and the establishment of an advisory committee of legislators, police representatives and community representatives.

Eleven states have already passed legislation banning racial profiling (California, Connecticut, Kansas, Massachusetts, Missouri, North Carolina, Oklahoma, Oregon, Rhode Island, Tennessee and Washington). Another thirteen states are considering such legislation. As mentioned, the House passed the End of Racial Profiling Act of 2001 sponsored by Congressman Conyers, although the Senate has not yet acted upon this bill. Other members of Congress have also set forth similar bills. In the Senate, one such bill would prohibit a "pattern of official misconduct" (sponsored by New Jersey senators Norman Robertson, R–Passaic and Wayne Bryant, D–Camden).

Two police departments, in Arlington, VA, and in Lincoln, NE, are using technology such as wireless notebooks and Palm Pilots to record the race and gender of drivers involved in traffic stops. In Oklahoma, police officers may be criminally charged for engaging in racial profiling.

Police at universities are also now beginning to look at racial profiling. Michigan State University has developed a comprehensive 12-point plan to address racial profiling on their East Lansing campus. MSU's plan is the first and largest of its kind; other universities and colleges are considering similar proposals. Highlights of this program include the collection of campus traffic stop data being analyzed for patterns by the university's criminal justice professor, forming police-student partnerships by which they "shadow" one another and spend time with each other both in terms of professional as well as personal lives, and the maintenance of a web page describing to students what they should expect during a traffic stop. The plan will cost Michigan State University approximately $25,000.

Solutions or Bigger Problems?

One of the proposed solutions to the practice of racial profiling is to collect data on traffic stops and examine these data for discriminatory patterns, a solution that has not gone without criticism. Police departments in several jurisdictions have already begun such data collection. The idea is that minority traffic stops should reflect the percentages of minorities in the population. If blacks represent 13 percent of minorities in the jurisdiction, it follows that they should represent 13 percent of all traffic stops. If there is a statistically significant difference, then this is supposedly evidence of race discrimination.

There is, however, an assumption that is being made which may not be valid since that assumption has not been empirically tested. The assumption is that there is no difference between whites and minorities in their driving. There are obvious differences in driving patterns among these groups as, for instance, in seatbelt use among the elderly and between black and white drivers. Until there is evidence that demonstrates that there is no difference in the driving patterns among the groups, then simply stating that traffic stops should be proportionate to each group's representation in society is ill-advised.

Secondly, because of past and present discrimination in the economic arena, younger minorities might be driving older vehicles that violate a traffic code, such as driving with a cracked windshield, a loud exhaust or burned-out taillights. A traffic stop based on such a violation is not one of racial profiling but a function of economics. The traffic stop would be a legitimate one. Racial discrimination would be argued, however, if the officer didn't stop white motorists with cracked windshields but only stopped minority motorists. But if minorities are more likely to drive cars with cracked windshields and loud exhausts because of their economic status, then the number of traffic stops would reflect this fact. In a three-week study of the Detroit inner-city freeway use by black and white drivers conducted by Tom Vacca and "Lindy" Lindell of St. Clair Shores, Michigan, in 2001, the authors discovered that older and broken-down cars driven by black motorists were unmolested as long as they stayed within Detroit city limits regardless of how fast they drove; however, once those vehicles crossed "the invisible line" north of Interstate 75 or Interstate 96, both of which arteries lead to the more exclusive suburbs where "white flight" had occurred in the decades earlier, these motorists were 8 times more likely to be pulled over after exiting the freeway. "It's as if a huge crevasse opened up at Eight Mile Road and swallowed these vehicles [driven by blacks]," said Vacca. "They simply disappeared." By confining their cars to the major spokes like Gratiot Avenue well south of Roseville, they were safe from police cruisers.

Consistently overlooked is the fact that race is a social construct, not a biological one. By mandating that the race of a motorist be recorded, an officer is expected to make a determination on a social construct. The same problems regarding "the race box" that befell the U.S. Census Bureau can be argued to exist in these mandates as well.

The impact that legislation banning racial profiling will have is yet to be seen. The proverbial jury is out. Despite the criticisms that have been leveled against current legislation, these attempts to correct a social injustice are a step forward. It is naïve to think that because a law has been passed behavior indicative of racial discrimination will be eliminated. Nonetheless, the dialogue on profiling, once begun, must become part of the national discussion.

References

Bush, George W. Memorandum for the Attorney General. 28 Feb. 2001. June 10, 2001 <http://www.whitehouse.gov/news/releases/2001/02/20010228-1html>.
Callahan, Gene, and William Anderson. "The Roots of Racial Profiling: Why Are Police Targeting Minorities for Traffic Stops?" *Reason* 33.4 (2001): 36–43.
Harris, David A. "Driving While Black: Racial Profiling on Our Nation's Highways." ACLU Freedom Network. June 1999. June 2001 <http//: www.aclu.org/profiling/report/>.

Kocieniewski, David, and Robert Hanley. "An Inside Story of Racial Bias and Denial: New Jersey Files Reveal Drama behind Profiling." *New York Times* 3 Dec. 2000 late ed., sec. 1: 53.

Leo, John. "Cincinnati Cops Out." *U.S. News & World Report* 30 July 2001: 10.

Lindell, Richard, Don Thibodeaux, and Tom Vacca. "Report to Stuart Kirschenbaum: Race-Profiling and Detroit's Inner-City Freeway System." St. Clair Shores, MI: Double L, 2001.

Ramirez, Deborah, Jack McDevitt, and Amy Farrell, comp. *A Resource Guide on Racial Profiling Data Collection Systems: Promising Practices and Lessons Learned.* Department of Justice. Washington, DC: USGPO, 2000.

Ruderman, Wendy. "Documents on Racial Profiling Reveal Much." *Record* [Bergen, NJ] 26 Nov. 2001: n. pag.

Thevenot, Chad. "Crises of the Anti-Drug Effort, 1999." The Criminal Justice Policy Foundation. 18 Mar 1999. 12 Aug. 2001 <www.cjpf.org>.

Whren et al. v. United States of America. No. 95-5841. US Supreme Ct. 1996.

18
Introduction

PAUL L. GASTON

The events of September 11 make particularly urgent the message of our speaker today. David K. Shipler, a Pulitzer Prize winning author, has repeatedly taken as his subject the issues and circumstances that divide human beings: Arabs and Jews, Soviet citizens, blacks and whites in America. Through sharing his understanding of schisms, we can glimpse also his vision of the possibility and the promise of community.

Of his most recent book, *A Company of Strangers: Blacks and Whites in America*, Bill Bradley wrote, "It will challenge you to look into yourself not as a white person or a black person but as a human being, and to recognize that … in the pool of our common humanity,… we will find a reflection of a brighter future."

While Mr. Shipler's values are clear and his grasp of principle is strong, he does not emphasize theory. His works educate us by showing us real people grappling with real problems: the law school dean balancing honest speech with a commitment to affirmative student recruitment, admirers of Thomas Jefferson struggling to come to terms with his bleak appraisals of the potential of African-Americans, an African-American military commander in Alabama encountering unofficial prejudices at his official welcome reception, a Louisville child trying to understand the strange import of skin color. But his books move beyond illustration and anecdote to lead us to a broader understanding of both current realities and the heartening possibilities beyond current realities. In short, he is an inductive social scientist and a captivating writer.

Mr. Shipler is a graduate of Dartmouth College. For more than 20 years, he worked as an award-winning international reporter for the *New York Times*. He has served also as a guest scholar at the Brookings Institution, as a senior associate at the Carnegie Endowment for International Peace, and as a professor of Journalism and Public Affairs at Princeton University.

It is my pleasure to introduce a perceptive observer, exceptional reporter, and compelling speaker, David K. Shipler.

19

"When I Go to Work, I Have to Leave My Culture at the Door…"

David K. Shipler

Introductory Remarks

I am quite honored to have a colloquium devoted to some of the ideas that I wrote about in *A Country of Strangers*. My head is full of thoughts having heard people talk about these issues and their coming to them from many different directions. But I have to tell you that foremost in my mind is, and I'm sure it is true for all of us, I've been emotionally exhausted for the last few days from the horrible events of September 11th.

When Timothy McVeigh was arrested for the bombing of Oklahoma, I was quietly relieved, even though he was the same race and gender as me. I knew that neither I nor any other white American male would be targeted for retribution by other people, being blamed for something that someone else of the same ethnic, racial group had done. In these days after Nine Eleven, we've seen incidents throughout the United States— graffiti on stores, windows smashed, assaults on individuals and desecrations of homes, mosques, businesses, the terrorist bombings occurring daily in the Middle East — feeding the worst of the stereotypes— how powerful are these impulses that generalize and stereotype and blame whole groups of people for the murderous acts of a few.

We can learn a lot about ourselves by looking at our own behavior at times like this. Our behavior so far has shown the best of us and the worst of us. It's a test for civility and civilization both. One of the reasons I did my book about blacks and whites was that, in spite of the multitude of ethnic and racial relationships in this society, I sincerely believed that, if we looked at the most problematic, the most troublesome and historically difficult relationship in this country (the relationship between blacks and whites, of course) and if we unraveled this one, we could learn a lot about the others and perhaps unravel those too. There's such a diversified society here and there are so many boundaries and borders and frontiers between us. If we think about the patterns of stereotyping and behavior toward Arab Americans and Muslims that some people exhibit, you can see similar patterns having existed for a long time between blacks and whites. Coincidentally, many of the remedies that suggest themselves are not very different either.

Recently I had an email from the Defense Equal Opportunity Management Institute. It's a Defense Department agency headquartered at Patrick Air Force Base in Cocoa Beach, Florida. Their whole job is to try to manage diversity in the armed forces. They spend a lot of time and a lot of effort — I wrote rather extensively about this — looking at racial issues, gender issues, teaching people, putting people through training, monitoring, surveying, advising commanding officers — all to make the military an open place where people are not discriminated against and don't have doors slammed in their faces because of their race and gender. You can make different judgments about how successful they are, but the military does spend a lot of effort on this. And the email that I got surprised me. Because I had done a lot of work with their staff down there, they sent me an email being circulated now in the military. Here is an excerpt (remember that it is the military, after all):

> In times of disease it is easy to try to make sense of the unsensible [sic] by channeling our rage toward one particular ethnic group. Although there has been speculation, no party has come forward regarding the bombing, and we must be careful not to condemn an entire group of people by actions taken by a heinous few.

The writer goes on to basically plead for tolerance, particularly for Arab Americans. The World Trade Center and Pentagon tragedies have left Americans around the world shocked, saddened, traumatized, angry, and vengeful. We know from experience what can happen when Americans feel internally threatened. The internment of Japanese citizens is a striking example. Have we learned a lesson from that experience? The sensational rhetoric in the media linking the devastation and tragedies to the entire Middle East clearly makes most Arab-American citizens and immigrants in the USA very uneasy. Some Americans are suspicious that an Arab neighbor or work colleague may be involved. Cultural revenge against those involved in the attacks only heightens the sense of fear and the search for an easy target. Most Arab Americans and other immigrants live productively in this country, but they are not as productive when they feel threatened by prejudice and insensitivity. Managers and employees need to do whatever is possible to avoid victimizing Arab employees.

Then there's something that was circulated also in private industry and now has been picked up by the military, which gives a list of suggested activities:

Hold a general employer or community meeting that focuses on beginning the process of helping everyone get through this diácult time.

Educate yourself and others on the contributions of Arabs living in the USA.

Learn about the difficulties Arab people face in the USA as a result of being Muslim, having stereotypical physical features of Arabs, speaking Arabic.

What we see happening is both tragedy and hopefulness. To me it is safe to say that this country, at the moment, is very different from the mood after Pearl Harbor. Most Americans are not old enough to remember this, but I would say that, although civil liberties might be threatened in the wake of something this momentous, the chance of Arab Americans being rounded up and put into internment camps was never discussed seriously. The fact that it had been discussed in a negative way — because of what Japanese Americans had experienced as a lesson that America cannot repeat — suggests how much this society has changed since then.

This is something that I would like to discuss— how much this society has changed and how much more difficult, in a sense, it has become to confront racial prejudice and discrimination than it used to be. This is ironic, perhaps, but after spending five years traveling around the country interviewing blacks and whites about the issues across racial lines, I began to see precisely the change, the progress and evolution of this society; in fact, some of the problems now contained are more complex and more difficult to deal with.

I grew up in an all-white town in New Jersey. It was after I graduated from high school and went to college that I realized what a disability it had been, because I never had the opportunity to speak with a black person about race until I got to college. The first black person I talked to about race was Martin Luther King, Jr. He came to Dartmouth where I worked for the radio station, and I interviewed him before elections began. I'm ashamed to say that I don't remember very much about that interview except for one anecdote he later included in both "I Have a Dream" and "Letter from Birmingham Jail." It was that poignant passage where he mentions his daughter, who was very young at the time and who kept agitating him every time they would drive past an amusement park outside of Atlanta. She kept asking him if she could go and if he would take her. He kept avoiding the subject. So finally he had to say to her that she could not go because she was not white. I remember that vividly because he behaved very much like a father would, any father trying to protect his little girl from that terrible truth. He was a towering figure, and yet there he was— an ordinary mortal, a human being, a father. He was so pained by his own daughter's pain that he tried to explain to her something that, of course, had no rational explanation.

Bigotry then, as conspicuous as it was, was very explicit and quite overt. You didn't have to guess about it. It was there, and it proved ultimately brittle enough to be broken by the force of America's conscience and law that was mobilized by, in part, Martin Luther King, Jr.

We're in a different phase of our history now. Racial prejudice, for the most part, has gone underground. It is not that there are *not* overt acts, as we have seen against Arab Americans; and I was told about the cross burned on the lawn of a biracial couple here in Ashtabula. These vile acts do continue here and there, of course, and society condemns them. Yet there are more important manifestations of racism that are infinitely subtler because they are encrypted; they're more difficult to identify; they are shape-shifters; they attach themselves to convenient and somewhat acceptable points of view. And so those are the ones I would like to talk to you a little bit about because this is where all of us have ground we can meet on, and we will for the rest of our lives as we go out and do different things, meet different people, work in different settings.

Roger Wilkins and Wilbert Tatum

About ten years ago when I started working on *A Country of Strangers*, I went to see Roger Wilkins, an old friend of mine. He used to be a journalist; he's a professor of law; he's an historian — indeed one of society's Renaissance men; he is also the nephew of Roy Wilkins, who founded the NAACP. I went to see Roger to get some ideas.

I asked: "How should I go about researching a book on race? What questions should I ask? What issues should I try to look at?"

Among the things Roger said was this: "Well, one thing you should look at is the way white people address black people."

I said, "What do you mean?"

He said, "Well, for example, that they use their first names very often as a way of condescending." For example, he said he was in a Senate office building the other day and he had seen John Danforth, then Senator from Missouri, walking toward him in the lobby. Roger went up and put out his hand (he had never met Danforth before) and said, "Hello, Senator. I'm Roger Wilkins." Danforth said, "Hello, Roger."

I said to Roger, "Wait a minute. You mean you're telling me that Senator Danforth is calling you by your first name because you are black?"

Roger said, "Yeah."

I replied, "Wait a second, Roger. I mean, a twenty-two-year-old secretary in Washington called *me* by my first name without having ever met me — and politicians always do — I don't buy it." Roger then said, "Well, yes, but Danforth is a well-bred, highly-educated Episcopal priest from my home state of Missouri, a border state that has gone through a very difficult racial history. He certainly knew the implication of calling a black man by his first name. You'll hear whites do this, as a way of looking at and putting them at a lower point in the hierarchy."

I was skeptical, although I understood that what Roger Wilkins was saying in theory might well be true. In the South there is a long tradition of calling blacks by their first names — and certainly in the era of slavery that was always the case — but I was really not sure Roger's was an example of that.

But I did get to listen. I went around the country, and I listened. I asked about this, and I found some other corroborative examples. The first black justice of the Virginia State Supreme Court, John Charles Thomas, told me when going to a government reception with the rest of the justices, people would say, "Hello, Justice this, or Justice that." When they got to him, they said, "Hello, John."

I even met a black psychiatrist in Baltimore who told me that, when she was a resident intern, her white supervisor refused to address her as "Dr. Jones." It was always "Miss Jones," and thereby with the change of one honorific, he removed from her all the years of her accomplishment and learning.

Such cases show how uncomfortable whites feel about blacks in power relationships where they have more authority or equal authority. I heard many such stories. I believe Roger Wilkins had a point; but still I was skeptical about his example of Senator Danforth. Reporters check things out, however, and so I had a problem because I could not call Senator Danforth and say, "Senator, when you called Roger Wilkins by his first name, did you do that because you are a racist?"

I didn't know what to do until I ended up at a luncheon where Danforth was the speaker. I myself had never met him. So after lunch, I went up to him and I put out my hand, and said, "Hello, I'm David Shipler." He said, "Hello, David."

Now it could be that he was prejudiced against people with beards, but as it happens, I figured that Roger had taken a pattern from history and projected it onto the present in a way that really was not accurate. Later I told Roger of my meeting with the senator. He conceded a little by saying, "Okay, I can see politicians seek to diminish the distance between them and the public."

But then he quipped: "Still, Danforth should have known better."

The thing about this is that Roger Wilkins was wrong about Danforth, but he was right about a broader historical pattern. He was right and wrong at the same time. This is what makes dealing with race so very difficult now. You can be right and wrong at the same time. Where does one put race into the equation of our relationships? What weight do we assign it? How does it figure into the pattern? What is the chemistry? It is never easy to decode a behavior when race is there somewhere lurking about as a factor.

The other significant thing about this particular little incident — and I began to realize it only after a while of interviewing — is that it indicates how differently blacks carry history around with them from how whites do. When I came back from the Middle East, a region steeped in history, imprisoned by history, I was struck by what I had found and thought was America's ahistorical attitudes. We seem to have no historical memory. We never seem to have much regard for the power of the past in influencing our behavior in the contemporary time.

And when I started to interview African-Americans, I soon realized that my view of America's amnesia and lack of regard for history really was not so much about America, but about white America. Of course, there are white American groups with very deep attachments to the history of their own particular strains or family clan. You're Irish, you're Jewish, you're Polish, you're a little bit of everything. Pick one or the other. You're Italian. Of course, you can keep some regard for that particular strain of history. But as a whole, as kind of an amalgam, by and large, most white Americans are very impatient with references to history in our past. We even have it built into our language. We say, "Ah, that's history," meaning,

"Let's get over it; let's get past it." In other parts of the world, people say, "That's history! Don't forget it!"

I remember hearing a report from Bosnia where a reporter said that he went to someplace where there had been a violent incident a day or two before. He went to interview a Bosnian Muslim, and asked the man, "What happened here?"

The Muslim said, "What happened here? Well, in 1193 …" and the Muslim began to recount the entire history of the region.

I believe many African-Americans have a deeper sense of history as a powerful force in time. They hear the echoes of history, which reverberate. That is why one often hears African-Americans use slavery as a metaphor and make allusions to slavery to explain something in the present. It is, conversely, why whites get very impatient because this seems like a personal attack—like an indictment as if blacks are saying, "*You* are responsible for slavery." Obviously, none of us living are responsible for slavery. So the kind of historical divide is a very deep one. Blacks and whites carry history around in profoundly different ways, which difference creates all kinds of misperceptions and clashes of attitude that are extremely difficult for us to resolve when we meet as strangers. We often talk past each other.

What Roger Wilkins was hearing when he heard John Danforth say "Hello, Roger" was not just Senator Danforth; it was whole generations of white people behind him saying it too.

When things which they interpret as expressions of racial stereotypes happen to black people, they do not receive that person's mere words—they often see a whole pattern. And they will see an incident as a part of that same pattern. The vast majority of us whites have to begin to get inside that frame of mind as well. In other words, we need to *hear* ourselves, and *see* ourselves and what we do, *note* the way we speak, regard how we think as part of a long-standing pattern in the United States.

To say that, however, does not mean we ought to be imprisoned and inhibited. Let me illustrate this with another story. I know a white psychologist in the Air Force who was telling me he has a very close black friend; they were sitting in a bar together. Magic Johnson had just come on television. The psychologist happened to be a specialist in racial issues in the Air Force, in fact. He wanted to talk about basketball with his black friend, but he was afraid that, if he did that, his friend would think that he, a white person, thought that the only thing that blacks could talk about was basketball. He didn't want to make that kind of mistake in their relationship, and so he shut up. But he recognized later that he was tying himself up in knots trying not to offend. We all need to loosen up a bit. Even with race, we need to keep a sense of humor.

I offer a pair of stories from my travels about America. The first is brief. I met a black woman from Jackson, Mississippi. She worked in an insurance office and she had become a great friend of a white woman who also worked there as a receptionist. One day *Gone with the Wind* was on television. The white woman had just seen it, came into the office, and said dreamily, looking at the elegance of the Southern plantation manor house, "Ah, don't you just wish you lived back in that time?"

The black woman paused a moment and said, "Well, no, not exactly, because I would have been your slave."

And the white woman said, "Oh, my, I'm so sorry."

The black woman had laughed about it; instead of cutting off the friendship, which would have been an option. She just felt that it was comical, so they continued to be friends. Both sides need a sense of humor because it helps.

My next anecdote concerns a black man I have known for years, Wilbert Tatum, publisher of the *Amsterdam News*, who told me this story. You should know that Bill Tatum is never hesitant to attack racism when he sees it. He said that he had gone to a party on a yacht hosted by Robert Maxwell, the media mogul, a few years before his death. The most prestigious of media types were all there. When Tatum boarded the yacht, everyone was asked to remove shoes. So he did. He was shuffling around in his stocking feet for a while when he noticed that many white people were given slippers. Now he had not been given any slippers, so he did a slow burn about this until, finally, unwilling to tolerate this racism a moment longer, he approached an attendant and demanded, "How come you gave all these people slippers and you didn't give me slippers?" The attendant said, "Oh, we're giving slippers just to people with holes in their socks."

By the way, I told this story to an all-white audience in New Hampshire a few years ago. Afterward, a white woman from Mississippi, who happened to be visiting in the area, came up to me with a very concerned look on her face. She was dismayed by my Bill Tatum and Roger Wilkins examples. She said to me, "You know, did you feel a wave of relief that struck across the audience when you told those stories? And they think, 'Ah, you see, it's just all in their minds—this racism stuff. It's not real.'"

I replied that she had a point, but the stories illustrated the difficulties of whites and blacks communicating with each other. I asked her what she thought I should do. She thought a moment and said, "Well, tell them toward the beginning of the speech."

So that is what I have done.

How to Measure Prejudice

Prejudice is very difficult to measure. Pollsters and surveyors have tried this and there are all kinds of formulas that have been used over the years. But it is especially difficult to measure in American society, where we are all well-defended against accusations of being bigots, for we loathe the accusation, and will not label ourselves as racists even in the seeming security of an anonymous poll. As a result, when questions are put, such as "Answer the statement *True* or *False*: "Blacks are lazy," etc., we almost always go into knee-jerk mode to respond with "False," even though, maybe in the back of our minds there might be just an iota of resistance to that usual response. So even though we might think to ourselves, "Ah, maybe there is a little truth to that," we won't permit ourselves to say what we believe.

The National Opinion Research Center in Chicago, however, devised a poll that is different and sophisticated. The designers created scales from one to seven and asked respondents to place various groups somewhere along each scale for a particular criterion — "lazy," "hardworking," "unintelligent," "intelligent," and so on. They did not ask respondents just about African-Americans — that would be the other technique — they asked them about many groups: whites, Southern whites, blacks, Jews, Hispanics, and Asians. The pollsters hoped that would create an "environment" in the questionnaire that would enable people to express attitudes in a subtler way without having either to signify or not to signify a blatantly bigoted statement. In other words, it absolved them momentarily of their biases so that they could answer the questions as "honestly" as possible.

Some of the results of this poll come close to exposing the degree to which people have these embedded stereotypes about other groups. For the record, the respondents were a representative sample of the demographics of the U.S., pretty much what is used in Gallup polls that measure potential voting patterns — a scientific sampling of men, women, all races, and religions. There were blacks included in this as well. Of course, most were white, based on the national population.

They did not merely tabulate the results in raw data form — that is, isolate the percentage of people who put blacks at this level or that level of respondents. Rather, they compared the way the respondents rated blacks to the way they rated whites and thus arrived at a comparative picture. In effect, it revealed not just that blacks were in this or that category but where they were seen in comparison with whites.

Here are the results of a couple questions. The percentage nationally who said that blacks were "less intelligent" than whites was 53.2 percent.

The percentage that said blacks were "lazier than whites" was 62.2 percent. Furthermore, the percentage that said that blacks were "more likely than whites" to prefer to live on welfare rather than to be self-supporting was 77.7 percent. That is, nearly eight out of ten people who responded genuinely believed blacks were more likely than whites to *prefer* to live on welfare than to be self-supporting, to work for a living.

By the way, this poll was done in the early 1990s, and it has not been repeated exactly this way, so there is no way we can compare to see whether attitudes have changed recently. They did ask a couple of these questions, but in a slightly different form. However, they did not ask about all groups, just about blacks and whites. As I mentioned, we have alarm bells go off whenever we are asked about the relations between blacks and whites. We invariably think, "Aha, they're trying to get me here."

Here are the results. The percentage that said blacks were less intelligent than whites dropped from 53 percent to 26.4 percent; and the percentage that said that blacks are lazier than whites dropped from 62 percent to 42.4 percent. They didn't ask the welfare question.

So what is going on here? One might infer that people are becoming less prejudiced. That would be nice if that were indeed the case. Or maybe there were problems in the way the survey was done, differences in the way the questions were asked. My point is that we are trying to measure something that is very hard to measure.

Prejudice, after all, is only a thought. If 62 percent of the population does think that blacks are lazier than whites, does that necessarily mean that 62 percent of the population will not hire blacks? Must it mean they would rather hire a white? First of all, we may safely assume that these people are probably not in positions to do all the hiring. Secondly, this society has erected a whole superstructure of obstacles between the thought and the deed, between the stereotyped idea and when the translation of that idea might go into action. We have discrimination laws; we have affirmative-action programs; we have diversity training; we have personal ethics; we have family values that in some families contribute to open-mindedness; we have institutional rules and regulations; we have self-interests of institutions, such as corporations and the military and universities that see their own interests being served by diversity, by promotions of minorities and women, and feel that without that or with less excess of that they are failing. All these proven, viable means constitute the superstructure of obstacles to expressing prejudice.

Racism's Intangible Reach

But of course this is not an airtight superstructure. That is, there are ways in which percolating, buried images and unwarranted expectations about other groups can leach through one's consciousness. Getting at that is the tricky part. It's not even easily definable. I'll give you a couple of examples where it may be visible.

I talked with a black B-52 pilot in the Air Force, a graduate of the academy, an interesting man, a winner of a White House fellowship. I asked this lieutenant colonel, "Why is it that, despite the military's avowed emphasis on opening doors and creating opportunities for minorities, there are so few black pilots in the Air Force?" Of about 15,000 pilots only 300 were black. I said, "Did they not get accepted into flight school?"

He said, "Well, yes, but I mean a lot of them wash out of flight school."

I asked why that was.

He said he had a "theory": "There's an objective part of the flight training — testing, and so forth — and there's a subjective part. In the subjective part, you're in the cockpit as a trainee with a flight instructor and you're flying. And the flight instructor has to make split-second decisions about whether you're flying capably. If he thinks you're not, he's going to grab the stick and take control.

"Now if the trainee's black, and the flight instructor is white, and virtually all of them are white, and if this flight instructor has somewhere buried in the back of his mind a notion of blacks as inferior mentally, not as intelligent, not as capable, not quite as good, it may be that he will act just a little more quickly in the case of a black trainee than he would in the case of a white trainee and take control of that aircraft. If he does that repeatedly, the black trainee will never advance to the next level of training."

This is a very interesting hypothesis, probably not provable, because in this particular case, you have a life-and-death situation in which you cannot ask the flight instructor to bend the rules and risk himself and his trainee, the plane and everything else. It is it up to the white flight instructor, and if he does have this kind of working suspicion that blacks are not quite as good as whites, then maybe that is a significant reason why there is a dearth of black pilots. Now play what-if with me for a moment: take this situation, remove it from a high-risk setting and transplant it into a university setting or a corporate setting where life and property are never at risk. Does it take much introspection to see how insidious this kind of subtle racism can be? More: think of all kinds of methods that would be used to overcome that particular problem.

Just as police departments have been forced to monitor traffic stops and gather data, so companies and universities monitor their own promotions of hiring and recruitment of students to keep track as a way of testing themselves to see how they are doing. Because people are human beings, hiring and promotions cannot be done by computer. People bring much baggage to their evaluations of others, a number of attitudes and expectations, so they see another person across a distance, without any introspective examination of their own feelings, and depending on how much like them the other person is, this distance is greater or lesser. For instance, I feel a sort of kinship to a middle-class white man like me automatically. But if I see or meet a black woman, say, especially if she's dressed in traditional African garb that demonstrates her identity, I might have to work to overcome the distance between us.

It's been understood now for a long time that people tend to hire and promote people they're comfortable with; and people they're comfortable with are people who are like them. I talked to a black man who works for IBM; he told me that he discovered after working there for three years that at five o'clock every afternoon a happy hour was going on in a bar down the street. But it was only the white men in the office who were gathering to have a few drinks; women were never invited and people with color were never invited. This would have been merely offensive if it had been merely social — but it was more than social, because they talked about work. They networked; they traded information. They put each other in a loop and knew what was going on, and the result was that the women and the minorities in the office were really out of that loop and weren't seen as knowledgeable, or efficient enough, or just good enough to be promoted. He finally quit when he realized this was not a place for him.

If one assumes those white guys gathered in the bar were not racists—which is an assumption, but for the sake of the argument, let us make it for the moment — there is a solution. The solution is what has been loosely called diversity training, where companies will hire somebody to come in and take a look at the dynamics in the workplace. They would have discovered the obvious: "Well, you see what's happening is you guys are retreating at five o'clock every day, and you're doing business, and you're excluding other people from your office. Therefore, you're giving yourselves an advantage or each other an advantage." It's like a baseball team where only some of the team gets to practice, and the other members of the team don't. What coach is going to play the latter?

I believe that self-awareness is taking place in many workplace settings nowadays when it didn't ten or fifteen years ago because corporations understand that in the global economy with a diverse customer base and diverse workforce, they need people who are capable of interacting across cultural and racial lines and who can get along with people who are different from them.

A vice-president of AT&T who manages a huge operation within the company told me quite frankly that, if he had two equally qualified white males whom he was considering for promotion and one of them had a good record working with minorities and women, but the other didn't, he would promote the one with the good record. It was simply not in his interest or in the corporation's to have somebody in place who was going to create problems.

Universities, then, have a direct interest in putting all of their students in a very diverse community in which people can interact and learn from each other. Unfortunately, I don't know how it is on the Ashtabula Campus of Kent State, but it wouldn't surprise me to learn that you cluster along racial lines. In every other campus I have been to, that is always the case.

I usually try to tell college students that you have an opportunity now that you are not going to have again in life. Because right now, you are in a community in which people who are different from you racially, ethnically, are peers. There is no hierarchy. You are all at the same level. You're all students. This is a great chance to get out of your comfort zone — to get out to the edge of what seems convenient for you. Take some risks, and walk over to the other table, or make friends across racial lines. Make a sincere effort at it and don't be afraid to be rebuffed.

This goes in all directions, not just by whites with blacks, but by blacks with whites, Asian Americans, Spanish-speaking peoples and other nationalities. Because once you get out into the so-called real world, the working world, the chances are that your peer relationships, depending on what you do, will be formed at the same stratum as in the workplace; it will not be much different racially. Therefore, you will not have as much opportunity once you get out into the working world as you do when you are in college. Where you live is also an important issue. Where you live, whether you live in a racially mixed neighborhood or not — there are not many racially mixed neighborhoods in the United States even after all these years — many schools are, in fact, still segregated. So these are not years to waste, clinging to your most comfortable friend. They are years to fight your own shyness or your own nervousness and get out of that comfort zone.

Having considered one of the most sensitive of racial issues — the intelligence issue — and the cruel stereotype of blacks being less intelligent, I remember that I once came across a white couple in the Bay area who had adopted a biracial girl, one biological parent being white, one black. The white adoptive couple had two biological children, both sons, and they were all close in age. The siblings all went to the same public school around the same time. The boys were a little older, the girl was the youngest, and was seen as black and was accordingly labeled that way. Her teachers and the other kids all thought of her in that way. Her friends were mostly black and Latina or Latino.

And the parents told me that when their sons who were white slipped behind in school, notes came home from teachers, telephone calls came from the guidance counselors. But when their daughter who was black slipped behind, there were no notes, no phone calls. The teachers just had written her off. Teachers might have 135 or 150 students, and there'd be 5 or 6 classes a day; they are busy; they have limited energy. They focus on the kids whom they think they can do something for. They decided this girl was not helpable.

The parents were advocates for their children, and they really were in the school all the time. They were trying to get some help for their daughter, but they basically felt that they had failed. The school just did not take her seriously as a student. I said to them, "Picture one other factor — that is, the male versus female one." But they both said that they really felt that here it was a question of race, not gender. They had seen white girls in the school get a lot of attention.

I know there is a whole pattern of this going on every day, everywhere in America's schools. These were not teachers who stood in the schoolhouse door and wore Klan sheets or burned crosses in yards or anything like that. They wouldn't be considered racists by the most drastic definition of the word. But they were doing something very damaging to this girl. So the racial component can work its way, burrowing deep, in a lot of very damaging ways. It's in there; you cannot get rid of it.

The Dynamics of Power Relationships

Let me consider one final subtopic of *A Country of Strangers*: power relationships. Readers know that I have divided patterns of prejudice into five different groups with each one getting its own chapter. One has to do with body (the way people look and all the attributes that are ascribed to people based on the way they look). A second is morality (the judgments that are made about people's morality based on their race). A third is violence. We really do stereotype each other — blacks very often see whites as violent. Whites see blacks as violent. But one of the most important but least understood has to do with power. The power relationships are very important because they are not often discussed in America. We tend to focus on issues of overt discrimination; for example, not allowing blacks into a restaurant, a club, or some racist comment, or cross-burning or, worst of all, police shooting a black man when he pulls out his wallet, assuming it's a gun. But these are really overt and traumatic examples. Yet a whole series of discreetly practiced power relationships exist that really do spin off what Roger Wilkins was referring to when he talked about the manner of addressing people.

I discussed this at a talk I gave in Washington, DC, one evening. I spoke about how there are some white people who are uncomfortable with blacks who have authority over them. And you hear, sometimes, how people express this. Most often, they don't. Richard Arrington, former mayor of Birmingham, Alabama, for many years, a black man, told me that white staff members of his used to get questions all the time, such as "What's it like to work for a black man?"—as if this were some novelty, some strange thing.

One white woman said to Mayor Arrington, "You know, Mayor, you have to understand that this a strange kind of phenomenon down here in Birmingham." She said that she was disciplined and kept in line and made to do her homework with a threat from her parents: "Watch out! If you don't do your work and do well in school, you're going to have a nigger for a boss." No matter how well you progress in the decades, when a vile word like that is uttered, and no matter how open-minded you assume you have become, it stays with you. You cannot ever get rid of that. It stays with you. You may not believe it any more, but it's like a scar that fades but never quite disappears. I mean, *nigger*, come on—that opens a dangerous threat.

So I told this story and I talked about this, and afterwards, a black man came up to me. He was in a lawyer's suit—a very dark, pinstriped vest—and he told me that he was an attorney, that he worked in the federal judiciary system, and that he was put in charge of a particular six-month project. Two months into the project, a white woman in his office with whom he was very good friends came to him and said, "I just want to tell you something. When this project began, Emily (not her real name, another white woman), said to me, 'I can't stand taking orders from a black man.'"

The black lawyer thought, "Now I understand what's been going on, because Emily has been torpedoing the project." She had been passively resisting, just not doing things right, and undermining his authority. So the end result was Emily was fired. Now the black lawyer was really offended that his white friend had waited for three months to tell him.

So I asked, "Well, how is your friendship?"

He replied, "We're working on it."

What you have here is kind of a wonderful little encapsulation of so many contradictory currents in race relations in America at this point. It indicates both a change and what has not been changed. What is significant in the long view perhaps is that a black man in the federal judiciary system is put in charge of some important project. Twenty years ago it would never have happened. A black man is an object of prejudice to a white woman, but the white woman hesitates to rat on her white sister. She finally does it, but she doesn't really want to do it. Friendship is such a complicated thing between races.

A white woman actually says that she can't stand taking orders from a black man and actually says that to another white. Some whites will admit that we white people have antennae. You can figure out whether another white person is going to take your racist joke well or not. You figure it out, and you sort of sense it, and maybe they will, maybe they won't, and if you think they won't, you just shut up. If you think they will, and you're so inclined, you might make the comment, or tell the joke. This is a dirty little secret about white people that I'm telling.

This woman, Emily, must have figured, "Well, this sister here, she'll take this from me. I wonder what she thinks. I'm going to say this to her." So here she was, subordinate to a black man and willing to say that she didn't want to take orders from him. The black man who had a lot of authority got her fired. So you can see how contradictory the currents are in this society now about race. Turn the clocks back twenty years and none of this would have ever had an opportunity to happen, because that black man would not have been in that position to fire anyone. And surely enough, the white woman wouldn't have been fired for that.

So, now, where are we today in America? We're here, there, and everywhere, and trying to figure it out and decode it and navigate our way through all of this. It's fair to say it is still true that different standards are applied between black people and white people when the former are evaluated, for example. I've seen this myself in a particular organization I'm a member of trying to get minorities into this particular group that has some authority.

There were two black women that were candidates a couple of years ago; and I didn't know either of them, but one of them was regarded as "abrasive." So I pointed out that one of the white males on this panel was really abrasive. I mean, he was just rude; but he also had a very good mind. He could cut through a lot of the junk and get down to the business, and he was valuable if you could get past his rudeness. But if the criterion was that we don't want anyone "abrasive," and they are going to apply it to the white man, he never would have gotten on this panel.

The other black woman was regarded as not knowing anything about this particular field we were dealing with, and I pointed out that when I was put on, I also did not know anything about it. In fact, if that had been the criterion, I wouldn't be on the board.

I think it happens very often in hiring faculty. I am sure that it happens in promoting people in corporations that the same characteristics that are admirable in a white man are seen as negatives in minorities, and white women, too, to some extent. A white man is "independent." A black or a woman is "not a team player." A white man is "forceful"; a black or a woman is "militant." A white man is "confident in a group"; a black is "pushy."

So these are two sides of the same coin, same characteristics, same behavior, evaluated very differently because of where you're coming from, what race, and what gender. These do matter. There is a great privilege to being white in America. Someone earlier today mentioned it. I had started with it in a sense, telling you that I didn't have to worry about being attacked or vilified because Timothy McVeigh was of my race and gender.

We Whites Sat

When I finished working on this book — I thought I had finished it — I went to a workshop in Washington on diversity. And I learned a tremendous amount that day. It was a good indication to me, a good illustration how you never stop learning in this subject. It's so interesting, fascinating, really, this racism in America. You never really finish learning because it is a lifelong process. One of the exercises that was done there was to have all of us, there were about 50 of us there, walk around the room silently, and pick a partner without exchanging a word. Pick a partner who was different from us, to sum it up. So a young black woman and I picked each other, and we sat there on chairs facing one another, and then the facilitator led us through a structured conversation in which we attempted to find out why it was we thought we were so different from each other without ever having exchanged a single word beforehand. And so, obviously, we came to the conclusion that it was because she was black, I was white; I was male, she was female. But, of course, we might have shared a lot, in terms of politics, musical tastes — who could say? We didn't know; we just thought we were different.

And then the facilitator led us through an exercise in which he made a statement, and we were supposed to respond to it, true or false, by standing or remaining seated.

"I never have to worry about my credit card or my check being refused at a store because of my race."

Only we whites stood, and he left us standing there for a long time while everybody looked at us and we looked at each other.

"I can be pretty sure that the next President of the United States will be a member of my race or ethnic group."

Again, only we whites were able to stand.

"When I go to work, I have to leave my culture at the door."

All the Latinos stood. Many of the African-Americans and Asians stood.

We whites sat.

Then he asked a question that, in all my years of roaming the country interviewing people for the book, I had never thought to ask. He asked people to stand if they agreed that "I have considered not having children because of racism." The young black woman sitting across from me rose slowly to her feet. I looked up at her and she looked down at me across a huge gap — a huge gulf. To feel the decision not to have children forced on you from without feels like the saddest thing possible.

Later she and I talked and she was crying. She said her husband had wanted children, but many of her friends felt that having a child now, especially a male child, was very, very difficult in this society; it was very hard to raise a black son in America. This was a question I had never thought to ask, and an answer I never expected to get.

What we have to do in America is to make sure we have a society in which, when that statement is made, nobody stands.

About the Contributors

James R. Birch is an assistant professor of speech/theater and education, a lecturer in the Teaching, Leadership, and Curriculum Studies Department of Kent State University, and director of the Education Program at Kent State Ashtabula. His research includes pedagogical theory and arts-based approaches to educational research.

Irene Jung Fiala is a former assistant professor of sociology and director of the Kent State University Ashtabula Justice Studies Program. Now a professional consultant and criminalist, she presented papers at international forensics conferences in 2000 in Toronto and Sydney.

Paul L. Gaston, provost of Kent State University, earned his doctorate from the University of Virginia, where he was a Woodrow Wilson Fellow, a DuPont Fellow, and a Woodrow Wilson Dissertation Fellow. He is the author of two books and of articles on subjects ranging from inter-art analogies, poetry of George Herbert, and the fiction of Walker Percy, to the assessment of educational outcomes. In 1989, his presentation at the 50th Anniversary Celebration of the Baseball Hall of Fame was cited by *USA Today* as one of the five most effective pieces of writing on baseball.

Stanton W. Green is dean of the Arts and Sciences College at Clarion University of Pennsylvania and a professor of anthropology. He has authored dozens of articles in anthropology and archeology and coauthored *Archeological Boundaries and Frontiers* (1995) and *Interpreting Space: GIS and Archeology* (1990).

Irene Sheryl Hammer of San Francisco is the one hundredth person accepted into the Sterling Room for Writers in Portland, Oregon.

Timothy M. Kalil received his doctorate in ethnomusicology from the University of Chicago and teaches music at Kent State University Ashtabula. He has published on ragtime, jazz, and the history of black influences in popular and religious music. He founded and directs the campus' Classical Concert Series.

Thomas Kaufman is an adjunct faculty member in the English departments of the University of Toledo and Lourdes College. He earned a B.A. in history at John Carroll University and M.A. in English at the University of Toledo. He is currently at work on two projects concerning the lives and writings of American authors Henry Blake Fuller and Brand Whitlock.

Lynda J. Lambert is an assistant professor in the fine arts and humanities of Geneva College, Beaver Falls, Pennsylvania. Also a Commonwealth Speaker for the Pennsylvania Humanities Council, she gives numerous presentations on African-American poetry and art. She teaches studio art and coordinates the annual Geneva Artist Exhibition program as well as a cross-discipline course every summer in Salzburg, Austria.

Elaine Lechtreck retired from teaching English and history at Lauralton Hall, Milford, Connecticut, and holds three master's degrees from Pepperdine University, Fairfield University in Connecticut, and SUNY-New Paltz. She is currently studying for a doctorate in U.S. history at the Union Institute and University, Cincinnati, Ohio. She recently presented "Lessons in Social Justice: The Story of a Union, Evictions, Two Interracial Cooperative Farms and Racist Infamy" at a higher-education conference sponsored by Wilmington College, Ohio.

Roy Lechtreck is a professor emeritus of political science, University of Montevallo in Alabama and has been a guest columnist for the *Montgomery Advertiser* and the *Shelby County Reporter*, Alabama. He has published numerous articles on the civil rights movement and presented "Paths of Progress: Why Some Social Activism Doesn't Work" at the Friends Association for Higher Education Conference in 2002.

Thabiti Lewis is an assistant professor of English at Willamette University in Salem, Oregon. He teaches literature, creative nonfiction, composition, African-American culture studies, sports, film, and popular culture. He has also worked as a journalist, talk show host and editor at Third World Press in Chicago. He received his Ph.D. from St. Louis University. His current research includes a collection of essays exploring race, sports and contemporary American culture and a biography of Toni Cade Bambara.

Michelle McCoy is an assistant professor at Kent State's School of Journalism and Mass Communication, Stark Campus. She teaches performance for television and many other media courses. An AFTRA member, she holds a long list of national and regional freelance credits. Michelle served as a commercial TV host for WAOH/WAX in Northeast Ohio for more than five years. She has received numerous awards, including excellence in teaching and several Emmy nominations. She is president of the American Association of University Women/Kent State and college university chair for AAUW, Ohio. Her current research focuses on media and feminist/diversity issues.

Noah O. Midamba is a former associate dean for the Office of Institutional Diversity for Kent State University and is currently executive director, Center for International Studies and Programs at Youngstown State University. Prior to his current posting, he served as associate dean in enrollment management and student affairs. Dr. Midamba earned his Ph.D. in international relations from the University of Denver. He is also a former executive youth officer for the United Nations, deputy executive director of the Senior Resources Center in Denver, a senior planner for the Denver Regional Council of Governments and a management consultant for a division of Merrill Lynch Realty.

Edward J. Murray is director of the psychology program at Kent State University Ashtabula. A licensed psychologist and doctor of psychology with a private practice and board memberships in mental health, he has published articles in cognitive psychology and presented at international conferences.

Carol Puthoff-Murray is assistant professor and director of the Kent State University Ashtabula Human Services Technology program. A licensed counselor, she has twenty years' experience in mental-health counseling and chairs the campus Diversity Advisory Council.

Todd Sallo (University of California, Santa Cruz, 1983), has served as consultant for the California Higher Education Policy Center, and the National Center for Public Policy and Higher Education, and is editor of *National CrossTalk*, a higher-education policy quarterly.

David K. Shipler is an award-winning journalist with more than twenty years' experience with the *New York Times*. He is the author of *Russia: Broken Idols, Solemn Dreams* and *Arab and Jew: Wounded Spirits in a Promised Land*, for which he received a Pulitzer. He was Ferris Professor of Journalism and Public Affairs at Princeton University, a guest scholar at the Brookings Institution, and a senior associate at the Carnegie Endowment for International Peace. His book on race, *A Country of Strangers: Blacks and Whites in America*, was published in 1997.

Gregory K. Stephens is a writer, teacher, public speaker, DJ, and activist who has spent more than twenty years advocating and participating in diversity and equal rights issues, multi-ethnic art forms and sustainable lifestyles. Stephens is currently a visiting scholar in the "creating the Transnational South" Rockefeller Fellowship at the University of North Carolina, Chapel Hill, doing ethnographic research among Spanish-speaking immigrants. Stephens was a lecturer in American studies and mass communication at the University of California, 1997–99. He wrote *Knowing What Diversity Means: The New Culture of Frederick Douglass, Ralph Ellison, and Bob Marley* (Cambridge University Press, 1999).

Susan J. Stocker is the interim dean of Kent State University Ashtabula, associate professor of nursing and former director of its nationally recognized nursing program. She was elected twice as president of the Ohio Nurses Association, has won the Distinguished Teacher Award from Kent State University and has authored dozens of articles on psychiatric nursing.

Jeffrey J. Wallace is an associate provost and holds the title special assistant to the president for campus diversity, University of Akron, Akron, Ohio.

Terry White is the assistant dean of Kent State University Ashtabula. As assistant professor of English, he compiled bibliographies on espionage and legal fiction, edited a colloquium proceedings based on poet Robert Bly's *The Sibling Society*, and assisted Richard H. A. Blum of California in publishing the memoirs of Carlton A. Sheffield (*John Steinbeck, the Good Companion*, Berkeley: Creative Arts, 2001).

Robert A. Widen holds an economics degree from Stanford and is adjunct faculty in history and political science at Prescott College in Arizona. He most recently taught government courses aboard the USS *Lake Erie*, a guided missile cruiser. He is now completing the manuscript *Whatever Gods May Be*, which considers the impact of the world's great religions on socio-economic theory.

Index